GPS TO HEAVEN

GPS = God Prayer Scriptures

Bedelia Ann Hilburn

THANK YOU

First, I must thank God for His unselfish, unconditional Love. Thank you for saving me from damnation. I Love you, Abba Father, and I need you in every area of my life. Jesus, I thank you for your obedience to our Father by being the final sacrifice on the altar. Your obedience saved all of mankind. Thank you for your love, and Jesus, if you are not there, I don't want to be there.

Holy Spirit, my comforter, thank you for doing all that you do by providing me with the instructions given to you by Our Father. I love you and need each of you in my life. Thank you for your blessings, for experiences that seem and feel good, and for some that hurt and cause pain. I have learned to count it all joy, and I understand that this is part of life's journey here on earth. Thank you, Father, for the Bible, your "Book of Instructions Before Life Eternal."

QUOTES

"An eye for an eye only ends up making the world blind." -
Mohandas Gandhi

"Life is like a game of cards. The hand that is dealt you
represents determinism; the way you play is free will." -
Jawaharlal Nehru

"Comparison is the thief of joy." - *Theodore Roosevelt*

"Everyone should be respected as an individual, but no one
idolized." - *Albert Einstein*

"There is only one thing that makes a dream impossible to
achieve: the fear offailure." - *Paulo Coelho*

"How can I soar like an eagle when I'm surrounded by
turkeys?" - *Bedelia Hilburn*

"Do give books-religious or otherwise, for Christmas.
They're neverfattening, seldom sinful, and permanently
personal." - *Lenore Hershey*

"All the Great things are simple, and many can be expressed
in a singleword: freedom, justice, honor, duty, mercy, hope." -
Winston Churchill

INTRODUCTION

In today's age of wonder, speed, and technology, make your life easier. The GPS has become a frequently used tool in navigation around the planet. Here are the GPS coordinates for guidance on your life journey. Using this way, finding directions can be found in having a relationship with God through prayers and the scriptures in the bible. The Word of God is effective both in the spiritual and natural realms. When used will lead you to establishing a relationship with God, through His Son Jesus, leading you to Eternal Life.

Following this Spiritual GPS navigational system provides, protects, and helps you to stay in your own lane in peace and not in pieces. Enjoy your journey. Move over and let "God, the King of all roads," have His way!

CONTENTS

EPILOGUE

The Amusement Park of Life

I am now age 74, and I have come to the conclusion that both the natural and spiritual journey path is that of an amusement park. Why? You may ask, and my reasoning is that this life to me is like an amusement park. It will make you shrill, cry, scream, fall, laugh, get up, stand up, lie down, be frightened, enter into darkness, walk blind, not knowing where you are going. Following a path that you can't see and are not familiar with.

Right away, you see long lines filled with people of all ethnicities and genders, while you yourself are an infant. Having no direction, growing in the atmosphere you are given. Who, too, are learning still on their life journey. There are lines where each person has to open and walk through a guardrail. Many enter in groups, some alone, some in couples, not knowing each other, merely intermingled with each other as they ventured through the open rail gates.

Roaming in, each person takes a ticket from a table, where there are organized stacks, where a sign above it saying take one, with no additional explanation. Once you take the ticket, it evaporates into a mist. Before you know it, you are faced with many different doors, all looking the same with door knobs. Once you open the door, what's on the other side are different scenarios of life's journey where you and others step into them.

An amusement park is not really a place or atmosphere of peace. It is noisy, chaotic, full of trickery and confusion, being quite frightening to both young and old. Surrounded by all types of different characters walking and lurking around the fairgrounds. Strange people, odd things, demons peeking out from tents, and unusual dwellings. Beckoning you to come in and experience something that may scare you to death, modify you so that you experience trauma from the ordeal, circumstance, events, or situations. Open your eyes and see the clown that has an angry smile or face under the heavy makeup. When you are alone in a place like this, so many things are frightening to you. When you have someone who loves you holding your hand, even walking with you, the park is not so bad.

Yet, each has different experiences for each individual who actually opens the door. Some of the doors have people, items, and more to give you an experience that may even kill you, but it is all of the life you become part of. There are some areas where you don't even get to choose what you want to do and experience. You just get what you get and move on. You may cry, throw up, laugh, enjoy, or wet yourself. You may experience love, loss, births, ruin, illness, happiness, and all that the "Amusement Park of Life" has to offer you, including addictions, horror, and poverty. All are part of what life has to offer you. Everyone and everything has a purpose and plays a part, although you don't know what to expect. Who, what, or where? Some rides in the amusement park of life can hurt you so bad you call for your mama and daddy by what you go through, see, learn, and experience. They are all part of the games and adventures of the Amusement Park of Life (APOL) experience.

Several tall poles and directories are located throughout the park, with arrow-shaped names of the "Amusement Park of Life's" rides, games, merchandise, sunglasses, and refreshments. Locations, songs to be heard, roads, fun, and adventures are all denoted by the arrows pointing in each direction. There are rides, trains, Ferris wheels, games, labyrinths, peculiarly shaped houses, rest stops, mazes, and many different arrayed foliage walls, some with flowers, some with seeds, some with fruit, and others with each leaf having something written on them. Beautiful flowers, trees, plants, and all of nature's wildlife, as they, too, play a part in many of these life adventures. Eventually, for some, their eyes are opened to see things that are not as they seem. While others walk blindly in foolishness. The park is always open, with different people, animals, birds, and atmospheres, which all have parts to contribute to life journeys; even the wildlife behaves the same as people.

Once you begin, it is a non-stop world of amazement, surprises, disappointments, mayhem, cheer, prosperity, and more. Just waiting for you to live life unknowing where, why, what, when, and who you will encounter in this park of mystery, trickery, folly, surprise, wonder, loss, joy, misery, and even hope and hopelessness on the journey. Awaits, filled with all that life has to offer you.

As you walk, you learn to run, on some occasions, from what you undergo. There are icy roads around the park; some of the roads are muddy, some are made of concrete, with tunnels and bridges made of wood, metal, and other materials. Walking past the rail gate, you see before you all sorts of rides and refreshments. There are both food and beverage booths, which allow you the choice of eating all you want and as much as you want until you regurgitate. Giving the experience of the consequences that come with the choices you make. In the distance, there is a Ferris wheel called "Sky High." You now have the choice of selecting the rides you desire to experience.

All you do is just walk up to a ride, and you gain access. You merely sit down in a seat before the ride automatically begins. Taking you who knows where, as there are no labels or titles on this ride, you learn as you travel. There are also booths and areas where you have the choice to try consuming alcohol, drugs, food, and vitamins as you choose which ride or trip, with various ingestive opportunities bringing you experiences. All the rides offer things that you have never seen or experienced before. Once you make a choice, you are not able to change it. You must experience whatever may come, causing you to go through whatever it is.

There are scenarios that allow you to sit and dine with others. Who you may think are your friends, that eventually will either be great friends or foes in the future, who knows? There is a game called "Spin the Wheel," which consists of a wheel mounted vertically, having several slots, each with something written on it.

You are given three darts to throw at the wheel, wondering what slot it lands on, as it affects your travel in the park of your life's journey. There are haunted houses that carry your past, guilt, regrets, and shame. There is a fun house that makes you think it's fun, but you find out that it isn't at all, and far from it. There is a merry-go-round for those who want to play it safe, only to find out that. Trying to mount a horse that moves up and down is not so easy when you have distractions, such as others trying to take the horse that you are trying to get on.

There are times when the floor dips, and you end up somewhere, maybe alone or with others who, too, are having an adventure, where you are now part of it. You see folks with 2, 3, 4-sided faces. Some are smiling, some faces that are crying, some that look angry, some mean, with others that are horrifying.In the park are many types of people: some with limbs missing, some tall, some with handicaps, some dwarfs, some people are obese, some have rosacea, and some are skinny; the park is a melting pot of living souls. There are even experiences of being in need of a lawyer and other positions with titles of worldliness in your life journey. You can hear laughter, crying, screams, loud conversations, and mixtures of sounds, accompanied by odors and scents that are pungent, while some carry aromatic and pleasant fragrances.

Somewhere, sometime, in this place, you hear the whispers of God through the Holy Spirit, calling out to you. Something you know nothing about, all is new to you. Here you have a choice to listen and follow, or to ignore and do what you are doing. Your strength is tested, along with your hearing, and so is your heart, mind, and soul. There is the "House of Mirrors," where you are offered the opportunistic choice to see what is real and what is an illusion. It also shows the word <u>live</u> when seen in the reverse reflection of the mirrors, showing the word <u>evil</u>.

You come face-to-face with the reflection of your true self, or is it? In the mirror, it allows you to know and see your true identity as you face the imagination of the mind, including self-evaluation of one's self. In the Amusement Park of Life, you get rained on, no matter who you are, giving you the freedom to make decisions and choices about what you want to do. You walk through rain and encounter various types of storms, some natural, some through circumstances. There is drama, unwanted attacks by the devil, giving false hope, and being laughed at when the joke is on you. Gossiped about by acquaintances you felt you could trust. You experience betrayal, war, hailstorms, tornadoes, floods, and unexpected objects falling out of the sky, down upon unsuspecting individuals, both in the natural and spiritual. There are hot spots with sinkholes you can fall into. Hurricanes and more are awaiting us all.

In the Amusement Park of Life, there are races where you run to get to the secret place of peace. That, in the end, is what everyone wants: true peace. There are some rides that make you sick, and some cause you to be thirsty, only to be fed what appears to be a delicious banquet, but due to the choices (s) you select to consume may destroy you. There are tall foliage fragrance walls that, when you lean in to smell or touch them, you fall right into another realm where you have to try and find your way out. Filled with roads and walkways, some rides and choices you make will sicken you, causing you to vomit or even die. Some of the rides on the path in the amusement park of life have a secret at the end of your last turn style, which is where you have your ticket punched, and you are no longer in the natural but in the spiritual realm.

With several stops before the occasional stops because you decided to repent and try again to make better life-changing choices. There is the ride, "The Whip," which does just that: it whips the tears out of you from disobedience, pride, arrogance, adultery, blasphemes, wickedness, worshiping

21

yourself, murder, debauchery, unrighteousness, having as you have no integrity, whipping you to your right sense. The Bitter Bumper Car ride is very rough and dangerous; each bump releases anger and unforgiveness, being very harsh when you ride this one. With the renewal of your mindset, your ride becomes the "Better Bumper Car," causing your life ride to change for the better because of your choices.

There are numerous rides, games, and mystery doorways with Enter or Not. In some of the haunted house(s), you have choices; you may select the "World-Famous Non-Stop Roller Coaster to Hell" due to continual "spiritual destruction through unrighteousness. Another choice is the Roller coaster of "Repentance," which does have stops because some people do repent, giving their lives to God. Then there are those who backslide to go back to the way that is Hellbound." Which, to me, is being physically born. We walk aimlessly around the Amusement Park of Life with no direction, being subjected to trickery, fear, chaos, confusion, deceit, illness, and financial ruin. Relationships broken, death, mayhem, situations, circumstances, and loneliness. Made to feel less than, incurring health issues.

Disappointments, addictions, discouragement, and mental illness. Suicides, failures, hate, alcoholism, domestic violence, aging, and child abuse are all found. Everything that you can and don't imagine happens while you are walking on the premises of "The Amusement Park of Life," grounds. In this park, which is really the world, you will experience bigotry, happiness, homelessness, temporary gladness, a feeling of being safe just to be harmed, and bigotry injured, ostracized, and not being understood, all leading to unknown surroundings. Large lions walk freely to devour whom they can by opening their large mouths and showing their teeth, inducing fear.

The longer you live, running the race to get to the Heavenly Kingdom, the closer you get, and the more experiences test you with lessons, trials, tests, and tribulations. Others, on their journey, branch out in lieu of what they will encounter in the experiences of life to come. There is a maze made of foliage that you go into after you get through the basic introduction. You walk into a maze that is taller than you. Once you reach a dead end and see the maze wall, while you stand in front of it, an opening is shown to you, and you walk in. What's on the other side of the Maze wall?

There may be people waiting to enfold you into their life journey. Same for all others, some reach a dead end, the foliage opens, and you see no one, so you start or continue your travel alone. Later, to have others join you in your life journey. You meet people, and you interact with them as they are on their own private journey.

After a period of time with these individuals, you will call them family, consisting of countless mixers of individuals, pets, and siblings. After a time of being in each other's presence, you are separated from your surrogate family, and a door appears to enter. You do so alone; there is a chair to sit down in the room that has walls made of foliage. Once you sit down, a screen is on the wall in front of you. It shows you and your family interactions and shows the words that you spoke, and how they affected those around you.

You see how you failed to edify those around you, and that devilish tongue you have does have great power to curse or bless. You feel some kind of way, but not sure what. There is another screen that appears, showing you speaking with love and being kind, and how that affects you and your family life. Next, the screen is gone, and you stand up to go to the next doorway. You look back and see all of your family members in line to enter where you just left. None of you gets a manual; you are just learning and growing as you travel on our road. You walk further and see a revolving door. Pushing the door and entering a room, you see a table with an open book on it.

Above it on the wall is a sign that says, "Read all you want, and take all the time you need." This is food for your soul and water for your spirit. You begin to read the already exposed pages, and it is John 3:16, but you really don't understand its meaning. You may even smile a bit and laugh, enjoying the experience and revelation of just reading it. Either because you understand or you just enjoyed what you read. There is a main stop, for all the trains meet at the depot called "Conduit." It's called that because when each of the trains rolls out, they each have a different direction, which leads to something more energizing for your spirit, soul, mind, and heart.

Depending on where you choose to stop, select the ride, food, and people that are added to your life journey. In a flash, you may be married, with children, or a World-renowned chef with your own cooking show. Having a dog and living in a city. The stop is the walkway to the "Rise Above Escalator." It allows you to see the roads that are available for you to choose from below. Some are wide; some are crooked; some are wide; some are dusty; some are in good condition, while others appear to be possibly hazardous, even toxic, depending on what the air smells like in the area that you are in at that time.

In order for you to understand the reason why you had to go through the situations, it was to get you above and out of the park. There is a train of "Delay" that goes around the entire Amusement Park of Life. It takes you all around the entire park, exposing you to different scents, terrains, dwellings, natural disaster sites, stores, people of all diversities, and animals.

The train ride is also with choices to be made. You may choose to get off at specific stops, like seeing tornadoes, flooded areas, or purchasing a home without knowing what will come of it. Is it dangerous? Is it out of your financial reach? The train of "Delay" is also an opportunity to observe different disasters in the air, man-made and natural, including mysterious sights and wonders. You may see hail fall from the sky. The "Ride of Fools" goes round and round, turns the rider upside down, shakes and jerks you in all locations, and has sporadic stops that may just leave you hanging.

This is the ride for those who are fools and say there is no God. It is also a ride for those backsliders who continue to do the same thing with the same outcome. Life has many games, rides, adventures, swamps, valleys, mountains, rivers, slime pits, and sinkholes in life's journey. Depending on your choices, that leads you to paths. You may see tornadoes, snow, lightning, birds falling from the sky, and flooded areas that are beautiful with landscapes to match. There are sinkholes that just appear. There is the smell of smoke, tar, feces, and stagnant water, and smoke.

There are all sorts of areas with some type of choice, which may bring disappointment, pain, surprise, and happiness. Even hurt, pain, and death, which are all part of the experiences of the Amusement Park of Life." Some places have people there, already allowing you to join in on their run and walk of life. Having each one of you facing your own battles, learning to maneuver the best way you can. Offering your wisdom if you are one of the people who were selected to stop at that area and gain knowledge. Everyone has their own Run. There are dead roads; there are signs that beckon you to come and see. There are areas where there are secret sins behind doors and floating above to land on some unsuspecting individual(s).

There are pictures that move within their frames, usually depicting an image of you being part of some action in a story. There are active volcanoes in sections actually spewing hot lava. There is a tour trolley that takes you to the "Free Fall Bridge," where you can make a choice to dive into the unknown quickly, using a Zipline to enter, then dealing with the consequences that come from your actions. The trains have a stop at the Highway of Choices. As with most amusement parks, the lines vary in the pace at which they move, with some moving slower than others, all being tests of patience. There is a stop for "Knowledgeable Lane," where you can learn and gain wisdom with the key of understanding and having the desire to learn with a teachable spirit.

There are speedways where people decide that they can't wait on God, so they go it alone, doing it their way, which leads to a catastrophic experience of testing and trial and circumstances. There is a stop for the "Line of Enough." When you say, "I'm done no more," this is when you feel you cannot deal with anything else. You make a choice of what you want to do or pray for what you need to do. The are several trains on the move, like the train of "Doubt," which is slower in some areas. It awards you to get off when and wherever it stops with the unknown. There is a road for the Lost and Found, for those who were lost but are found, for those who are seeking the Heavenly Kingdom.

There are sections of the part where the sun shines and smells wonderful, but what evils lie in the midst of it? You are constantly going around, seeking what you think is best for you to make you happy. But the real happiness is knowing who you will serve on the life Journey, Man or God? Having the freedom of will, you make the choice throughout your life journey. You choose which roads you select and want to be on, not knowing what awaits you ahead. Then, by some decree of order, you arrive at a pivotal time period in your life where you make a decision to seek and listen to God or not; the choice is yours.

Either way, you are in the park until your time is met. Whenever you want to stop on any ride, you just raise your hand, and the ride will stop. The only way to enter is when the light inside you begins to glow. The brighter your inner light is, the closer you are to entering the Heavenly Kingdom of God. The goal is that when you become so fluorescent, others must cover their eyes or wear sunglasses to look at you, which is a sure sign you are walking in the Holy Spirit of God.

Beautiful rivers and waterfalls cascade down the cliffs and mountain ranges that intrigue you with wonder and bliss. You may also transfer to another train going in another direction if you choose to. Receiving the Kingdom of God is receiving Eternal life for some. These are factors that are all part of the entire experience. There is a sign that says "The Golden Rule" as you exit the Amusement Park of Life. Your life span has come to an end. Now, you are to be judged by El Elyon, God, the only true judge. Here, all of your actions, words, deeds, and sins will be reviewed. This causes the direction your soul will go in eternity.

GPS>[Philippians 4:5-7; John 8:44; 1 Timothy 6:17; Ecclesiastes 8:15; Ephesians 2:10]

CHAPTER 1

Do You Know That God Loves You?

Do you know that God loves you? He loves you so much that he gave his only begotten Son to be the atonement for all of humanity's sins. God's Agape love is unconditional and everlasting. He is always available to you. If God had a refrigerator, he'd have your picture on it. That's how much he loves and cherishes you. GPS>[John 3:16; Romans 8:38-39]

God's love is the air that you breathe, for God is Love, Jesus is the vine, and you are a branch. You can do nothing detached from the Vine. God is a spirit that is omnipotent. He created everything in the world: what's in it, what's below it, what's inside it, including what's above it. God created the heavens, what is above the heavens, in the heavens, and below it. Your great creator made everything and all that exists visible in the natural and Supernatural. He also created what you cannot see using your natural eyes. Anything that has life, God caused it to be. God is a Spirit and is physically untouchable; He cannot be touched, corrupted, or contaminated by anyone or anything. He is God, not your next-door neighbor or coworker whom you can walk over to and ask to help you move on Saturday.

The Love that God loves you with is in a supernatural capacity. The truth is, God, the heavenly Father, is life itself. He created both Adam and Eve, which was the beginning of mankind. From that time on, each and everything on and off the earth needs oxygen, in some way or another, to live. God is the oxygen that you breathe continually, throughout your life span on earth. When God breathed into Adam's nostrils, He gave Adam a life force, which is what God is made of. When you were born, the first thing you did after you were out of your mother's womb was to take a big breath, gasping for air.

Regardless of whatever life form or species on earth was created by God, it needs air to survive. It is a unique part of God's Divine Design for mankind. GPS>[Genesis 1:31; Genesis 2:7]

AGAPE LOVE

What is Agape love? Agape love is pure love that is unconditional and perfect. No strings are attached; nothing is expected to give Agape love. It is a spiritual awakening of the love essence that was given to you when you were created by God. The physical way that Agape love causes you to feel is that of a child under four years old, seeing anything for the first time. It is a wide, eye-opening, mouth-dropping, dropping-in-awe experience. This love opens both your eyes to the natural and the spiritual realms. Agape love is filled with compassion and mercy. Compassion also consists of the giving and receiving of God's Love. It means that the love God has placed in your heart is to be given freely to others. In order to be able to give love, you must have a heart that is open to receive it. Having a heart that is filled with bitterness, unforgiveness, and unrighteousness is not capable of receiving love. Your heart must be clean of all darkness, with no bitter stones in it, and also loving unconditionally. God has so much compassion and love for humanity that he sent His only Son, Jesus, to tell you that you are loved dearly by the Heavenly Father. **GPS>**"For God so loved the world, that he gave his only Son, that whoever believes in him should not perish but have eternal life." **[John 3:16]**

Being compassionate is having an inner feeling that convicts you to help, sympathizing with the victim(s)in solidarity to understand their plight. Agape love is putting light and good air back into your struggles of worldly situations. Agape love has comforting attributes that are non-stop.

Condolences, support, assuage, hearten, uplifting, willing to help others in any way that you can. Agape Love is not a sexual thing; it is a completely spiritual, pure, uncontaminated love. Having Agape love is realizing that love is bigger and more powerful than you or anything else. "What the World Needs Now Is Love, Sweet Love" is not a mere cliche. Love is what you need in this world, where the entire planet and mankind are in turmoil continually. There have been times when good old love saved a life, a relationship, a business, a family, including terminally ill people. The only way to explain this factor is that it is by supernatural Spiritual power. Agape love is a pure Spirit within you, accomplishing the glory of God.

Agape love is filled with Mercy; it's given gladly without any qualms. Mercy is showing the Omnipotence of God; in practice, there are never harsh words, blame, jealousy, offense, or worldliness. There is no putting others down. Agape love is the ultimate love of "The Great I Am," in all its glory; it indeed is not a love of this world. This is a love that comes from the spiritual realm of the supernatural. Because of the Mercy of

Agape love, there is a feeling of being free, having an illustrious light shine through your entire being, allowing both your spiritual and natural eyes to see everyone and everything in its true beauty. Enhancing your ability through a pure heart and spirit. To actually fill and see the beauty and glory of God. It is intended for everyone, allowing mankind to exchange worldliness to come back to their Heavenly Father by expressing their love to God.

Agape love is the ultimate embodiment of God's supreme power of discipleship in Jesus Christ. When the disciples asked Jesus what the greatest commandment was? Jesus said, **GPS>**"You shall love the LORD your God with all your heart, with all your soul, and with all your mind." With the second commandment, "You shall love your neighbor as yourself." **[Matthew 22:37-40]** It is a tracker that God has breathed into you. It is a very important and priceless part of your spiritual relationship with God. Though you cannot touch God with your bare hands, you are able to show your love and obedience through your behavior by imitating Jesus.

GPS>[Colossians 3:12-14; Ephesians 4:22-24; Deuteronomy 6:5; 1 Corinthians 13: -4-8; Romans 5:7-9, 12:10; 1 John 4:19, 15:13]

CHAPTER 2

The Blessed Trinity

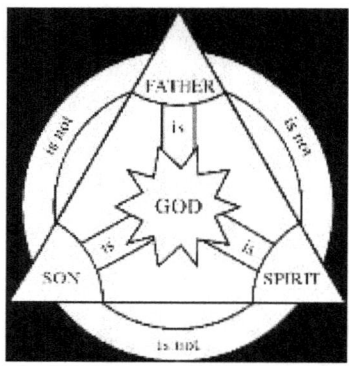

The Blessed Trinity consists of three different persons who are all part of the Godhead in Christianity. There are three persons in one. The Father, The Son, and the Holy Spirit. Each position is unique for its specific purpose. The Father wears 3 hats. They are God the Father, God the Son, and God the Holy Spirit. It is similar to what positions you hold in life. Take, for example, before you got married, you were a son and a brother. Then you got married and became a husband, now wearing three hats; you are a son, brother, and husband. Once you share your seed with your wife, she becomes pregnant. You became a father to the child that was born.

Now, wearing four hats, when your sibling gives birth, you become an uncle. This is how the concept of the Blessed Trinity is. It is God having three different roles he plays, just like you, being a son, a brother, a husband, a father, and an uncle. Each of these positions has different responsibilities and characteristics. Same for a woman; she being a daughter, a sister, a wife, a mother, an auntie, a grandmother, and it continues. Each title fits the physical position you are filling at that time. **GPS>**"Yet for us, there is one God, the Father, from whom are all things and for whom we exist, and one Lord, Jesus Christ, through whom we exist." **[1 Corinthians 8:6]** The first position of the Holy Trinity is that of "God the Father." God has this title because He is the Creator of all things. He is the Lord of history; he is the beginning and the end. He is El Elyon, the Judge; God the Father is the Alpha and Omega. GPS>[Revelation 22:13; Matthew 19:26]

JESUS CHRIST, THE SON OF GOD

The second part of the Blessed Trinity is Jesus Christ. The Son of God is he who was created of a human woman and impregnated through the Holy Spirit, replacing a male human. Jesus Christ brought the Word of God, the Father, providing guidance for all of humanity on earth. Instructing how to live and survive on Earth. **GPS>**"Do not believe that I am in the Father and the Father is in me? The words that I say to you I do not speak on my own, but the Father who dwells in me does his works." **[John 14:10]** The Son of God, Jesus Christ, became a living sacrifice, as the Lamb of God took away all the sins of the world. Jesus is the Way, the Truth, and the Life. Becoming your needed Savior, bringing salvation and redemption to all. While renewing your mind, freeing you from all condemnation, bondage, and Spiritual death. Jesus came as a servant to all, being obedient to the will of His Father. Jesus is also your advocate when you pray to the Heavenly Father. It is the face of His only begotten Son he sees when you error. God does not see any unworthiness in you. Read your Bible, and you will see all the blessed titles that define the Power and Authority of Jesus. In order to be part of Jesus, you must have the Spirit of Christ within you. Allowing him to speak to your soul, giving you life in the Spirit, and walking in the Spirit. Causing you to be spiritually minded, bringing life and peace.

GPS>[Psalm 100:3; Mark 16:15; Luke 9:20-22; Mark 13:2; John 3:16; Ephesians 2:10; Romans 8:1; Philippians 2:9; Romans 6:6, 8:]

GOD THE HOLY SPIRIT

The third part of the Blessed Trinity is the Holy Spirit upon leaving earth to return to sit on the right side of His Father. Jesus has compassion for you, knowing that he will no longer be walking among you. Asked the Father to send a comforter. God did, sending the third part of the Blessed Trinity as the Holy Spirit. The purpose of the Holy Spirit is to confirm the existence of Jesus Christ. Enforcing the Word of God, which Jesus taught while he was on earth. He is to remind you of what you have heard, read, learned, and know about the Word of God through Jesus. Encouraging you to apply all the teachings of Christ to your life journey. The Holy Spirit answers prayers that you have not spoken.

He hears your groans and moans, including silent and seen tears. He knows what you need. Acknowledge your sin and ask God to shower you with Righteousness.

GPS>"But you will receive power when the Holy Spirit has come upon you, and you will be my witnesses in Jerusalem and in all Judea and Samaria, and to the end of the earth." **[Acts 1:8]** The Holy Spirit is your conscience, guiding you into all Truths. He guides you with wisdom for both the natural and spiritual journey you travel. Jogging your memory to follow the Spirit walking by faith and not by sight. Helping you defeat the sinfulness of worldly living. Prompting you to remember who you are in Christ Jesus.

GPS>[Psalm 119:105; Proverbs 3:5-8; Philippians 4:8; Matthew 5:3; Revelations 1:4-6; Roman 6:1-34]

FEAR OF THE LORD

Good Fear of the Lord#1

There are two types of "Fear of the LORD." One type is when you show homage to your Creator, which is God. **GPS>**"The fear of the Lord is the beginning of wisdom, and knowledge of the Holy One is understanding." **[Proverbs 9:10]** Giving thanks is a way of acknowledging that He, God, does exist. Just as anyone appreciates being told that they are loved and given recognition for their qualities. Most are often communicated by word of mouth, physical gestures such as applauding, singing, dancing, giving notes/cards, pats on the back, and gifts. Showing the honored one praise and respect for something they had done. Having no catch, just unconditional admiration, recognition, sincere praise, and love for them.

These same mindsets and exhibits are most definitely also due to God! Fearing God is knowing God, and this is where true wisdom lies. It teaches you that you must submit to God's will, and by doing so, you acquire wisdom that leads you to higher spiritual growth in walking in the Holy Spirit as a follower of Jesus Christ. Through the death of Christ, you are now the adopted child of Abba Father, through Christ Jesus. Having this mindset is the correct way of having "Fear of God," as being respectful, obedient, a loving heart. Seeing God's guidance as a blessing provides help when you follow it. There are different ways that you can express your genuine love for Him.

The good type of Fear of the Lord is wanting to have a deep desire to know, love, trust, and serve the Lord. Having a fear of the Lord is the same as having a fear of your parent(s). This type of fear is a mixture of having respect that causes you to be obedient to the rules and guidelines that have been given to you. Having the understanding that if you disobey, you will have to deal with the consequences that are to follow, varying in methods of discipline. The Lord does chastise you, his child, because he cares and loves you.

Always wants only the best for you, for he is faithful. Protecting you from the pits of hell and the snare of temptations due to a worldly lifestyle. Your heavenly Father wants to protect you, just as your earthly parent(s). This is a good kind of fear of God, which is of awe and wonder, having a holy respect and reverence for Him. This type of fear of God is a mixture of discipline, homage, tribute, and having respect that causes you to be obedient. This is the same type of fear that Jehovah, your Creator, expects from you. The Ten Commandments are an excellent resource for gaining an understanding of the Lord and a healthy way to fear God in love and amazement. Having the understanding that if you disobey them, your life journey will be blessed.

There should be a daily relationship with the LORD. Yahweh must not be treated as if He is only a parent with weekend privileges. Jehovah is a Full-Time Father 24/7; when you sleep, he is still working, providing for you in every area of your life. Today, tomorrow, and tomorrow, be wise and learn to submit to God's Will, for you are a seed sent from heaven. Now, here on earth, with the purpose of being an agent of the Lord. Helping your brothers and sisters get back to where they belong, which is in the mindset of Christ, leading them to Eternal Life. Understand that there are actually two jurisdictions in play while on your life journey. One is the jurisdiction of "The Kingdom of Light," where Jesus is the door to enter through, finding Jesus, the doorway to Eternal Life. The second jurisdiction is the "Kingdom of Darkness." Due to a lack of knowledge, your imagination is corrupt, leading you to confusion and fear.

Where Satan rules, this jurisdiction of evil. Whenever you are in a jurisdiction, being Light or Dark, rules apply, with all in the spiritual realm knowing and obeying them in accordance. **GPS>**"For God hath not given us the spirit of fear; but of power, and of love, and of a sound mind." **[2 Timothy 1:7]** GPS>**[Proverbs 15:32]**

Erroneous Fear of The Lord #2

The other type of "Fear of the Lord" is when you have been disobedient, not listening to the Holy Spirit. This is an incorrect mindset of having a fear of God. It consists of being afraid of God, seeing God as cruel, controlling, mean, unforgiving, and a dictator who is uncaring, selfish, and far away. Wreaking havoc in your life. This is a stronghold, which is an incorrect way of thinking.

Possibly, you see God as mean and a bully. This type of thinking is ideal for the enemy. Satan, who actually sets you up for failure, wants you to see God as a punisher. Having this kind of fear of God is that of an enemy, which is good be you yourself. As in the spelling and sound of the word enemy, it could be [in is me or in me]. Meaning that you lack knowledge and understanding, and your heart is lacking in love. You may have heard the saying, "Knowledge is power." Knowledge is truly powerful. It can take you from darkness to light. The antidote for ignorance is wisdom. When wisdom is applied to both earthly and spiritual needs, it is the light in any situation. Many people are lost because of their lack of knowledge and lack of understanding of God's Word. You lack wisdom, which is, for certain, a sure way to fall into a ditch of demise in the world. While you are blind spiritually, Jesus says, for those who lack knowledge, ask.

Your Father in heaven is like your human parents. He gives you ample chances, including various types of warnings, to address the action, behavior, or path that you are following. Your heavenly Father will step right in and pull that rope that's been given to you as free will, allowing your ability to make choices. You can tell when you have been acting unrighteous. That is because all of humanity has been given a conscious. That shows you right from wrong. This is through the Holy Spirit. The Holy Spirit is not your friend! He is the Truth of God. Many of the circumstances that you encounter are because of your being in the dark and liking it, because you are trying to hide your sinfulness.

GPS>"For everyone who does wicked things hates the light and does not come to the light, lest his works should be exposed. But whoever does what is true comes to the light, so that it may be clearly seen that his works have been carried out in God." Your Father in heaven is like your human parents. He gives you ample chances, including various types of warnings addressing the action(s), behavior, and paths that you are following. You can tell when you have been acting unrighteous. That is because you were given a conscious by Jehovah, enabling you to know right from wrong.

Be aware, tho, that the Lord will step right in, pulling that rope of free will that He gave, allowing you to make choices when you have gone too far. God will chastise you, learn, and become wise from them all. **GPS>**"A wise man will hear, and will increase learning, and a man of understanding shall attain unto wise counsels." **[Proverbs 1:5]** Many of the various circumstances that you encounter are because of your being in the jurisdiction of sin and death.

Opening a way for evil to enter through your corrupt imagination, which causes you to be hoodwinked by the devil, sabotaging you from receiving blessings, which you can only receive by repenting. Having a sincere, heartfelt remorse for all of your sins, being willing to be held accountable for them, confessing them to God, asking for forgiveness, and making a vow [Covenant]with God to turn completely around from all sinfulness. Facing Jesus, letting him lead the way to righteousness, truth, and life. Becoming baptized in the name of Jesus and accepting Jesus Christ as your Lord and Savior.

GPS>[Psalms 121:1; 1 Peter 3:14; Proverbs 1:5-7, 9:10-12, 15:5-15; John 3:20; James 1:5-8, 4:3-12]

CHAPTER 3

God's Grace, Mercy & Compassion

What is Grace? Grace is giving you something that you don't deserve.

It is something that you cannot earn, and it is a spiritual gift from God. Through the grace of God, you receive love, eternal comfort, and good hope. Jesus' mother, Mary, who was engaged to be married to a man named Joseph, was full of grace as it was declared by the angel Gabriel, who was sent by God. GPS>[Luke 1:28-32] **Grace Consists of Five Divine Portions:**

[G] God's generous goodness

[R] Restoration through His Resurrection

[A] Authoritative Power

[C] Compassion for He Cares and Cherishes

[E] Eternal Life given through His glorious essence

The goodness of God brings back the authority that you lost when you sinned, causing a separation from God. Through the Resurrection Power of God, you are restored to righteousness, shown compassion, and guided to eternal life. Grace causes you to attain Spiritual attributes that build your character in honor, Spiritual growth, thanksgiving, wisdom, and love. It establishes in you an enthusiasm that wells up as that of an overflowing spout of "Living Water." Purifying you to excel in helping others, being nonjudgmental, and being in obedience to the will of God. Showing love to anyone, anytime, anywhere, regardless of their circumstances.

Although these characteristics are each unique in themselves, when put together, they equal Grace. Grace is the essence of God; it is all of what He is, which is Love. Encompassing salvation and truth, for without a scrupulous love, there can be no Grace. A global trumpet has blown, notifying you of only half of what God wants to do in the world. You may not realize it, but you are overwhelmingly blessed. God is a "Now, God! Faith is now! When you walk by faith and not by sight, you are experiencing this miraculous power, for by grace, you have been saved through faith. You have been given a portion of grace from the Father that gives you hope. This, indeed, is not by your own doing; it is a gift of your Creator. It is not a result of the work you've done, so there is no way you can boast. Declare these things; exhort and rebuke with all authority. Let no one disregard you. Stay prayerful, grateful, and receive the grace of God, which is good for your soul and you.

GPS>[Titus 2:11-14]

MERCY

What is Mercy? Mercy is giving you something that you don't deserve. Mercy is having the authority to inflict punishment for failing to meet the agreements of a contract. Instead, you show leniency, choosing not to enforce any sanctions on the person. Mercy shows compassion and grace to anyone. There are times when someone is in need, and you contribute whatever you can in a generous manner, wanting no accolades. Mercy shows tolerance when needed in situations where exhibiting patience is required. Mercy is being sympathetic and supportive to others.

Edifying them by encouragement and lifting up their spirit through God's Word. Mercy is having forgiveness regardless of the sin. Mercy allows love, charity, softhearted, and wisdom to flow freely, blessing all through a domino effect of love. Between the parties, magnanimity is established through kindness and forbearance. Mercy has no self-indulgence; it is grace for all humanitarian purposes. Let the lights of tenderness, pity, humility, and the love of God be used to bring Him peace. All of these things describe the infinite Love of God that He shows to you daily, giving Him all the Glory. Regardless of your sinful nature, at each daybreak, God gives you new, limitless Mercy. Declaring that you are worthy of his Mercy and love.

GPS>[Matthew 18:23-35; John 3:16; Colossians 3:12-14]

Compassion also consists of the giving and receiving of God's Love. It means that the Love God has placed in your heart is to be given freely to others. In order to be able to give love, you must have a heart that is open to receive it. Having a heart that is filled with bitterness, unforgiveness, and unrighteousness is not capable of receiving love. Your heart must be clean of all darkness, with no bitter stones in it. Compassion is also loving unconditionally without motive or trickery.

God has so much compassion and love for humanity that he sent His only Son, Jesus, to tell you that you are loved dearly by the Heavenly Father. Being compassionate is having an inner feeling that convicts you to help, sympathizing with the victim(s)in solidarity to understand their plight. God's love is putting light and good air back into your struggles and worldly situations.

GPS>[Ephesians 4:22-24; Colossians 3:12; John 6:1-14; Deuteronomy 6:5; 1 Corinthians 13: -4-8; Romans 5:7-9]

CHAPTER 4

Not Trusting God

Many people don't trust God. This is so amazing because wheneveryou start a new job. It usually requires you to work for two weeks before you get your first paycheck. Yet you trust these people you do not know. You don't even get a written or verbal confirmation that you will get paid. It was a given, and you were just like a mute, shaking your head in agreement. Extending your hand to shake with the person who said you werehired. Isn't it ironic how you don't trust God?

Some say it is because they can't see Him. You don't see who is processing your check(s), but you trust them. When you make purchases online, you are given a date by which the items are to bedelivered. You have no qualms. You can easily trust what the computer screen shows from the vendor. Requesting *payment first* before receiving the item(s).Here, you trust both an unknown and unseen person[vendor], who has programmed the computer to interact with you, gaining your trust. Trusting them, you provide your most personal and valuable information to a stranger.

That good ole debit card number, charge account number, including the *secret* CVN number. Now you've not seen nor even heard the voice of anyone. Yet you have given your most pertinent and private information by phone or any mobile device, including your computer. Yet you trust them! Hoping to receive an order confirmation number, which is merely a floating promise from an unseen and unknown stranger from anywhere on earth. Confirming that your order request has been received, acknowledged, and will be processed.

Though there is a given (ETA) estimated time of arrival still there are times when the arrival date is not honored. What do you do? You wait, hoping that the item(s) ordered will come when it is supposed to be delivered. What happens when you don't receive the item(s)on the ETA date given by the vendor's programmed computer system? Sometimes, there is not even a new ETA; what then? Sure, you can complain by calling you reach out to the vendor's customer service department.

Though there is no guarantee, again, you trust unknown sources that have already taken your money from your debit or charge card. Now, what do you do after trusting the vendor, not once but twice, waiting again for your paid items to be delivered, are a no-show? Metaphorically, there you are, sitting like a little baby on the floor with a wet, itchy diaper. That is not yet able to walk, so you rock on your little fat thighs, scooting around on the floor. You are upset, wet, and uncomfortable. You start to cry while flapping your little baby's hands, making gestures of a bird flapping its wings.

You feel frustrated, angry, and anxious, yet you trusted the unknown, unseen vendor. So why can't you trust the one who actually created you, GOD?" The one who knows your life story because He had established it before you were physically in existence? "God is the author and finisher of your faith." Yet you have trust and hope for the best in man and in the world, which neither have a love for you; all they have to give you is disappointment, painful situations, doubt, betrayal, loss, and all the issues of life, which are all to kill, steal, and destroy you. Trust God; He knows your needs and is the source to pray to and ask for help regarding all matters and circumstances that you will encounter.

You can trust an unseen person with your earthly treasures, but you don't trust GOD? You trust the trash pickup men who pick up the trash. Sometimes, there are unforeseen reasons why your trash doesn't get picked up. You believe that it's going to rain when that knee that has arthritis in it starts to ache when it gets colder. You trust this guidance, yet you won't trust your heavenly Abba Father. He knows all your aches and pains. Still, you trust those who say that they will help you and be with you in your time of need, be it emotionally, financially, physically, or in any way that they can. But when you do need them, what can they do?

They are human, just like you, experiencing their own journey of trials, tribulations, tests, and fears. No one can help you like Jesus. Just saying the name of Jesus has the power to turn any chain of bondage that you are facing into being broken, removing you from darkness to light. Trusting God is a commitment to having a relationship that is pure.

GPS>[Jeremiah 17:5; Deuteronomy 1:31-36; Micah 7:5-6; Proverbs 28:26; Hebrews 3:12; Psalm 37:7]

A Fool Says There Is No God In His Heart

How ludicrous is this? Just waking up in the morning that in itself a definition of the power of God. Try holding your breath for a couple of minutes. You can't! Because it is not yours to begin with. God gave you the "Breath of Life." When He breathed His breath into you, you became a living creature. You are His creation of His workmanship. You did not make yourself. Even when you propitiate, God is in the midst of that entire process from the beginning of life until its end. What about nature? What causes it to know when to blossom? How does the ocean know how far it should go? Look at the ants, the bees, the birds, how all have been exquisitely, wonderfully, and fearfully made by God. **GPS>**"O LORD, how great are thy works! And thy thoughts are very deep. A brutish man knoweth not; neither doth a fool understand this." **[Psalm 92:5-6]**

Even if the egg came first, it had to be created by some higher power, and that is God, your Heavenly Abba Father Hallelujah! There are scientists who have scientific explanations (s), but where did the knowledge come from to provide them with the ways to know how to calculate, learn, and see these things? God makes "all" things happen. There are others who believe a big explosion in outer space caused the universe to be created. If so, then who caused the Big Bang? Where did the matter come from? Surely, they see the sky every morning unless they are physically blind. Even hearing the birds chirp says this is bigger than you. What is sustaining you right this moment?

All your accomplishments aren't because you climbed the ladder, knew the right people, had the right education, and have made millions. All of these earthly accomplishments have been synchronized and orchestrated through the direction of God. Many are the plans in the mind of a man, but it is the purpose of the LORD that will stand. True, you worked hard to get where you are, but God put you where you were supposed to be at that time. God gave you the ability to learn how to use the talents that you have been given, which are a gift(s) to you when you were born, to bring Glory to Him.

Think of the arrogance one has to think they have caused everything to line up perfectly in their lives. They are in a mindset of pride, showing disrespect to God, the Creator of all things. Maybe non-believers see themselves as a god. Believing that he, a mere man, has made his destiny. It is so foolish to think this way. Seriously, nothing is an accident or a coincident, nor is luck involved in your life journey. It is all directed by God. **GPS>**"The wisdom of the prudent is to give thought to their ways, but the folly of fools is deception. "Fools mock others that are repentant to God for the guilt they feel for sinning, but goodwill is found among the upright." **[Proverbs 14:7-9]** God is alive just as Satan is, and it is God who has the ultimate control over all, including Satan.

Satan has no power over God. "A fool says there is no God." Yet Satan is their God. Satan is a wannabe; he is God's messenger, his heavy, carrying out the wrath of God. Satan can only do what God allows him to do. Satan is a fallen angel from heaven due to his wanting to be above God. Satan fell to earth, where he is now in charge of all the foolishness, sin, wickedness, and darkness in the earth's realm and others. Satan has been assigned a limited amount of time to get as many souls as he can before the Rapture," begins. There are "fools" that don't worship God the Father nor Satan; they worship themselves. The description of a fool is a silly or stupid person, a person who lacks judgment or sense. Formerly kept by a person of royalty or nobility around for amusement, such as the "Court Fool."

Don't be led by a fool, scriptures say, **GPS>**"The blind leading the blind; both fall into a ditch." **[Matthew 15:14]** Therefore, when you follow someone who is ignorant of a subject, such as knowing that God loves them. You both are spiritually blind, lacking knowledge and understanding, having no wisdom. Providing a way for the enemy to corrupt your mind by keeping you in darkness and foolishness. Where you are being guided by someone else who is equally uninformed as you are. Bringing fear and disobedience, exposing ignorance of the light and love of God. There is no excuse for staying in ignorance. God has provided you with the righteous way to gain Spiritual wisdom by just asking. **GPS>**"If any of you lack wisdom, he should ask God, who gives generously to all without finding fault, and it will be given to him, but let him ask in faith, nothing wavering. For he that wavereth is like a wave of the sea driven with the wind and tossed." **[James 1:5-6]**

Know that you have the ability through God, asking Him in faith, believing that there is only one true God. Having no doubt. Accepting Jesus Christ, the Son of God, as your Lord and Savior, the way, the truth, and the life. Confessing your sin(s) with a truly remorseful and repentant heart. Asking God for forgiveness, vowing to turn your back on your sinful mindset. Following the Holy Spirit, walking in faith and not by sight, no longer obeying the flesh. Receiving God's love, blessings, and truth leads to Eternal Life. God is always with you, always providing a way for you to find a way through any fear, trouble, trial, and tribulation. God is faithful and true, not at all whishy-washy. God is faithful and is true. He is the same today as he was yesterday and will be forever.

GPS>[Psalms 14:1; Hebrews 10:23,13:8; Revelation 1:8, 20:1-3,7-10; Isaiah 14:12-14; Ephesians 1:11; Proverbs 1:7-9, 22; 23:7-9; 115:5-8]

No One Can Serve Two Masters

This verse from the Bible is teaching you about loyalty. What is Loyalty? Loyalty is having a sincere commitment to something or someone that causes you to stand by them and your decision about them. Being loyal means you don't care what anyone says or does; you are standing firm in your belief, which you are adamant about.

Regardless of the outcome, no matter what others may say or believe. Loyalty is placing others before yourself, devoting yourself to someone or a possession. Being loyal means you feel that you have a duty to that person or thing in serving. Loyalty may also be directed to a credence you have. It doesn't matter if it is good or bad; in this bond, your sincere dedication is to oblige that person or thing faithfully in all areas. Loyalty is the willingness to die for a person, having a strong commitment, in selflessness, honesty, trust, faithfulness, a belief, or a thing.

When you are loyal, you have placed all your belief, hope, and dedication toward a doctrine, person, or possession. Pledging your allegiance to that cause affects your way of thinking. The Blessed messages and promises of God are proven and real. Jesus is your Savior and the Way. He is the Solution to every problem and attack. Jesus is what loyalty looks like, giving His life willing for the cause, which was to save humanity from damnation. You should be giving God the highest level of exaltation. He is Glorious, that is loyalty. The loyalty that Jesus has for you is priceless. There is no way that you could ever achieve the ability to repay Jesus for His Loyalty. Jesus served one master, and that was his Father, your Creator.

There is no way you can have that type of devotion that can be divided to give to another so intensely. In fact, if there was another person or thing that demanded this type of devotion, you would resent them for putting pressure on you. Believing that money and material things can bring you complete happiness is ludicrous. When you die, you cannot take anything with you. The Egyptians proved this with records of their elaborate burial rites and beliefs that after death, they needed material props that they had in the natural world. Little to say, they were wrong, and many artifact collectors and grave robbers have gotten wealthy on those precious items they felt were so important for the next life.

Money is great to have when used for good things. God wants you to be wealthy. He wants you to be a witness to His power, might, majesty, and Glory. Don't put money first to purchase props that God has allowed to be placed in your life while on your life journey, when you put money or anything in front of the one True Living God. Making other items your god and idols. If you are not serving God, then who are you serving? You, your friend(s), trying to please and impress them? Beware, God is a jealous God, and he will get your attention one way or another. He will cause you to let go of temporal idols and props, asking His forgiveness. Read the scriptures in the Holy Bible; they are life for your survival.

It is the Power of God through Jesus and the Holy Spirit, which is a righteous life vest for you to wear, leading you to Eternal Life. The Word of God is loyal to you, for God is faithful. He is the same today, yesterday, and tomorrow, not like the so-called friends of this world. This is the loyalty you are to show God by being loyal to His Blessed Word with unwavering faith. The one that you are dedicated to is the one that you tell your most personal secrets to, let that be Jesus. So, choose this day as to who you will serve, God or man? Give God your loyalty, standing firm in your belief in Him.

Show your dedication and love through Jesus being a willing servant and warrior for humanity. Loyalty may require compromise and even sacrificing one's personal needs or priorities at times. Nevertheless, the result makes a tighter moral and Spiritual relationship. Loyalty also helps promote very strong emotional, healthy, and psychological direction in obedience, leading to righteousness.

GPS>[Matthew 4:3-11, 5:1-26:24; Luke 10:19, 16:13; Proverbs 3:5-6; Joshua 24:15; John 16:33].

CHAPTER 5

7 *Gifts Of The Holy Spirit*

The 7 Gifts of the Holy Spirit are Spiritual Gifts given to those who believe in God. Each gift is named for the specific blessing of wisdom and guidance it holds. These gifts benefit both the natural and supernatural realms, teaching you how to walk in the Spirit.

The Gift of Wisdom provides you with intelligence in handling various situations with tact and love.

The Gift of Understanding grants comprehension in situations, allowing you to grasp concepts that guide intelligent behavior.

The Gift of Counsel removes your ego, helping you recognize when additional help is needed. It relates to the mind, knowing when to step back and seek assistance from those with more experience and wisdom than you.

The Gift of Fortitude gives you the patience to believe and trust in God's deliverance. Through courage, perseverance, and strength, you will witness the fruition of solutions, bringing victorious outcomes to any situation.

The Gift of Piety is a virtue involving respect, teaching you how to treat others with reverence and humility.

The Gift of Fear of the Lord is the beginning of wisdom, granting you access to the promises you have the right to ask for, leading to an abundant life and, ultimately, Eternal Life.

All of these gifts help you influence others by being an example of wisdom and counseling instead of pridefulness. They strengthen you to persevere and succeed, giving you the spiritual ability to see the ultimate power and might of God working in all situations. This strengthens your faith in trusting and believing, allowing you to thank God even before your victory. He is the author and finisher of your faith. He is to be honored, obeyed, loved, and feared. He is the Creator of All Life, and all is to give Him glory.

THE FRUIT OF THE HOLY SPIRIT

The Fruit of the Holy Spirit is singular, but it has 9 different segments, like an orange, each bearing its own distinctive spiritual virtue as a guide for living a godly and righteous life, walking in God's love and wisdom. In essence, it is the gifts of the Holy Spirit that are the result of the 9 segments of the Fruit of the Holy Spirit. These virtuous wedges are what you digest spiritually, providing you with nutrients and enabling you to gain the revelation of "Christ's knowledge," guiding you to deliverance and salvation.

GPS>"But the fruit of the Spirit is love, joy, peace, long-suffering, gentleness, goodness, faith, meekness, temperance: against such, there is no law." **[Galatians 5:22-23]**

You are enabled to solve all your problems by using these gifts and applying them to the issues of life. They bear fruit in helping you gain an understanding of the deep truths of God. These gifts help you confidently apply what you've learned, sharing love, joy, and peace with your family and others. Long-suffering is a fruit that you may shun, but it is through this virtue that you become patient, strengthening your character in learning how to endure with and without.

These fruits cause you to surrender all your concerns to God in faith, empowering you to make decisions no longer using the world's chaotic and sinful ways. You now follow the ways of Christ. Though your path may be narrow, it will lead you to eternal life. All of these attributes help you grow in virtuous character, adhering to the ways of Christ and advancing His truth and wisdom through the emerging Fruit of the Spirit. In the Fruit of Love, you find true love.

Be sure to set your GPS for the first stop: Heaven, which leads to your final destination—Eternal Life. Through the consumption of the Fruit of the Spirit, you will not perish while on your journey. These pieces help to restore your mind, spirit, and soul as you travel on your Life Journey Road. There may be times when the GPS seems incorrect due to circumstances beyond your control, connected to the spiritual warfare happening in and around the heavens.

Now, you've reached a pivotal point on your journey. Indulge in consuming the Fruit of the Spirit, applying them in your travels, and sharing them with others you meet along the way. Be a humble servant on your journey, giving glory to God and being obedient and faithful to others on their journeys. Show genuine repentance while establishing a relationship with

God. Make sure to have your favorite scriptures to guide you as you travel on your spiritual life journey. Be filled with the Fruit of the Spirit. Ensure that you have all the tools needed, seek wisdom at all times, and be rooted and grounded in faith. In obedience, walk by the Spirit through the grace, mercy, and love of God, serving as an ambassador of Christ.

From the Bible, memorize scriptures that will serve as your peace, strength, and everything you need for Eternal Life.

GPS>[Romans 8:31; Galatians 5:22-23; Hosea 4:6; Philippians 4:12-13]

CHAPTER 6

The Ten Commandments

The Ten Commandments are pertinent teaching tools addressing ethics, health, scruples, respecting others' property, honor, and conscience. Comprised of the first four commandments addressing God. Along with the remaining addressing mankind. The laws were to establish and bring order to everyone's life. They are pertinent directives providing guidelines for living on earth in peace and victory. **GPS>**"For the commandment is a lamp, and the law is light, and reproofs of instructions are a way of life." **[Proverbs 6:23]**

Study these to help be a basic guide while navigating both your physical and spiritual journey. These same commandments have not changed over the ages and are still just as powerful when given to Moses on Mount Sinai, demanding obedience in following these sacred ordinances given by God, which are:

1. You shall have no other gods before me.

2. You shall not make or worship idols.

3. You shall not take the name of the LORD your God in vain.

4. You are to remember the Sabbath day and to keep it holy.

5. You are to honor your Father and your mother.

6. You shall not kill.

7. You shall not commit adultery.

8. You shall not steal.

9. You shall not bear false witness against your neighbor.

10. You shall not covet thy neighbor's wife nor their goods.

GPS>[Exodus 20:8-11; Deuteronomy 4:2; Malachi 3:6; Isaiah 66:23; Genesis 2:2-3; Leviticus 27:1-34]

WHAT IS THE PURPOSE OF PRAYER?
P=PRAISE, R=REPENT, A=ASK, Y=YIELD

Prayer is communicating with God the Father; it is a means of having a relationship with him. Prayer is a solemn expression of requesting help and offering praises to God. Prayer is done to draw nearer to God, having an intimate relationship, expressing your soul to the Lord. Prayer is not seeking your own will but seeking to align yourself with the will of God. There are many forms of prayer, such as prayers of praise, thanksgiving, help, repentance, confession, honor, love, worship, forgiveness, and paying homage to God. Prayers may be done alone or in groups, expressed through walking, singing, standing, playing instruments, whispering, dancing, kneeling, speaking in tongues, crying, shouting, hymns, talking, respectfully, tearfully, and in reverent fear, and clapping, to name a few methods of praying.

Acknowledging Jehovah, in adoration, using both your voice and Spirit to speak praises, in humility acknowledging and giving glory to who He is, the Creator of heaven and earth, "The Great I am," "Alpha and Omega," "The Beginning and the End," shows that you love, cherish, and worship your Abba Father. Prayer is how you can present your requests, thanksgivings, adoration, and faith, knowing that you are His child and that He is faithful in hearing and answering your prayers as they are counted as incense before Him.

Prayer is powerful and effective, giving God glory and helping you to receive forgiveness. **GPS>**"Let my prayer be counted as incense before you, and the lifting up of my hands as the evening sacrifice!" **[Psalm 141:2]** Just as an individual who is the target of affection looks down seeing his child's arms lifted up, this is what God your heavenly Father sees when you, his child on earth, lift your arms up, including when you cry out, in hope, trust, acknowledgment, and homage, saying Abba Father! This is how you are to pray, expressing your love for Jehovah, your almighty creator.

Raising your arms is a gesture of surrender, a demonstration of trust, an act of asking for help, for love, for attention, for giving recognition, or just to be lifted up higher than you were, which makes you feel better. This is the same concept as a toddler crying out for whatever reason(s) to get noticed. This method is the same for you as an adult to use. **GPS>**"Rejoice evermore. Pray without ceasing. In everything, give thanks: for this is the will of God in Christ Jesus concerning you." **[1 Thessalonians 5:16-19]**

Prayer is a combination of repentance, which, once you are forgiven, makes way for you to ask in humility for the yielding of the favor of the Lord, blessing you with more abundance in every area of your life. Your Beloved Abba Father must not be treated as the parent that has only visitations from you, due to date and time restrictions, allocated in order to have a relationship with Him! Your Heavenly Father is not a weekend-only parent. He is available twenty-four hours a day. Prayer is paying homage to your Abba Father, your Creator, your Daddy, your God, who is the Solution and conduit to all of life. Having faith in all of our petitions to God with the belief that HE hears us, and for any request you have, you know that it will come to pass if it is in God's will for you. Giving praise and worshiping the Father should be done daily, throughout the day. The primary purpose of prayer is to change you, not to change circumstances.

GPS>[1 Timothy 2:8; Hebrews 4:16; James 5:16; Jude 1:20-21; Philippians 4:6]

THE OUR FATHER PRAYER AND ITS MEANING

[Matthew 6:9-13] Also known as the 7 Petitions]

1. OUR FATHER, WHICH ART IN HEAVEN, HALLOWED BE THY NAME.

This sentence acknowledges that God is our Heavenly Father, giving Him honor, praising HIM for who He is, and that His name is Holy. This sentence acknowledges that God is our Heavenly Father, giving Him.

2. THY KINGDOM COME. THY WILL BE DONE IN EARTH, AS IT IS IN HEAVEN.

Here, you pay homage to God for His infinite wisdom, authority, and power over all the universe. That there is a Heavenly Kingdom, and in that Kingdom, God reigns. It is His will that rules and that His will be done both on earth and in heaven, under God's will. God's Will is done, as He reigns both on earth and in heaven.

3. GIVE US THIS DAY OUR DAILY BREAD.

God is our complete provider for every sector of our lives, so we are asking Him to continue to provide our needs. He is the guidance for our life journey.

4. AND FORGIVE US OUR DEBTS, AS WE FORGIVE OUR DEBTORS.

Asking God to forgive us for our sinful nature, knowing that only He can do this, in obedience, we forgive those who have sinned against us.

5. AND LEAD US NOT INTO TEMPTATION, BUT DELIVER US FROM EVIL.

Aware that there are all forms of temptation all around us, we ask God not to tempt us.

6. BUT DELIVER US FROM EVIL.

Asking God to rescue and deliver us from destructive behaviors and all forms of sinfulness.

7. FOR THINE IS THE KINGDOM, AND THE POWER, AND THE GLORY, FOREVER.

It is God's Kingdom; His absolute authority, mightiness, power, and magnificence reign are endless.

AMEN

**Means all men are in agreement with any prior statements. Note: There is a shorter version in Luke

THE LORD IS MY SHEPHERD PRAYER [PSALM 23]

The Lord is my shepherd;

God is my provider; He supplies all my needs, and He is my protector. He would give His life for you. He is a protector and defense.

I shall not want

You need nothing.

He maketh me to lie down in green pastures:

God gives you a place to rest that is peaceful and is abundant in resources, and lush.

He leadeth me beside the still waters.

God takes you to a serene, peaceful place that allows time to focus on God.

He restoreth my soul:

God's Holy Spirit rejuvenates you when you are in need

He leadeth:

God guides you on the path of salvation and deliverance.

He leadeth me in the paths of righteousness for his name's sake.

God guides me on the roads of uprightness because You are one of His children. You have the name of I am. [i.e., I am a child of God]

Yea, though I walk through the valley of the shadow of death,

Yet, I have gone astray from following the path that God set me on. Now, because of disobedience, I am facing worldly issues that can lead to my demise.

I will fear no evil:

I am not afraid of any wickedness, for God is with me and has given me the victory.

for thou art with me;

God is always with you

thy rod and thy staff. They comfort me.

The power and authority of God soothe your soul, giving you peace.

Thou preparest a table before me in the presence of mine enemies:

Your heavenly Father sets up a beautiful buffet and charcuterie board for you. Your Father invites all your foes, so-called friends, to your banquet. Showing your reward for being obedient.

Thou anointest my head with oil;

God, your Father, places His hand on your head with the consecrated crown of glory, caring and emitting divine blessings. [The Lord gives strength to his people; the LORD blesses his people with peace. Psalms 29:11]

My cup runneth over.

You have an award along with numerous spoken prayers, anointings, dedications, accolades, and honor, and you have an overflow of great promises, goodness, mercy, forgiveness, prosperity, wisdom, protection, and all that one would want.

Surely goodness and mercy shall follow me all the days of my life:

For certain righteousness, compassion, grace, and leniency.

And I will dwell in the house of the Lord forever.

Also, I will reside in the presence of God, settled in spirit, worshiping Him eternally.

THE SERENITY PRAYER

God grant me the serenity. To accept the things I cannot change, Courage to change the things I can; And wisdom to know the difference. Living one day at a time; Enjoying one moment at a time; Accepting hardships as the pathway to peace; Taking, as He did, this sinful world as it is, not as I would have it; Trusting that He will make all things right If I surrender to His Will; So that I may be reasonably happy in this life and supremely happy with Him Forever and ever in the next. Amen.

RHEMA WORD

Have you ever heard a word in your head that came out of the blue? This is what a Rhema word is: a word that is spoken by God to a specific individual. The Greek word rhéma simply means "any spoken word." In the New Testament, there are two different Greek words used to identify words from God: logos, which are written words from God. The single powerful Rhema Word is made alive in your present day through the Holy Spirit, bringing guidance to you for your specific request and need. Peter never walked on water by reading about the Israelite crossing the Red Sea.

Peter requested Jesus to command him to walk on the water. **GPS>**"And Peter answered Him, Lord, if it is you, command me to come to You on the water," and Jesus did just that one time. Peter heard the Rhema Word, "Come," **[Matthew 28-36],** and faith came only to Peter, hearing Jesus answering his specific request, stepped out of the boat, and began to walk on the water, as Jesus was doing. The other disciples did not respond, as the Rhema word was not for them. Jesus did not call them to walk on the water. Jesus knew that they didn't have the faith or necessarily had the desire to do as Peter did at that moment. Even Peter's faith through fear wavered, as he saw himself miraculously walking on the water.

Becoming a wave-driven and tossed by the sea, doubled-minded, in panic, and lacking faith, Peter began to sink. As he cried out, Jesus saved him, brought him out of the sea, and into the boat. And so that miracle was over for that specific time, as faith comes by hearing and hearing by the Rhema Word of God. Trusting in the Lord, wait on the Lord daily, so that you may receive your inspired Word. Jesus spoke of this truth when He said, **GPS>**"Man does not live by bread alone but by every word that comes from the mouth of God." **[Matthew 4:4]** Listen for your Rhema Word daily; it will fill you with the Holy Spirit and life. When you have a prayer request or some situation that you need help with, unable to make a clear decision, wait on the Lord, and you will hear the Rhema word. In the Bible, there are over seventy Rhema Word usages.

GPS>[2 Peter 2:3; John 6:63, 15:7; Romans 10:17]

CHAPTER 7

What Is Religion?

The members are called believers and faithful in expressing their belief in a Supreme deity, which controls all of mankind's existence. There are numerous religious denominations throughout the world, all with their own set of rules for their religion's Supreme deity. Through rituals and traditions, the various deities are shown homage. In each religion, there is a governing party known as the Corporation of the church. Through its help, the church's Corporation decides what devotions, prayers, curriculum, and music are approved. Everything is governed by their own specific agendas related to community outreach programs, the churches, and their practices.

In most religions, there is a contract for the members of the congregation to sign, establishing what is permissible and what is not acceptable behavior in the church, in your home, and out in public. The contract is similar to that of a private club. The pastor distributes the contract to the congregation, instructing them to read it, and if they accept the rules, then they are to sign and return it to the minister. This is what religion is. Its doctrine is keeping you under the Old Testament at its laws, which attaches you with condemnation under the laws of death. Religion causes you to fear, frightening you with such doctrines, which carry punishments of sin and death.

Religion methods that teach fire and brimstone to those who do not follow the teachings of their church are erroneous.

Often sending the message of how you are to get away as fast as you can from Earth. In religion, it also has you running away from Earth. You've heard someone say, "The end of the world is coming!" or seen signs. This is a method used by religion to frighten people. They are not teaching about loving one another, while you come to realize what purpose God has for you to do. Religion doesn't teach you about being under God's grace, having no condemnation, walking in faith, and not by sight. Scriptures in the Bible say. **GPS>**"There is, therefore, now no condemnation to those who are in Christ Jesus, because through Christ Jesus the law of the Spirit, who gives life, has set you free from the law of sin and death."

Being that the law (Old Testament) was powerless to do so because it was weakened by the flesh. Therefore, God sent his own only begotten Son, in the likeness of sinful flesh, to be a sin offering, condemning sin in the flesh for all of humanity. **[Romans 8:1-6]** Those who are clergy and heads of churches, under the guidelines of the Corporation of the church. Have placed themselves as judges over others. There is only one true Judge, El Elyon. Who is not made of corrupted flesh but is "God Most High," a Spirit, having superiority in power, strength, and authority, all in truth and light.

GPS>"There is only one lawgiver and judge, he who is able to save and to destroy. But who are you to judge your neighbors?" **[James 4:12]**

GPS>Proverbs 27:2; Jeremiah 9:23-24]

WHAT IS CHRISTIANITY?

The fundamental belief in Christianity is believing and following the teachings of Jesus Christ of Nazareth. Christianity believes that Jesus Christ took all of humanity's sins by dying on the cross, being buried in a tomb, and, on the third day, being resurrected from the dead. Through the Resurrection Power of God, Jesus is the Savior of the world, bringing salvation to those who have faith in Him. Christianity is focused on having a close personal relationship with God. Rather than doing religion, which follows rules and rituals, which man introduced into their religious practices. Telling you what you can do and what you can't do. In Christianity, the main objective is to build and nourish a close Spiritual relationship with God, being in His presence. Believing that Jesus Christ is your living hope.

As Christians, you believe that faith comes by hearing and hearing the word of God. You do not lean toward your own understanding. **GPS>**"Trust in the LORD with all your heart and lean not on your own understanding; in all your ways acknowledge him, and he will make your paths straight." **[Proverbs 3:5-6]** You understand that there are mysteries of the universe that you don't understand, and that is alright. Some things you as a human don't need to know. Your mind is too small, fragile, and limited to absorb the magnitude of life, existence, death, and beyond.

Christianity is more than that of being a follower of Christ; it is more than belief. It is giving your mind, soul, spirit, and heart to God. It is the maturing of yourself in Christ Jesus, being born again, having a new beginning as a new person, renewed, restored, forgiven, and being baptized in both water and the Holy Spirit. Being a Christian requires you to focus on applying the teachings of Jesus. Let his words guide your behavior, heart, faith, and love. There is no forcing you, strong-arming you, or shaming you into becoming a Christian. It's your own choice when you decide to have a personal experience in spiritual growth gained by receiving the Gifts of the Holy Spirit. Manifesting the Fruit of the Spirit, that you accept of your own accord, in your own timing. In faith, love, trust, and wisdom, having a testimony of the Goodness of God in your life journey.

The Word of God is from Heaven; this is where Jesus came from, bringing the Word of God with Him. Providing you with information and guidance through scriptures in the Bible, which are directly from your heavenly Father. Christianity, no matter the problem(s) you are given, through God, whatever the situation is, God has already set you free from it. God has given you a way to survive any and all temptations, challenges, chaos, and circumstances. He has given you victory. All that's needed is belief, faith, prayer, and trust in God. God is not a liar. He is the same today as He was yesterday, will be tomorrow, and forever. Know that as long as what you are praying for is in God's will, your prayer(s)will be answered.

There are times when the prayer request does not manifest in your life. Knowing that delay or not seeing something you want come to fruition immediately does not mean that God hasn't answered your prayer(s). Christianity educates you in trusting God's senses to imbue knowledge that everything that God does or allows to happen is for your good and His timeline. In Christianity, you are taught to follow the Ten Commandments of God, loving your neighbor as yourself, in forgiveness and unselfishness. Its doctrine is to help others, using your experiences as an eyewitness, declaring the Good News of the Gospel by which you have been victorious through the Word of God and the scriptures in the Bible. Being an example of how to be a disciple of Christ Jesus. Although you don't see it or understand, trust God and pray for understanding.

Christianity teaches you that God is Love, and you should walk, talk, and act in love, for love is the key. Seeing that before Jesus came, it was the kingdom of Satan, where humanity pledged allegiance to that kingdom, walking in darkness. As a result of Jesus' coming, he brought light, God's Love, and the Word. Giving you the freedom to ignore the power of darkness. Having the virtue to witness the illumination of God's Word, building you up, guiding you closer to Eternal Life. Pledging allegiance to God's Kingdom, having the mind of Christ, and not of Satan. In God's kingdom, you must follow the law of love. For through Christ, you have been made free. In view of the fact that in every human, there are two separate natures at play.

In Christianity, the promotion of God being the, when you are a partaker of the Divine nature of God's holiness, you have Holiness in your heart, your mind, and your emotions. Therefore, when you are a partaker of the Divine nature of Satan, in Satan's kingdom, there you experience fear due to ignorance and foolishness that goes on in that kingdom. You have Wickedness in your heart; your flesh leads you, following your corrupt mind and imagination in sinfulness. In Christianity, the promotion of God being the "Sea of Love." Full of compassion, grace, mercy, wisdom, faithfulness, having all that you need to become righteous, living in peace and love.

Christianity, following the scriptures, believes, **GPS>**"And Jesus looking upon them said to them, with men this is impossible, but with God all things are possible. But with man, can do nothing in his own strength or power." **[Matthew 19:26-27]** In Christianity, you believe, trust, and rely on God to take care of everything. You believe that God is your Creator and that His Son Jesus is your Savior's Redeemer. Christians believe that you are in error when you sin, never using the terms "that you are bad, or wrong."

In order to defeat the various daily darts of Satan, his demons, imps, and servants of his court. These are Powerful tools that Christians use.

1. Put on the Whole Armour of God.

2. Whenever you talk, speak God.

3. Honor God.

4. Love God, not love the world.

5. Believe in God's decrees of His Love.

6. Have an appetite for God and His Word, not an appetite for the world.

7. Serve God, stop serving yourself

8. Worship God,

9. Glorify God.

10. Praise God.

11. Thank God for all He has done in your life and is doing in your life.

Christianity teaches you to embrace the love of God and love your neighbors as you love yourselves. Christianity requires forgiving in Grace and God's Agape love. Love your enemy, remembering that you must forgive others as you want to be forgiven. As a Christian, you strive to walk in righteousness, forgiveness, truth, faith, and love. Forgiveness is a seed that God sends to your heart. That is why you ask God to help you forgive, because you cannot do it on your own. Jesus was the only one who could forgive, being that he was the Son of God.

In being a Christian, the virtue of forgiveness is a virtue of high standing. Promoting love, harmony, goodness, understanding, and empathy. This is not easily done; it really requires a renewal of your mindset. Christianity means to be more like Jesus and have an intimate connection with Adonai Jehovah. Since sin causes you to go three steps back, regardless of where you were or at the place you are now on your life journey.

Christianity teaches you that you are free through Christ Jesus, but it doesn't mean that you can do anything you want. You are to see Jesus, your Good Shepherd, in front of you, leading you while you walk behind. Letting him take you away from your ugly thoughts and behaviors. Guiding you to Eternal Life through forgiveness and repentance, for the Kingdom of Heaven is at Hand."

GPS>[Matthew 16:24-26; 1 Corinthians 1:6-8, 2:8; Proverbs 27:2; Jeremiah 9:23-24; Romans 8:1-3; Matthew 3:2; John 14:13; Proverbs 13:12]

WHAT IS SIN?

Sin is deemed in Christianity as the enactment of actions that deliberately go against the laws of God defined through the "Ten Commandments."

A sin is an immoral act of evil done purposefully against the divine law of God through wickedness, crime, and offenses. Sin is always against God, showing irreverence, sacrilege, misdeeds, and irreligious behavior. Sin is meant to offend God; it is an immoral, premeditated, and purposeful act(s)in violation of the will of God.

Shown through acts of transgression. Sin, in the eyes of God, is doing evil. According to the Bible, sins are always mortal sins(s) quite severe. There are three different categories of sin: the lust of the flesh, the lust of the eyes, and the pride of life. In order to sin, you first allow your mind to be willing to have sinful thoughts. Focusing on that thought until it controls your actions to commit sin.

GPS>[James 1:19-22; Philippians 4:4-7]

CHAPTER 8

Get Out of Your Own Way!

Some of you, I'm sure, have heard the phrase "get out of your own way." If you haven't, this is what it means. Have you ever wondered why things are as they are in your life? You are not seeing positive change. Possibly, it could be you being you, self-sabotaging yourself. Often, you don't realize that you are blocking your own blessings, spiritual growth, and prosperity. Maybe you don't realize that your thinking process, attitude, and interest can put you in a weak position. Are you delaying having a relationship with God?

God wants to bless you, but you continue to get in your own way, choosing not to change your mindset. You talk a lot, missing important Spiritual guidance. Be quiet when someone speaks, listen attentively and patiently, letting them get every word out. Then, when they are finished, gently speak in love. Never block a blessing someone is giving to you verbally. Often, this happens when you are experiencing the issues of life. You ask for counsel from those who have more knowledge than you do in this matter. When you receive some relief, you immediately start to exclaim, becoming distracted and rambling on and on so much that no one can get a word in edgewise. No longer focused on the main issue you were originally seeking prayer for.

GPS>"My people are destroyed from lack of knowledge." **[Hosea 4:6]** Get out of your own way; stop being a stumbling block to yourself. Renewal of the mind is needed for you to walk in the spirit and not in the world when dilemmas arrive. Check yourself. Do you have problems with having good relationships with others? Do you continually wind up having frequent breakups with suitors? Maybe you are afraid of commitment and have trust issues. Being a procrastinator is a hindrance to your blessings in growth, peace, wisdom, and prosperity. Not upholding your promises or giving your word leads to distrust, the ending of friendships, a lack of respect, and chaos. Causing your quality of life to suffer.

Now, because you have a tendency to let people down, your character is marred, becoming tarnished, causing murmuring, gossip, complaints, and trouble. People realize that you cannot be depended upon. This may lead to offense being taken by individuals whom you reneged on. Possibly, there may be a project that you need to do, and you know it needs to be done. Yet, instead of doing the project, you go out and party. Promise yourself that you will do it first thing tomorrow. Beware that tomorrows are taken away as a thief in the night. You may have self-doubts; doubt is a distraction, fearing you will fail. Fear is nothing but False Evidence Appearing Real! This is what Satan relishes; he loves it when you have doubt; it is a distraction to your progress.

If so, you may have the mindset and attitude that you are afraid to be happy because you believe the relationship will fail or that you don't deserve to be happy. Could you be sabotaging yourself? You need Jesus. I am not being funny, but you really do. Having Jesus in your life by following his teachings from

God is sure to bring you joy, peace, and love. Do you feel that you are unworthy of having nice things in your life? This thought pattern is also a self-sabotaging issue, which can also be changed when you follow the word of God. Maybe you feel that you are not worthy of being happy, having a happy life, and being loved by others. This is self-loathing, which delays and blocks you from receiving the blessings that God wants to give you.

Get better, not bitter. This is not a cliché; in order to get love, you must have love for yourself. Stop hating yourself; in order to receive the Love of God, you require a heart that is open to forgiveness, ready to receive. God also says that you are worthy, you were created by the Creator of the universe, and made perfect in every way. All grace is in Christ Jesus, which qualifies you to partake in the inheritance of the Saints in Light. First, seek God in every area of your life, and wait on the LORD, believing and having a genuine repentant heart. Confessing your sins to Him, surrendering all, showing that you trust Him. God will forgive all of your sins. All obstacles are removed that were in your way. Through continual fellowship with God, reading and applying the Word in your life journey. It will manifest great things for you spiritually, which is sure to improve your life journey.

GPS>[Matthew 18:7]

CHAPTER 9

How Are You Walking, Running in The Race?

How are you walking in your Spiritual Journey? Are you hearing the Holy Spirit speak to you by convicting you? If so, listen and do. Being obedient is the key to having a life that is more abundant. Causing you to eat the good of the land. It's time for self-evaluation of yourself spiritually, mentally, and physically. How is your hearing of the Holy Spirit? Are you on the right frequency to receive guidance, having a clear transmission of the Holy Spirit communicating with you? How about your vision? Is it 20/20 focused on Jesus and his life? Reading the Bible will guide you to all the truths that apply to everything that the world throws at you.

It shows you how to live in peace by walking in the Holy Spirit. Being in the world but not of it. Using the examples of Christ. Jesus is the best example to follow because He, while on Earth, experienced what you go through daily. His love and compassion are so great that He provided scriptures to help you on your journey, the word of God. Righteous as you remain focused on Jesus? How are your loins? Are they covered and girded with the Truth of the Spirit? And what about the shoes you're using for the race? Are the shoes of Peace completely covered with the Good News of the Gospel?

How is your Heart doing? Is it able to receive the Love that God has for you?

Do you have stones of sinfulness blocking your receipt of God's Love? Remember, only through repentance are you able to receive from God forgiveness, through "Resurrection Power." How do you get to your final destination? Do you run slow and cautiously through the dense foggy wilderness on the winding Life Journey Road? Do you know that everyone has a life journey, and all are participants, some striving for Eternal Life? Others do not know where they are going, what they are doing, or what they need for their journey. All are on a journey of life, making a choice to have Eternal Life through believing in Jesus. Or have no belief in living with no direction. Run in such a way as to get the prize. Everyone has a life journey to complete, which requires various learning and training sources. You are not to run aimlessly, nor like a boxer beating the air, but to run with rejoicing in receiving "Eternal Life."

GPS>[Hebrews 12:1-13:1; Corinthians 9:24-27; John 16:33; 2 Corinthians 5:7; Isaiah 119:19-20]

RESOURCES FOR YOUR LIFE JOURNEY

In preparation for your life journey, several resources will help guide you along the way. Through Bible Scriptures, wisdom, and the Holy Spirit, you are on the right path to Eternal Life.

Have a fully charged Spirit and Heart filled with Peace, Love, Righteousness, Wisdom, and Joy. Remember to recharge daily by taking time to read the word, speak the word to yourself, and practice the guidance that God has provided through the scriptures in the Bible. Associate yourself with people who are in good rapport and followers of Jesus. Apply what you read and learn from the scriptures, for they relate to both your earthly and spiritual life daily. Keep a prayer on your lips and in your heart. Praying regularly provides all that you need. Keeping you in the right mindset causes your spiritual battery to be charged with the energy of the Holy Spirit. Make sure you are infused with faith. Sometimes, your spirit needs to be recharged, meaning you are disconnected from your Father and need to have a relationship with Him. Don't hesitate; He is always on call.

Travel within your own SPEED LIMIT: Travel at a speed that is best for you to reach the destination. Don't worry about others who have leveled up in Revelation of Christ Knowledge before you. You, too, started off as a baby when first introduced to the Word of God. The speed at which one becomes a true Christian takes time, faith, trials, prayer, and perseverance. Stay in your own lane, following the instructions that are in the Bible. In this world, the race is either to obtain wealth, power, or success. Take time to read the word so that the Holy Spirit will help you to have discernment. Helping you to understand, reiterating that Jesus is "The Good Shepherd," and you are a sheep of His pasture. Come receive the Living Water of God, which makes sure you are sustained, for he is faithful. Remember, everything you see on Earth is all temporal. You are in the world but not of this world. You are a spirit in a body with a soul. Don't be concerned with what others have, for your Father knows all your needs and will provide. GPS>[2 Corinthians 5:7]

Jesus is the bread of life; when hungry, stop and consume more of the word of God. It is nourishment for your Spirit and Soul: These scriptures assure you that by His spiritual water and spiritual bread, you will never hunger or thirst. Your spirit will be full, sustaining your conviction by the Spirit. You should have a hunger for the word, for this is your life. Nothing on Earth can provide you with the food that God gives, for it is Spiritual, coming from the heavens, your home and destination. GPS>[John 6:35]

Be certain that YOU, the Vessel, are spiritually and whole heartily believe and confess that God is real. Repenting from your old ways, turning to God's Word as guidance to get to heaven. Learn to follow the Holy Spirit. GPS>[Romans 12:1-2; John 6:35; Proverbs 23:19]

Have several means of light: to help you navigate in dark areas on your life journey while you are walking or running. There will be times when you experience feelings of hopelessness with no direction. Fear not, for God is with you. By the words of God, you can see where you are going as they throw a beam of light on your dark path through faith. God's Word is the light that shows you what is true. It will not misdirect nor mislead at any time, preventing you from seeing who you really are, which is a child of God. As you seek enlightenment, you begin to become more aware of the benefits of being selfless. GPS>[1 Corinthians 6:19-20]

Be sure to have your Spiritual vitamins: To give you strength when the road seems too hard to bear and you feel you are too weak to continue. Remember to reaffirm who you are and do a self-examination of your mindset and spirit daily.

Rejoice each day, for each day is a gift that is why it is called "the present."

GPS>[1 Chronicles 16:11-12]

SHOT OF B12 + 2 On YOUR SPIRITUAL JOURNEY

14 Bible Verses To BELIEVE

Man Says	God Says	Bible Verses
"It's Impossible"	All things are possible	[Luke 18:27]
"I'm too tired	I will give you rest	[Matthew 11:28-30]
"Nobody really loves me"	I love you	[John 3:16 & John 3:34]
"I can't go on"	My grace is sufficient	[2 Corinthians 12:9 & Psalms 91:15]
"I can't figure things out"	I will direct your steps	[Proverbs 3:5-6]

"I can't do it."	You can do all things	[Philippians 4:13]
"I'm not able"	I AM able	[2 Corinthians 9:8]
"It's not worth it"	It will be worth it	[Romans 8:28]
"I can't forgive myself"	I forgive you	[1 John 1:9 & Romans 8:1]
"I can't manage"	I will supply all your needs	[Philippians 4:19]
"I am afraid"	I have not given you a spirit of fear	[2 Timothy 1:7]
"I am always worried and frustrated."	Cast all your cares on ME	[1 Peter 5:7]
"I am not smart enough"	I give you wisdom	[1 Corinthians 1:30]
"I feel all alone"	I will never leave you or forsake you	[Hebrews13:5]

CHAPTER 10

I Feel Like I Don't Belong

How long has it been since you said or thought, "I don't belong here?" I'm sure you have had this thought at one time or another. You ponder, asking yourself, Why am I here? This feeling is correct; you are actually a visitor on Earth from the heavens created by your heavenly Abba Father God. Metaphorically, have you ever gone out of town on a vacation? If so, you recall how awkward it felt being somewhere you hadn't been before. This explains how and why you feel like you don't belong here on Earth. You are a Spirit in a body with a soul. You have been created by God, who is also the Spirit.

You were created for the purpose that God had planned for you. You are domiciled to reside on Earth, doing the will of God for a specific time period. You're feeling like you don't belong because you don't. This feeling of not belonging here is because you are a heavenly creature. You are a vapor inside of a fleshly body with a heart and soul all charged by God's energy, your creator. His Power, Glory, and Luminous light charge you up like a car battery. You are a visitor from the Heavens with a mission to spread the love of God, teaching that Jesus Christ is your Lord and Savior. Witnessing to the world, "To seek the Lord, and to repent, for the Kingdom of God is at hand."

Staying metaphorical, when you are on vacation, you smile and make the best of it, regardless of how the locals look at you, give you a stink eye, or wonder why you are so happy. The reason is that you know you are just visiting for a specific time, and then you will return to YOUR home and be comfortable again. You don't worry if your room is ready. You simply make the best of your surroundings and situations. You are on a temporary journey, though you may not realize it. Just as a vacation ends, so does your life journey. However, you are not feeling complete, so you begin to search for something that will make you feel whole. You seek money, things such as love, food, relationships, prosperity, and clothing, which are all temporal.

There is nothing wrong with desiring to have temporal props by using a righteous mindset and searching for the key. However, the key to attaining these things is all available to you through first seeking the kingdom of God through Christ Jesus. It becomes unrighteous when you use the ways of the world to gain these things. Which often leads to your behaving sinfully, leading to destruction, filled with disappointment. Which often brings some form of pain.

Now, it is not bad to have these experiences. By accepting Jesus as your Lord and Savior, you find the key to the treasure you have been seeking. It is the Holy Bible, Best Instructions Before Life Eternal. Informing you that you have access to all that you desire and need. The Holy Bible actually gives you guidelines on how to make it work here on Earth, including how to survive the crap you have to go through because it is inevitable that you will go through trials and tribulations. God is your provider; He placed you here on Earth.

He knows all that you need when, where, and how you need them. It is a part of growth for you to gain wisdom, helping you not to sweat the small stuff. Don't let earthly things and issues interrupt your peace. A way to prevent this is to renew your mind and start walking in the Spirit of God. You are to be a leader on this life journey, helping others by sharing your experiences, being a true witness of the Power and might of God, and giving Him the Glory. This feeling is as if you don't belong; well, it is because you are not connected to God, Your TRUE Father and Creator, so you feel off-center, like an orphan. Having feelings of no love, no ideas, no hope, without understanding. You are feeling loss is partially due to not knowing and understanding the word of God.

GPS>[Hosea 4:6; Matthew 6:25-34; Matthew 3:2; Thessalonians 5:23; Matthew 6:19-20; 2 Corinthians 4:18; Matthew 6:31-33; Hosea 4:6]

WHO AM I?

The Forty-One (41) I AM'S

Acknowledging by decreeing and declaring the [41] I AM on a daily basis will cause you to see yourself the way God sees you. The opinions of others don't offend you when you know who you are. You are loved by God, and that's who you are. Amen!

1. I AM a Child of the most High God [Romans 8:16]

2. I AM Redeemed from the hand of the Enemy [Psalms 107:2]

3. I AM Forgiven of my Sins through the Blood of Jesus [Ephesians 1:7]

4. I AM Saved by Grace Through Faith [Ephesians 2:8]

5. I AM Sanctified In Christ Jesus [1 Corinthians 1:2]

6. I AM Justified by Faith, having Peace with God [Romans 5:1]

7. I AM A New Creature In Christ [2 Corinthians 5:17]

8. I AM A Partaker of His Divine Nature, escaping the corruption of this world [2 Peter 1:4]

9. I AM Redeemed From the Curse of the Law [Galatians 3:13]

10. I AM Delivered From the Powers of Darkness [Colossians 1:13]

11. I AM Led By the Spirit of God for the Spirit of the Lord is upon me [Luke 4:18]

12. I AM A Son or Daughter of God, a Joint Heir with Christ Jesus [Romans 8:14]

13. I AM Kept In Safety Wherever I Go [Psalms 91:11]

14. I AM Getting All My Needs Met By God [Philippians 4:19]

15. I AM Casting All My Cares On Jesus for He Cares for Me [1 Peter 5:7]

16. I AM Strong In the Lord and in the Power of His Might [Ephesians 6:10-18]

17. I AM Doing All Things Through Christ Who Strengthens Me [Philippians 4:13]

18. I AM A flame igniting the Holy Ghost Fire in others, witnessing the truth of God [1 Corinthians 2:5-15]

19. I have Dominion over ALL the power of the Enemy [Luke 10:19]

20. I AM guided and obeying the Lord's Commandments [Deuteronomy 28:12]

21. I AM Blessed Coming in and Blessed Going Out [Deuteronomy 26:6]

22. I AM An Heir of Eternal Life [1 John 5:11-12]

23. I AM Blessed with All Spiritual Blessings [Ephesians 1:3]

24. I AM Healed by His Strips [1 Peter 2:24]

25. My body is a temple of the Holy Spirit; I belong to God [1 Corinthians 6:19]

26. I may approach God with freedom and confidence [Ephesians 3:12]

27. I AM the head and not the tail, and I only go up and not down in life as I trust and obey God [Deuteronomy 28:13]

28. I AM More Than A Conqueror [Romans 8:37]

29. I AM an ambassador from heaven, Establishing God's Word Here on Earth [Matthew 16:19]

30. I AM An Over-comer by the Blood of the Lamb and the Word of My Testimony [Revelations 12:11]

31. I AM Daily Overcoming the Devil [1 John 4:4]

32. I AM Not Moved by What I See [2 Corinthians 4:18]

33. I AM Walking by Faith and Not by Sight [2 Corinthians 5:7]

34. I AM Casting down Vain Imaginations [2 Corinthians 10:4-5]

35. I AM Bringing Every Thought into Captivity [2 Corinthians 10:5]

36. I AM Being Transformed by Renewing My Mind to the [Romans 12:1-2]

37. I AM A Laborer Together with God [1 Corinthians 3:9]

38. I AM The Righteousness of God in Christ [2 Corinthians 5:21]

39. I AM An Imitator of Jesus [Ephesians 5:1]

40. I AM The Light of the World [Matthew 5:14]

41. I AM The Salt of The Earth [Matthew 5:13]

Be assured, this is who you are, in Christ Jesus.

YOU ARE IN THE WORLD BUT NOT OF THE WORLD

What does it mean, "you are in the world but not of it?" It means that you are actually a spirit in a body with a soul. You are from heaven. You are an ambassador of Christ, being used by your Heavenly Abba Father to spread the Good News of the gospel to every creature. You are to tell everyone that God loves them and that the kingdom of Heaven is at hand. This life you are experiencing is only a small part of a big plan of God's.

Stemming from Yahweh, his agenda is your agenda. You are on a heavenly mission infused with some blessed gift or talent, which is to be beneficial to both you and others. These divinely designed attributes have led you to accomplish various feats and successes. All part of God's plan and will for you to be where He wants you to be, using your gift(s) for the betterment of mankind and His Kingdom. To those who have much, much is expected.

Nothing is free; even your blessings come with a cost. True, you are blessed, yet you are to be obedient in order to eat the good of the land. **GPS>**"If you are willing and obedient, You shall eat the good of the land; But if you refuse and rebel, You shall be devoured by the sword; For the mouth of the LORD has spoken." **[Isaiah 1:19-20]**

God provides help to you in every situation, circumstance, trouble, and test. There is a reciprocation for God providing a means of rescuing you from all of those things, which cause you to cry out to your Father in Heaven. This exchange is done by the challenges you encounter on your life journey here on Earth. There is not one person who is excluded from having to face the issues of life. They are part of being on Earth, living in the world, which is an introduction to hell.

There may be times when you wonder if this is Babylon. Know that the events that you experience are made to help you grow spiritually. Though you must go through things, these are blessings in disguise! In order for you to have peace, you must go through trials and tribulations that strengthen you, empowering you so that you are able to stand courageously as a chosen ambassador of God. Jesus is the way; your way should be the same as Jesus'.

GPS>[Ephesians:10;17; Luke:18- 19; Colossians 1:18; John 5:19; John 16:33; Col 1:18; Isaiah 1:19-20; Genesis 1:1; Jerimah 32:17]

CHAPTER 11

God Does Not Need You, He Gives You Purpose

Think about this: God is invisible. God created the universe. He created the Earth and all that is above, below, and inside of it. God can create anything He wants. It is God's will that is to be done. Yahweh is the Supreme Creator of all that is, that was, and is to come. All realms and existence are God in Himself. He is time itself. He can create life and take life. **GPS>**"Before I formed you in the womb, I knew you, and before you were born, I consecrated you; I appointed you a prophet to the nations." **[Jeremiah 1:8]** "I AM" means all Authority, Wisdom, and Power of God. The infinite Power of God controls after your body dies, where your molecules and atoms go. God's breath is returned to Him, the Source of all life forces. He has power over death and eternity. Jesus, the Son of God, was used by the Father to bring the Word of God to Earth. Jesus was a servant; while he lived among you, he was the Word, the Truth, and the Life. His purpose was to be crucified as a living sacrifice, die, and be buried, taking on the sins of mankind. Through the Resurrection Power of God, Jesus was raised from the dead.

He defeated Satan and death, became the Savior of the world, and fulfilled his purposes as a servant to God and Redeemer to humanity. Restoring the relationship between

God and man. God, being a Spirit, works in Spirit, selecting whom he chooses to find their way through Christ Jesus. God uses you to interact with others in their natural physical form. Making it easier to communicate from person to person and spreading the Word and the Good News of the Gospel to every creature. You are to walk by faith and not by sight, being led by the Holy Spirit in Truth as a servant of God. Through the experiences you endured and overcame, they have caused you to become an eyewitness to the power and might of God, giving Him the glory.

Jehovah can give you life, and he can take it back at any time he will. Being a servant accomplishing your God-given purpose, you are to use Spiritual words and thoughts and have a righteous manner in moral behavior. Speaking in truth and love, speaking life into all situations. God really doesn't need you. He uses you as his servant. God equips you for whatever task He has called you out to do. Equipping you with all you need to accomplish your task successfully, for you cannot provide it for yourself. When you begin to use the tools that God has given you to accomplish His task for you, it will not return to God void; it will successfully accomplish what it was sent out to do. In this scenario, it is an honor to be chosen by God to do his bidding.

In whatever capacity or area you are called to do, don't hesitate to accept it, giving thanks for being selected to be his blessed servant. Ask for guidance, and in prayer, do all you can to fulfill your calling. Yahweh knows that He can trust you and that you are faithful and obedient. Read the Bible, be saturated with God's Word, and let it get inside you. Seek God, praising, worshiping, and thanking him as you strengthen your relationship with Him. GPS>[Exodus 31:3; Jeremiah 29:11; Isaiah 55:11; John 14:15-24; James 1:2-4; Isaiah 55:11]

Do you know that there is a spiritual war going on right at this moment that never stops, in which you are in? GPS>"[Ephesians 6:10-14] There are several realms involved that are part of your life Journey. This GPS will help you travel through them. First, God has given you Dominion like a governor to rule over areas where you run the territory in light, spreading the love, spiritually and physically, the word of God to others, keeping that territory secure under God's rule, bringing the Kingdom of God. Teaching to repent for the Kingdom of Heaven is at Hand, wielding the power of God using the powers of purity and loyalty. While the enemy has principalities, such as generals who are fighting warriors in high places using aggressive tactics of spiritual warfare in the forms of aggression, temptation, unrighteousness, sin, wickedness, and evil to overthrow your dominion over your set territory. They have demons that come to possess human forms, not to fight for you.

Understand that there are rules, the same as in any war, where the Principalities seek territories and fight to gain and destroy, and they do not fear what is not legitimate power and authority. **GPS>**"Then certain of vagabond Jews, exorcists, took upon them to call over themselves to call over them which had evil spirits the name of the LORD Jesus, saying "We adjure you by Jesus who Paul preacheth. And there were seven sons of one Sceva, a Jew, and chief of the priests who did so." And the evil spirit answered and said, "Jesus, I know, and Paul, I know, but who are you?" And the man in who the evil spirit leaped on them, and overcame them, and prevailed against them, so that they fled out of the house naked and wounded.

[Acts 19:13-15] You are a principality of light in the Spiritual dimension in which Jesus is the Kingdom of Heaven. Teaching that you must be born again to gain eternal life.

GOD GIVES YOU PURPOSE

There is a portion you have that requires you to believe in God. God uses imperfect people to change the world; the apostles were a group of mere men, each on their own journey. You are not supposed to operate in worry, anxiety, or worldliness because the real you is a spirit in a body that has a soul. In God's freedom, you are to walk in obedience, having both your soul and body in alignment with your spirit, which is in contact with the Holy Spirit. Soul, you have been chosen by God to be a disciple. God has given you honor, rights, privileges, and grace in doing His Will. The Lord knows that you are of flesh and that you are always in battle with the Spirit.

God loves you so much that in scripture John 3:16, the word so means intensity. That word so is just as when you use it to express your devout intensity for whatever you are directing it toward. If God had a refrigerator, your picture would be on it! In God's intensity, He even provides help for you in the form of protection, guidance, goodness, mercy, and truth, which are weapons for your journey. Jesus is your caretaker, for he cares for you. In fact, in accomplishing your purpose, Emmanuel is with you; this is what Emmanuel means: "God with you." You are here on Earth to help others, spreading the Word of Salvation through the Lord Jesus Christ, seeking redemption. This is a wonderful gift that confirms the wonderful words of life from God to his chosen one. God's instructions, which have not changed, are for you to help others who are lost, being their good shepherd.

Showing them the right path to having a good life through walking in the Spirit of God. Your life journey illuminates the help for others as you have become a bright beam of truth. Through your stout example, showing evidence of what being obedient to God attains for you. Gratitude, praising God, giving him glory for all he has done and is doing, and faith for the things that will be done by him for you. There may be times when God tells you to do a certain task, and sometimes, along the way, it gets difficult.

Sometimes, it is so difficult that you convince yourself that you can't accomplish the task. You feel that it is impossible to do. So, you say, "This is too hard to do; it will not work." When you do that, you are calling God a liar. **GPS>**"With man, this is impossible, but with God, all things are possible." **[Matthew 19:26]** For anything that God calls you to do, you can believe it will be accomplished; when God gives you a specific purpose, you best believe that he has also given you the gift and all you need to complete your Holy mission. **GPS>**"So shall My word be that goes forth from My mouth; it shall not return to Me void, but it shall accomplish what I please, and it shall prosper in the thing for which I sent it." **[Isaiah 55:11]**

Your being obedient serves him best when you focus on his will and plans for you. Having the feeling of purposelessness is a form of hell. The devil will make you feel like you have to prove that you have a purpose in God. Satan, being the liar and deceiver that he is, knows that there is no reason you have to prove anything.

God has a purpose for you that eliminates the need for proof. Having a God-given purpose eliminates the need for proof. The blood of Jesus has already done that; instead of grumbling and envying others while comparing your issues of life to theirs. Stop and see all the blessings that are in front of you. You don't know who was praying for them generations ago; you don't know what sacrifices have been made for God's Glory by someone praying, asking God to bless them.

You don't know what God has and is doing in both your and their lives. Jehovah's agenda should be your agenda done in obedience, which is required of you in order to bless yourself and future generations. You have been given a gift of some kind of talent that is to be shared while you are on Earth. God equips you with all you need to serve him both on Earth and in the kingdom of heaven. You are anointed, both a servant and an ambassador of God. The Lord will reward you for being obedient.

GPS>[Matthew :36 -38, 25:21; Mark 9:23; Jeremiah 12:18-19; Psalm 57:2; Colossians 1:16]

GOD'S PROMISES AND PLANS FOR YOU

Did you know that there are over 7,000 promises that God has made toward you? God used Jesus to deliver HIS words, which are in the Bible. God's words were spoken by

Jesus Christ. Also known as The Word, The Way, The Light, and many more, all describing Him as the Son of God. Having ultimate power on Earth, Heaven, and Hell, as directed by His Father. There are three different categories for God's Promises. The first set of Promises is for everyone. The next set is for the Twelve Disciples. The last three are all the Promises from God to you and others. 9 Promises of God with Scripture, as you receive Spiritual blessings in Christ. You are blessed by God, the Father of your Lord Jesus Christ. Who has blessed you in Christ with every spiritual blessing in the heavenly places?

Before the foundations of the world, God chose you to be in His Son, Jesus, so that you will be holy and blameless before Him in love. God in love predestined us for adoption by Him as sons and daughters through the blood and body of Jesus Christ. In Him, you have redemption through his blood, which consists of the forgiveness of our trespasses, according to the riches of his grace, which He has lavished upon you in all wisdom and insight, making known to you the mystery of His will. **GPS>**"You are worthy, our Lord and God, to receive glory and honor and power, for You created all things, and by Your will they were created and have their being." **[Revelation 4:11]**

According to His purpose, which He set forth in Christ as a plan for the fullness of time. To unite all things in Him, such as things in heaven and things on Earth. GPS>[Numbers 10:29]

Promises From God Meant for Everyone

1. God, through the Holy Spirit and Word, is your teacher. GPS>[Matthew 4:4]

2. God is always with you; he will never forsake or abandon you. GPS>[Matthew 7:8]

3. God is Just, and forgiving does not hold grudges. GPS>[Matthew 5:45]

4. God is Love. He is the Way, The Truth, and the Life.

5. Jesus is the vine, and you are the branches. You can do nothing detached from the vine.

Promises from God are meant for the Twelve Disciples and you as an ambassador of God.

6. God is powerful and has given you power and authority to overcome various temptations, tests, and trials. GPS>[Matthew 18:18]

7. God is your Protector and healer. GPS>[Matthew 10:26]

8. God gives you empowerment over all the power of the enemy. GPS>[Luke 10:19]

Promises from God through Jesus for others

9. God is a way maker, rewarder, and promise keeper. GPS>[Matthew 15:28]

10. God provides help and strength. GPS>[Isaiah 41:10]

11. God is forgiving, compassionate, merciful, faithful, and loving, GPS>[Matthew 6:14]

12. God has promised eternal life to all who believe and confess that Jesus Christ is the Son of the one true living God and is their Lord and Savior.

God's promises never fail; He can be trusted. God will provide wisdom to you; His promises are set to give you an abundant life. God has made promises to help strengthen you when you need them. His words are all true. God's passionate, unfailing love and commitment toward you are limitless. His promises gird you with hope, peace, joy, undying love, and commitment to you. He is with you always and hears each prayer. Knowing and acknowledging each tear that you shed. He is a great and good God! He is your "Beloved Abba Father."

CHAPTER 12

Renew Your Mind with Spiritual Renewal

Renewing your mind is easier said than done. To renew your mind, you first need to decide if you want to change how you think. It requires discipline, constant practice, prayer, patience, humility, and love; changing habits you have acquired from the time you knew right from wrong is somewhat unsettling. Although it may be quite challenging, it can be done with the help and grace of God. Spiritual renewal instills a virtuous character, changing from old, ungodly thoughts and behaviors. It transforms the way you respond to challenges and offenses done to you by others. Spiritual renewal allows God to work unrestrictively, saturating you with his Spirit and cleansing you inside out. Reviving you back to life, showing the infinite authority, power, and might of God, renewing your faith, surrendering all ungodliness, and accepting Jesus Christ as your Lord and Savior.

You restore Spiritual direction with the renewal of your mind. Your mindset affects others through behavior, causing you and others to unnecessarily face issues of life alone, unarmed, without the Armor of God. Stubbornness causes many experiences with life issues to be harsher than they need to be. It's time to stop thinking selfishly and harboring stubborn attitudes. Your attitudes are from the mind, and when you let your imagination run wild, all sorts of wickedness are produced. Allowing Satan to torment you by guiding your thoughts. Keeping you in bondage, along with all manners of confusion, causing you to think that you are above God's knowledge.

In renewal, you begin to think in the new, learning to replace your old thoughts with the newness of life in Christ Jesus. There are so many gifts given to you by God through Spiritual resurrection and renewal. Rescuing you from the spiral of darkness, leading to loss and death. Restoring your faith and reconciling your relationship with God, your Father, is what renewal does. It leads to a modification in your old attitude, being replaced with the new, accepting the truth, and being set free. A renewed mind makes a renewed soul, spirit, and body, affirming the Resurrection Power of God.

GPS>Doubt and being double-minded play a large role in being lost on your life journey. When you choose to please man instead of God, you lose your focus on God, who heals you, who provides for you, who sent His only begotten Son to save you from damnation. A double-minded man is unstable in all his ways, reflecting the image of a wave being tossed to and from in the winds of life. Being unstable in your train of thought gains you nothing; trust in God and receive the benefits of His wisdom **[James 1:6-12, Psalms 119:113-120;1 Corinthians 9:27]**. Stop imagining things; your mindset plays a large part in your salvation, deliverance, and redemption. God says to cast all imaginations down.

GPS>"Casting down imaginations, and every high thing that exalteth itself against the knowledge of God, and bringing into captivity every thought to the obedience of Christ; and having in a readiness to revenge all disobedience, when your obedience is fulfilled." **[2 Corinthians 10:5- 6]** You may realize that things aren't working out, possibly due to the way you think, letting you make choices that lead to sinfulness. Metaphorically: When you know each time you walk outside, once you turn left, a bird poops on your head. Yet, you refuse to change your direction when walking. Instead of going in the same direction, doing things that have proven messy.

Turn around mentally and go the opposite way; giving that a try, what do you have to lose? Make a change in those habits that only bring disappointments and anger. In the world, you have two choices that you control. One is choosing to be righteous or to be unrighteous. The other is how you handle the consequences of the choices you have made. God is in control, giving you freedom of choice.

In the world, one sinful attitude that's popular is "having it **your** way! This is not the way to have peace and grow in the Spirit of Christ; this mindset shows a character of selfishness in your heart. God had already predestined your destiny before you were born. It is God's Will, not yours. Stinkin Thinkin is comparable to motionless water that doesn't flow but remains still in a puddle. When sitting too long, it becomes stagnant and stinks because it is not moving.

This metaphorically describes your walk when you are not changing, moving, being complacent, or growing in your sinful thinking and choice patterns. Satan wants you to think that you are worthless and nobody. But God wants you to know that by your being resurrected and renewed in righteousness, you are an important somebody who is supposed to tell everybody about the treasure you have found in Jesus through the Word, the truth, and the life. This is the only way you can evolve by renewing your mind from worldliness to Christ's likeness. Come to your right senses, repent. Cry out to God, confess your sin(s), ask for forgiveness with a remorseful and repentant heart, and acknowledge your sin.

Stay in faith, willing to turn around facing Christ, vowing not to repeat those sinful acts again. "How, you ask?" By reading the Bible and other spiritual doctrines based on Jesus Christ. Discover God's will in knowing Christ is growing and yielding fruit. The book you are reading is another stepping stone to guide your way to Eternal Life, presenting you with wisdom that can only be understood through both Knowledge and understanding.

GPS>[Scenario] Someone gives you a plane; you see it and acknowledge that it is a plane, but you don't know how to fly it. So, the next step is to read the instruction manual, which provides details on how to operate and maintain the plane you have received. Once you have read the manual, you will have an understanding of how to fly a plane. Now you have both ***Knowledge plus Understanding, and you now have Wisdom. [K+U=W]***

In renewing your mindset, think about things that are good." **GPS>**"Finally, brothers and sisters, whatever is true, whatever is noble, whatever is right, whatever is pure, whatever is lovely, whatever is admirable- if anything is excellent or praiseworthy- think about such things." **[Philippians 4:8]** In this mindset, you will find peace, love, and wholeness.

GPS>[Matthew 18:12-14; Romans 12:1-2; 2 Corinthians 5:17;2 Corinthians 10:5-6; Jeremiah 4:22; Jeremiah 29:11; Proverbs 23:7; 29:18; Philippians 4:11–13; 2 Peter 1:2; Mark 4:1-11] 2 Peter 1:2; Mark 4:1-11]

WHERE THE SPIRIT OF THE LORD IS, THERE IS LIBERTY

There is liberty in the Spirit of the Lord. No longer struggling with both worldly and spiritual issues alone. Freeing you of guilt, shame, and fear of what Satan or man will do to you. Freeing you from all worldly bondage from issues of life. Causing you to no longer be stuck in the bondage of sin, going nowhere. It transforms you into being pure again, surrendering your entire being to God, trusting him for your every need. Now, being spiritually stronger, you allow yourself to face boldly any chastisement, challenge, or trial you encounter on your life journey.

Allowing your heavenly Father to fight your battles for you, giving you the blessed victory in all trials, circumstances, and situations. **GPS** "Now the Lord is that Spirit; and where the Spirit of the Lord is, there is liberty. **[2 Corinthians 3:17]** When you are free doesn't mean you are free to do whatever you want. It means you are free to do what Jesus is doing and what God wants you to do. You are to continue walking in Christ's likeness in righteousness. Righteousness should be reigning in your body as you walk in the Spirit. The freedom of Christ has set you free, causing you to stand tall in the Spirit, breaking any chain of sin that may make way for the devil to enslave you again. Only when walking in the flesh does sin occur, causing you to believe only what you see. "If you can't see it, then you don't believe it."

This mindset is part of an issue in your heart. Exposing your bad attitude(s) and lack of faith, getting in your own way. Attitudes are a major problem; the flesh has you searching for physical worldly things. Those are just props for you to use on this life journey, which God has and is still providing for you. You have placed your faith and belief in the world and its ways. That's why you do not see what you want to manifest in your life; your wants are selfish and unrighteous. You are walking, looking down and all around, searching for what the world has to offer you, which is nothing good.

The only thing that is good in this world is the Good News of the Gospel, which is truth and freedom!" Look straight ahead, seeing Jesus, and focus on him as he leads you to Eternal Life. The Spirit of the Lord has set you free from guilt, shame, and all Spiritual traps. Empowering you with the Power and authority of God, standing tall and strong in faith. No longer easily chained in bondage by Satan through sin. Don't allow sin to have mastery over your life, for it brings death.

Seek the Kingdom of Heaven, calling on Jesus your Savior for help, knowing that the Kingdom of Heaven is at hand. Stay in obedience to the way and truth of Christ, for in them, you will find peace and a loving and close relationship with God. Protection from selfishness, improving your mind to achieve set goals. Transforming you both inside and out, causing you to make better life decisions. Gaining the ability to manage stress and temptations, enhancing resilience through the power, might, and spirit of God.

GPS>[Ezekiel 36:27; Romans 8:14-14; John 16:13; Isaiah 11:2; Proverbs 13:24]

GODS' LOVE, MERCY, GRACE & COMPASSION

What is Grace? Grace is giving you something that you don't deserve. It is something that you cannot earn, but it is a spiritual gift from God. Through the grace of God, you receive love, eternal comfort, and good hope. Jesus' mother, Mary, who was engaged to be married to a man named Joseph, was full of grace as it was declared by the angel Gabriel, who was sent by God. GPS>[Luke 1:28-32] **Grace Consists of Five Divine Portions:**

[G] God's generous goodness

[R] Restoration through His Resurrection Power

[A] Authoritative Power

[C] Compassion for He Cares and Cherishes you

[E] Eternal Life given through His glorious essence

The goodness of God brings back the authority that you lost when you sinned, causing a separation from God. Through the Resurrection Power of God, you are restored to righteousness, and compassion is shown, guiding you to eternal life. Grace causes you to attain spiritual attributes that build your character, such as honor, spiritual growth, thanksgiving, wisdom, and love. It establishes in you an enthusiasm that wells up as that of an overflowing spout of "Living Water," purifying you to excel in helping others, being nonjudgmental, and being geared in obedience to the will of God. Showing love to anyone, anytime, anywhere, regardless of their circumstances.

Although these characteristics are each unique in themselves, when put together, they equal Grace. Grace is the essence of God; it is all of what He is, which is Love. Encompassing salvation and truth, for without a scrupulous love, there can be no **Grace.** A global trumpet has blown, notifying you of only half of what God wants to do in the world. You may not realize it, but you are overwhelmingly blessed. God is a "Now, God! Faith is now! When you walk by faith and not by sight, you are experiencing this miraculous power, for by grace, you have been saved through faith. You have been given a portion of grace from the Father that gives you hope. This, indeed, is not your own doing; it is a gift from your creator. It is not a result of the work you've done, so there is no way you can boast. Declare these things; exhort and rebuke with all authority. Let no one disregard you. Stay prayerful and grateful, and receive the grace of God, which is good for your soul and you.

GPS>[Titus 2:11-14]

MERCY

What is Mercy? Mercy is giving you something that you don't deserve. Mercy is the authority to inflict punishment for failing to meet the agreements of a contract. Instead, you show leniency, choosing not to enforce any sanctions on the person. Mercy shows compassion and grace to anyone. There are times when someone is in need, and you contribute whatever you can in a generous manner, wanting no accolades. Mercy shows tolerance when needed in situations where exhibiting patience is required.

Mercy is being sympathetic and supportive to others. Edifying them through encouragement and lifting up their spirit through God's Word. Mercy is having forgiveness regardless of the sin. Mercy allows love, charity, softheartedness, and wisdom to flow freely, blessing us all through the domino effect of love. Between the parties, magnanimity is established through kindness and forbearance. Mercy has no self-indulgence; it is grace for all humanitarian purposes. Let the lights of tenderness, pity, humility, and the love of God be used to bring Him peace. All of these things describe the infinite Love of God that He shows to you daily, giving Him all the Glory. Regardless of your sinful nature, at each daybreak, God gives you new, limitless Mercy. Declaring that you are worthy of his Mercy and love. GPS>[Matthew 18:23-35; John 3:16; Colossians 3:12-14]

COMPASSION

Compassion also consists of the giving and receiving of God's Love. It means that the Love God has placed in your heart is to be given freely to others. In order to be able to give love, you must have a heart that is open to receiving it. Having a heart that is filled with bitterness, forgiveness, and unrighteousness is not capable of receiving love. Your heart must be clean of all darkness, with no bitter stones in it.

Compassion is also loving unconditionally without motive or trickery. God has so much compassion and love for humanity that he sent His only Son, Jesus, to tell you that you are loved dearly by the Heavenly Father. Being compassionate is having an inner feeling that convicts you to help, sympathizing with the victim(s)in solidarity to understand their plight. God's love is putting light and good air back into your struggles and worldly situations.

GPS>[Ephesians 4:22-24; Colossians 3:12; John 6:1-14; Deuteronomy 6:5; 1 Corinthians 13: -4-8; Romans 5:7-9]

CHAPTER 13

Be In Christ and Not in Crisis

To be in Christ is to believe that Jesus is the only begotten Son of God, accept him as your Lord and your Savior, and receive eternal life. Being in Christ allows you to surrender all your concerns to God, giving him control. No longer living in doubt, worrying about what you will eat, how you will pay your bills, and meet the life issues of the world. **GPS>**"Therefore, I tell you, do not worry about your life, what you will eat or drink, or about your body, what you will wear." **[Matthew 25-27,34]**

No one is exempt from experiencing a crisis in their lives. Even when you are a faithful Christian walking in righteousness, a crisis may come into your life abruptly, but be assured that the Lord will not forsake you. When a crisis arises, repent, have a repentant heart and belief, and seek the Lord through prayer and submission. Confessing your sins, asking God for forgiveness, ready to take responsibility for your sinful acts, including restitution and apologies to those whom you have hurt. Vowing to God that you will turn your back on sinfulness, turning to face him face to face. Because you are a Christian believing in Jesus, though you are in crisis, you stand strong in the power and the might of God.

Nothing can separate you from his love and protection. He is always ready to rescue you from whatever you need help with. God is faithful to you, being the same today as he was yesterday, and will be for you tomorrow. He is available, walking beside you and listening to your prayer. All in limitless forgiveness, power, and unconditional love, ready to provide you with every need.

Obedience and following the Word of God are very important in your life journey. Scripture says, "If you are willing and obedient, you shall eat the good of the land. "Through Christ Jesus, the Word, the Way, and the Life. Patiently and with humility and having no fear, you are able to face all circumstances, trusting that you will go through them all victoriously. As you now walk in faith and no longer walk in the flesh, you fix your eyes on what is unseen, knowing that it is Eternal. You spend time reading the Word daily, communicating in prayer with the Father.

Be thankful for the mercy and grace that he has bestowed upon you. Knowing, crisis, or anything can separate the love of God, in Christ Jesus, from you. You are at peace and not in pieces because you are in Christ Jesus. God uses your present suffering to prepare you for future glory, using anguish and pain to get your attention, to discipline you so that you may share in his holiness and grow in godliness. Being an agent of Jesus, you share and apply the love of God, which you have received, to others. Being an eyewitness to the Power, authority, and might of your Savior.

You see, experience miracles and blessings for being obedient and righteous. Every crisis you face in life is a turning point, for better or worse, working for your own good. No longer do you doubt, for you know that all things are possible with God.

GPS>[Isaiah 1:19-20; Philippians 2:8, 4:6-7; Romans 8:28,37-39; John 16:13, 33; Isaiah 35:4,41:10]

Give thanks for the mercy and grace that he has bestowed upon you. Knowing, crisis, or anything can separate the love of God, in Christ Jesus, from you. You are at peace and not in pieces because you are in Christ Jesus. God uses your present suffering to prepare you for future glory, using anguish and pain to get your attention, to discipline you so that you may share in his holiness and grow in godliness. Being an agent of Jesus, you share and apply the love of God, which you have received, to others. Being an eyewitness to the Power, authority, and might of your Savior. You see, experience miracles and blessings for being obedient and righteous. Every crisis you face in life is a turning point, for better or worse, working for your own good. No longer do you doubt, for you know that all things are possible with God.

GPS>[Isaiah 1:19-20; Philippians 2:8, 4:6-7; Romans 8:28,37-39; John 16:13, 33; Isaiah 35:4,41:10, 41:13; Psalm 56:3, 91:4-5; 2Corinthians 4:17-18]

TO BE IN CRISIS

What does it mean to be in crisis? It is a sudden situation that has imminent harm in it. This causes you to be under pressure to make abrupt decisions during a critical life event in which a solution is needed. In a crisis, you are facing a traumatic, life-changing calamity, which frequently induces a psychological effect connected with the loss of your faculties, making you mentally unbalanced. Often, from the impact of

116

the threatening situation, you start to question your purpose for living. Wanting to be as far away as possible from the ordeal you are encountering. Hating the breaking of a new day. You begin to wish you hadn't woken up rather than go through the torment. Many times, crises develop from offenses and sinful choices, bringing the consequences to be faced. You walk in the flesh, thinking that you can solve your own problems, thinking you know more than God, and following your own agenda.

However, you don't relish anything that forces you to change, doing things differently from how you might want to accomplish things. Trusting God's way always results in success. They connect you to the Word of God, the good news of the gospel, and help you receive the power that flows from the heavens through faith, because of the mindset you have chosen to follow the path that puts you into crisis. If you are a non-believer in Christ and do not adhere to the Word of God, he is not in your life to help because you believe not. You don't believe in him, so how can he help if he doesn't exist to you? Through your behavior of disobedience, selfishness, and arrogance, you have turned your back on Jesus. Causing nothing to be possible in your life because you live and think as the world thinks, undisciplined and selfish.

Although you may not have established boundaries in your life, the "Ten Commandments" are sacred laws that God gave to Moses. They are the best instructions before life is eternal. Providing guidance in attaining a quality of life filled with blessings, wisdom, and truth. Let go of your ego and pride, and turn to God for help in denying yourself of worldly lust and becoming unselfish, learning discipline through self-control, knowing your limitations, and abiding by them. When you become accustomed to discipline, you make better choices, learning and applying the Ways of Jesus through Spiritual instructions. Leading you to forgiveness, redemption, and deliverance through the Resurrection power of God. Discipline leads to strengthening your faith, and putting this mindset into practice daily truly helps to keep you on a righteous path. There are a few simple habits and practices that will assist you in the development of spiritual knowledge, understanding, and wisdom, strengthening and strengthening your faith in Christ.

Such as prayer, Bible study, meditation, fasting, confession, solitude, worship, and celebration. **GPS>**"With man, this is impossible, but with God, all things are possible." **[Matthew 19:26]** Being in crisis is lonely, dangerous, and a frightening position to be in. Even when using worldly resources and your worldly way of thinking. Seeking help, you find that no one is able to help you; no one can provide what you need. It is a major problem that requires more than earthly methods. You need a solution, but none is available to turn this crisis into a mere wisp, giving you peace.

Instead, you are in pieces, worrying, full of anxiety, confusion, and dread. You are forced to waddle in the complex, menacing world of life on your journey, seeking relief from your peril, finding none, only emptiness, uncertainty, hopelessness, and defeat. But God is a forgiving God. He will not leave you. He will deliver you from all crises victoriously. He has the power, and Jesus is the solution. If you are a non-believer, God does not hold that against you. He waits for you to come to your right senses after hearing the truth and the Word of God, causing you to believe in Jesus as your Lord and Savior, being led by the Holy Spirit. Come to God with a repentant heart, ask forgiveness for your sins, make a covenant with him to turn away from sin, turn to Jesus, and be reborn in Christ. It is a journey that elevates you to a level that is not seen, but has the belief that they do exist, such as the heavens.

GPS>[Hebrew 12:7-11; James 1:2-3; Romans 5:3-4; Deuteronomy 31:8; John 16:8-11; Proverbs 3:11-12] Seeking relief from your peril, finding none, only emptiness, uncertainty, hopelessness, and defeat.

But God is a forgiving God; He will not leave you. He will deliver you from all crises victoriously. He has the power, and Jesus is the solution. Being a non-believer, God does not hold that against you. He waits for you to come to your right senses after hearing the truth and the Word of God, causing you to believe in Jesus as your Lord and Savior, being led by the Holy Spirit. Come to God with a repentant heart, ask forgiveness for your sins, make a covenant with him to turn away from sin, turn to Jesus, and be reborn in Christ. It is a journey that elevates you to a level that is not seen, but has the belief that they do exist, such as the heavens.

GPS>[Hebrew 12:7-11; James 1:2-3, Romans 5:3-4; Deuteronomy 31:8; John 16:8-11; Proverbs 3:11-12]

LET GOD TURN YOUR TRIALS, TESTS, AND MESS INTO A MESSAGE

Ever since Adam and Eve disobeyed God in the "Garden of Eden, there has been a mess. Starting from Eve's speaking with the devil, tempting her, she took the forbidden fruit from the Tree of the Knowledge of Good and Evil." Adam and Eve's physical state was different as a result of their eating the forbidden fruit. As God had promised, they became mortal, placing a death sentence on all life forms on earth. They were now being contaminated and in a sinful state; both Adam and Eve were driven out of the Garden, never to return. That ordeal was the first mess done by man. In fact, the first sibling rivalry was between Cain and Abel because of Cain's jealousy of his brother's offerings to God, which led to Abel being murdered by his brother, Cain.

The first family feud in the Bible was due to Rebekah, the mother of Jacob and Esau, betraying her husband, Isaac, in order to cheat the oldest son, Esau, out of his birthright and blessing so that her favorite son, Jacob, would receive them from their father, Isaac, who was blind, and on his deathbed. Rebekah's betrayal, greed, and favoritism of one child toward another caused division to arise between the two brothers and the separation of the mother and her favorite son, Jacob.

Throughout the Bible, there are chapters full of messes people got themselves into and were delivered by God due to his loving kindness and mercy. His way of restoring you to peace is always done in such a way that it leaves no doubt that God's miraculous power was how you were saved, giving Glory to God. No man on earth is able to deliver you from any mess because mankind is part of your mess due to worldly thinking, frailty, and ways. You aren't able to help yourself out of a mess you've made; your mindset is walking in the flesh.

You being you is the reason why messes develop. Generally, because you just opened your mouth, saying something that you knowingly offend, in your sinful state of mind. Maybe you just walked in on others talking stink about you, causing you to feel hurt and betrayed. Wherever people are, messes can ensue from someone being offended by what someone said or did. The reason for you to be offensive toward others possibly stems from the disorder and mayhem that are in your life journey. Many messes manifest because your life is in shambles, having no harmony. Your mind is cluttered with unpleasant misconduct and fallout from past hurts, growing into seeds of bitterness in your heart. You are having difficulty finding peace because you are full of wickedness. Having covetousness and jealousy in your heart. You are selfish and arrogant, with a lifestyle full of muddles and blunders because of the way you speak to others. Your disposition is full of debris from anger, regret, and thoughts of revenge.

You have no respect for anything, being untidy and sloppy. Because of your attitude, people in your circle gossip about you. Making the mess of "he said," - "she said," which is a sin trap. Making it an act of retaliation, adding more fuel to the spark. These types of tests and trials can be avoided by following the Word of God. He knows what is going on in your life; he is your heavenly Father, and he wants you to stop whatever you are doing and be still, acknowledging that He is God. He answers your questions on why this mess is happening, speaking to you through the Holy Spirit. He then asks you a couple of questions. Do you see how you got into this mess? Then He asks, What is the lesson you learned? Then he tells you how to avoid a mess. Messes often have to do with your choices, your environment, your circle of friends, your mindset, heart, and lifestyle. You being you is the reason why messes develop.

Minding your own business and staying out of other folks' business is a way not to get into messes. That is called respect and loving thy neighbor as yourself, following the "Ten Commandments." God uses messes to get your attention, occasionally to reprimand you, showing you that you need to change your worldly ways. He is always with you, ready to provide all you need, including fighting your battles. Sometimes, you need to have drama and mess in your life to make you stop and reflect on what you are doing or have done to create this mess. God wants you to renew your mind and walk in the Spirit, letting go of thoughts leading you to sinfulness. **GPS>**"For you, O God, have tested us; you have tried us as silver is tried." **[Proverbs 66:10]** Tests, trials, and messes have messages in every single one. While you are in messes, you get a chance from God to sit and waddle in them. Seeing how unimportant it is, full of foolishness, listen to what the Holy Spirit is saying to you.

All trials and messes confirm that some sin has you in bondage, causing disorganization in your life due to your trying to serve two masters, making choices that have caused you to lose focus on God and place your focus on something earthly. God says to turn your burdens over to him. **GPS>**"Come to me, all who labor and are heavily laden, and I will give you rest. Take my yoke upon you, and learn from me, for I am gentle and lowly in heart, and you will find rest for your souls. For my yoke is easy, and my burden is light." **[Matthew 11:28-29]** Through messes, you become humble, fearful, and frustrated at wit's end. Finally, realizing that no human can help you due to their own frailty, using the ways of man, you see that you need more than physical rescuing, but also spiritually. God is your spiritual hook, pulling you back to your right senses.

In sincerity, full of remorse, fall on your knees, cry out to God in prayer with a repentant heart, ask forgiveness, confess your sins, and plead to turn your back on your sinful behavior. Willing to accept responsibility for the suffering you caused by restitution, apology, or both. God is your heavenly Father, willing to fight for you always in victory, giving Him the Glory. Messes come from a person whose affairs in life are in a state of confusion and laxity. As the world turns, so do messes, nonstop twenty-seven each day. There are no perfect families, people, churches, relationships, or marriages. Though you are not perfect, God forgives you of your sins, using you as an eyewitness to share what He has miraculously done for you through His power, giving him glory.

Messes are always about something imagined from what someone said or did, about something that is temporal, seen only with the natural eyes. Mess is are really distraction, inducing fear into your life journey. Causing you to be anxious, overwhelmed, and discouraged. Don't let messes, tests, and trials control you; let go of pride, ego, and sinful thoughts. These are all the thorns of mess, which usually call for you to be humbled, broken, unable to have, receive, feel, or see love. If you don't have love, how can you give it? If you can't, then you need your heart cleared of the sinfulness that is preventing you from receiving the love God has for you.

Do not lose hope when facing messes; remember that God is Love, trust, and believe in the Word with the help of the Holy Spirit, granting you wisdom and guidance. Turning such situations into teaching stones shows you ways to become stronger in faith and Christianity, teaching you discernment, to recognize the various lures of messiness, helping you avoid such pitfalls, helping you and others to remain in Christ, having selfless, loving hearts, minds, spirits, and souls.

There is a process that transfers the mess that you are into, becoming a victorious way out, allowing you to walk out of your mess victoriously, with God turning your tests, trials, and messes into a message for yourself and others through eyewitness testimonies and experiences. Sharing how the goodness of God and His Power saved you from your messy dilemmas, delivering you miraculously, presenting no doubt that to God be the Glory and praise, for he is your rescuer in His omnipresent ability, not man.

GPS>[Genesis 25:23-31, Genesis 27:15; Psalm 34:17-18, 46:1-3, Romans 12:12; Isaiah 41:10; James 1:12]

CHAPTER 14

Luck, Coincidences, And Accidents

What is the meaning of luck? It is "To prosper or succeed, especially through chance or good fortune; to come upon something desirable by chance." All your life, you have heard or even said these statements: "Good luck." There are no such things as luck, coincidences, and accidents. Wishing on "luck" is merely a word to make you feel, it will bring you what you desire. It is a ploy of Satan to give you false hope to believe in rather than to believe and trust God for your prosperity and destiny. Luck cannot exist because God knows nothing happens without the Lord's approval. There are no surprises, for He is Omniscience, knowing all things.

Yahweh, your heavenly Father, has planned everything that happens, whether you see it as good or bad. There are no accidents; each second of your life has been predestined before you were even born. Everything happens the way it is presupposed, being it is God's will for you. In reality, you are where you are meant to be every second of each day. This is what God does: He brings success through his mercy and grace. He is the one who gives favor and directions of the path that you are on, in every area of your life. Nothing is a coincidence; in the world, this word means" something that occurs, which is not planned or arranged but seems like it is."

The true definition is "God's will being done for your good," whatever it may be. Blessing you with experiences of awe, predestined by your heavenly Father. Whenever you find yourself experiencing something that seems out of the ordinary, but is amazing how it happened. It is truly the presence of the "Great I Am, showing you signs and wonders, causing you to openly acknowledge His name, "Amazing to identify these Supernatural events that occur in your life journey. Jesus says, **GPS>**"Unless you see signs and wonders, you will not believe." **[John 4:48]** There was a time when the statement, "If it be God's Will," was spoken all throughout the day by wise people.

Acknowledging the infinite Power and authority of Jehovah, paying homage through love, trust, respect, and reverence in God's ways, and being accepted. Just speaking those five words before taking action or doing anything is really a blessing being spoken over all your activities and thoughts. "If it be God's will" is acknowledging that God is God! In the movie "The Wizard of Oz," there is a great man behind the curtain in Oz running things. God is the "GREAT I AM," controlling everything on earth, on earth, above, below the earth, in the seas, and all the heavens, including all forms of life, declaring the existence of God. It is God that provides your every need; luck, coincidence, or accidents exist, and it is inappropriate to use those terms.

Here is what they both are in the Spiritual and in the natural. Hearing the prayers from the earth, God, in his mercy, love, and compassion, sends help to you through the means of using different things in a close enough vicinity, which addresses a similar issue that you have prayed yourself to sleep about. Now, you see the so-called "Coincidence" close enough for you or someone in your circle who will recognize the message, thereby experiencing the miracle(s) of God. Causing that, "Wow, I can't believe it! That's impossible! Moment. Is the Omnipresence of God, being who He is, the "Great I Am!" Answering your prayer(s), sending guidance on your journey, both spiritually and in the natural.

GPS>"But Jesus beheld their thoughts, and said unto them, with men this is impossible; but if they forsake all things for my sake, with God whatsoever things I speak are possible. **[Matthew 19:26]** Trust Jehovah, no longer having fear, receiving the promises and blessings of the Lord in love, and gaining wisdom.

GPS>[Jeremiah 29:11, 32:17; Luke 1:37-45; 2 Chronicles 18-19; Ruth 2:3; Genesis 50:20]

CHAPTER 15

Some Reasons Why You Get Physically Ill

Reasons why you get sick are due to many factors. Whenever I hear someone died from Cancer, I immediately deduce that it was either due to stress of employment issues, marital issues, a broken heart, or relationship problems. Children are hereditary, including self-hatred, anger, and bitterness. It all stems from a stony heart. I used to have one; I remember telling my Apostle that I could not love. He politely told me, "No, you can't love." You have to have to receive God's Love to give it." I was dumbfounded. Yet he was right; I was trying to love on my own terms. But that was not the right way to love. It should be with a pure heart and intentions that are not based on any condition.

When you get sick, something that is not helpful to your body stores excretions of poisonous chemicals that the body produces in response to your emotional state. Your body remembers that being unforgiving is the poison that you drink, hoping to kill someone else. Have you ever noticed someone you hate or don't like? How they are walking around, sashaying around you, living their best lives. While you are about to blow, festering at the sight of them. You are empowering them to cause you hurt, pain, and illness that can literally lead to physical death. Another thing that helps to kill you is fear, which plays a large role in your overall health.

Often, when you start thinking, speaking to yourself and others, that you are going to die because you have symptoms or a specific illness. You curse yourself by saying it. You are coming into agreement with what Satan has placed on you through sin. You must know who you are; you are a child of the Most High God, and you are healed by the stripes which Jesus endured for you and humanity. **GPS>**"But He was wounded for our transgressions. He was bruised for our iniquities. The chastisement for our peace was upon Him, And by His stripes, we are healed." **[Isaiah 53:5]**

A healing prayer is to say, "Lord, forgive me for my iniquities; I call Jehovah Rafaa to heal me. "I repent of my sins, and Lord, I denounce any wrong I have done knowingly or not knowingly, and I ask you, Abba Father, to heal me, for I am healed by the stripes of Jesus. I have sinned against you, and only you, Lord. Please forgive me and help me follow the path that you have planned for me. Thank you, Lord, for hearing my prayer and healing me. Lord, I love you, I need you, I am nothing without you. Lord, let your will be done, Amen."

Sometimes, you unknowingly claim things that people say to you and cause them to manifest, for example. You see someone who says, "Wow, you look sick. I heard you cough; it sounded really bad."

"It sounds like Pneumonia; you can die from that, you know?"

"I had a friend who had a friend that had a brother that sounded just like you."

Then you say, "Yeah, I do feel sick. I probably do have Pneumonia."

"I could die from this."

And there you go, cursing your own self due to fear and the foolishness of the world. Often, you are allowed to become ill because it shows that you should not be eating that, or you should not be there, warning you of your worldly ways. God allows sickness and death as the result of sin and the fallen world you live in. Because of sin and fear, you need a Savior, as sickness and death are a part of this temporary life. **GPS>**"Worship the Lord your God, and his blessing will be on your food and water. I will take away sickness from among you. **[Exodus 23:25]** Sometimes, as with Job, testing shows the faithfulness of a good servant to God. Sickness can come from a need for discipline, including a need to learn God's ways and decrees. Illness can lead you to pray more often and sincerely.

GPS>[Jeremiah 33:6; Romans 5"3-4; James 5:14-15; Isaiah 53:55; John 14:27]

THE BENEFICIAL EFFECTS OF DOING A FAST

Fasting plays a major role when walking in the spirit following Christ. You may fast, but you may not get the results you were seeking. Often, it is due to you're being spiritually clogged. Due to sinful thoughts and behaviors, the Living

Water of Christ is being prevented from flowing freely in your spirit. After a length of time, there will be a buildup of gunk that causes the hole to become smaller, causing less water to flow through freely, due to being clogged. This is the same concept for you. Metaphorically speaking, just as water flows through pipes, the contents in the Living Waters of the Word of God are life flowing throughout your Spirit. God wants to use you as a conduit, filling you with living water that will bring change and blessings to your situation.

When you are clogged, you are unable to receive God's words and spirit. It's as if you have overeaten, feeling miserable. This is the way it is for your spirit; you cannot receive because of being full of worldly crap issues. Having a worldly mindset, which is already detrimental, requires you to be purged of all that waste that is preventing you from hearing the Lord. Maybe you don't believe in God. Maybe you watch too much television, or maybe you play video games too much; the different bondage of captivity varies for each individual. But it really comes down to a lacking of self-control and discipline.

In order to receive the Lord's blessings and hear the Holy Spirit, you must be willing and obedient and have a righteous heart and mindset. Fasting helps you to break habits and removes you from having a clogged mind (pipe). This spiritual pipe must be cleared in order for you to be purified, sanctified, and renewed, allowing you to receive the guidance of the Holy Spirit. God cannot get through to you because you have eyes, ears, mouth, heart, and spirit, which are all clogged with worldly ways. It's as if you are physically consuming these hindrances, affecting you and others, both spiritually and in the natural.

131

There is a perpetual battle between flesh and spirit, with your mind influencing the choices you make continually. Fasting ignores the flesh, changing the effect it has on you and your circumstances. Fasting moves you into a better position regarding the Kingdom of Heaven, increasing your spiritual capacity. Establishing a closer relationship with God, strengthening you, bringing clarity, and authority on your journey. Your experience will change, and God will make you like a pipe that has been cleaned through prayers and sacrifices, allowing fasting to be an inhibitor.

Fasting requires spiritual discipline, helping to separate you from the distractions of this world. When you fast, you actually hear God better because you are focused on pleasing Him, setting up a covenant between Him and you. When you fast, you make a petition listing why you are fasting, in prayer, humbling yourself, denying yourself of worldly lust, including the pleasures of the flesh. Repenting causes you to be forgiven, find salvation and redemption from God, and become a living sacrifice for God's glory. The effects are that you become closer to God, being renewed and purified by the Holy Spirit, strengthening you in Christ, and defeating temptation(s). **GPS>**"When you fast, put oil on your face so that your fasting isn't obvious to others but to your Father, who is in secret. And your Father who sees in secret will reward you." **[Matthew 6:17-18]**

Doing a fast is very effective in causing breakthroughs over issues in the world that are causing you to feel hopeless. Putting the spirit first is an extra boost to get the attention of God! When you pray regarding your request, it must be done in supplication, realizing that malevolence is needed, enhancing the power that brings breakthroughs. To help you overcome your flesh, empowering the Spirit to do what it does, God will. Fasting is very powerful, giving access to the Spiritual realms and the supernatural. Your flesh is a bully, shoving you around with temptations of fleshly desires.

Your flesh is all about your relationship with yourself, in the natural, with physical cravings. These are selfish, leading to destruction if not acknowledged. Your mind, though, can overrule your body, giving you the capacity to meaningfully relate to others and the world while your spirit communes directly with God. There are some prayer requests that require additional dedication and outward shows of sacrifice, such as physical denial. Express love and worship to God. If you are not sure about the way you are fasting, and the reason for your petitions is possibly not Christ-like. Then ask God, for he says in the Bible.

GPS>"If any of you lacks wisdom, let him ask God, who gives generously to all without reproach, and it will be given him." **[James 1:5]** Most people can go without food for a day, but there are some who have medical problems and can't. Fasting is not always without food for the whole day. There are Intermittent types of Fast, allowing you to skip a meal, such as breakfast, or you can do a Daniel fast. Doing a fast doesn't mean abstaining just from food. You can fast by abstaining from sex (within marriage, of course) or abstaining from television and other electronics and activities. Allow the Holy Spirit to guide you, and always remember that fasting without prayer is not fasting at all. There are numerous resources to enlighten you regarding Christian fasting.

GPS>[Isaiah 1:19; Romans 7:13-23, 12:2; Daniel 10:3;1 Corinthians 6:19-20, 9:27; James 1:5, 4:10]

CHAPTER 16

How To Be a Good Steward and Servant?

How to become a good steward, which is also similar to a steward? Being a good steward is to know God, follow His Word through the teachings of Jesus Christ of Nazareth, be Faithful in righteousness, and let the Holy Spirit lead him to where your services are deemed. Take care of what God has already given you, no matter how minimal it may appear. Each item you see while on your physical and spiritual journey is merely a prop. They are all temporal, not part of your journey to Eternal Life. They are to provide you with comfort and provisions to help you along your journey.

Don't be lazy; appreciate everything you have, cherish all in natural, and take care of it. In everything that you do, do all things as you are doing them for God, in obedience. God knows a good steward, and He sees that you are taking care of what you have been given. Showing and speaking in thanksgiving and contentment. Jehovah will "Reward" you, elevating you because he loves you and sees that you are growing in love and wisdom. Bless you for being faithful, righteous, and walking in truth through Jesus Christ. Overflowing your cup with goodness and mercy in your life, always to stay in the house of the Lord forever. When you show that you can handle what you have and not complain.

You will be blessed and moved to something better. Elevated to a higher level of Christianity, increasing your wisdom and salvation. Because you have grown in your journey, not want for anything except to be closer to God. Being a good steward, God will upgrade you both Spiritual and in the natural. Just like a hotel, a plane ticket is done. You should use whatever gift(s)you have received to serve others as a faithful steward of God's grace in its various forms. **GPS>**"Every man according as his purpose that is in his heart, so let him give, not grudgingly, or of necessity; for God loves a cheerful giver." **[2 Corinthians 9:6-7]** As a good steward, you ungrudgingly pay the 10% tithes to the Head of the Church, being God." Through the clergy of that church, you fellowship. Paying Tides to a church is what God requested in the amount of 10%. God does not need any money. He is asking you to just give ten percent of your earnings as an acknowledgment, obedience, and willingness to give.

The word **tithe in Hebrew** means "a tenth part." Tithing is a donation, an offering, of one-tenth of your income for the service of God. Anytime you give, you give what you have decided in your heart to give, not reluctantly or under compulsion, for God loves a cheerful Giver. As a steward, you have life experience and empathy for others, all in God's love. You now have a heart that has been resurrected to all mercy, Spirit-filled, alive in the Spirit of God. Becoming a beacon of light as an example of how to be righteous.

As a Christian follower of Christ in the maturing stages of wisdom, the Spirit encouraged you to pray for others, taking everything to God, awaiting His Word, through the Holy Spirit. Jesus describes a good steward as diligent, hardworking, and willing to take reasonable risks. You are a well-seasoned

Steward, rooted and grounded in love. **GPS>**"There he will serve the Lord in gladness, for as a man thinks in his heart, so is he." **[Proverbs 23:7]** Not because of your age, but by the reminder of the Holy Spirit, causing you to remember what you know about Jesus. Having testimonies of the ways of the world leading to death. How he is being saved through grace, renewed in the Spirit of the Lord. Now rescued, reborn, letting all malice, confusion, and wickedness go in the name of Jesus.

God, having unconditional love, sees the face of Jesus, absolving you from all sin. He is such a loving God that he forgives you each time you fall back into sin. Nevertheless, through true repentance, having a repentant heart, you confess your sins to God, acknowledging them, willing to take responsibility for any pain and damage you caused to occur because of your choice. You make a covenant with God to turn around from your sins and be restored to walking in the Spirit, no longer in the flesh, surrendering to God completely.

In the Bible, there is the parable of the three stewards, how they managed what they were given by their master. Having him say that they were good stewards, rewarding them for their wisdom in managing what they had. There are many good stewards in the Bible, such as John the Baptist, Lydia, Mary, Moses, Paul, Nathan the Prophet, the Disciples, Job, King David, Joseph, and many others. Possibly, you may know a few good stewards yourself. You, as a good steward, are not selfish, using your life experiences in which you apparently fell victim to Satan's ploys of temptation, which led to your being in the bondage of sin. Now, not forgetting, you stay focused on Jesus, awaiting the right answer in and through prayer.

Realizing that anytime you have to rush and give an answer, it is always from the devil, along with confusion, is Satan's calling card. In wisdom and humility, you step back, letting pride and ego get in the way of saving a soul in righteousness. You seek wise counsel when necessary, keeping everything about the brother or sister you are helping in confidence. The knowledge you gain is applied to those whom you are helping, including yourself, on your life journeys. In love and obedience, you follow the Word of Yashua, walking in the Spirit.

GPS>[2 Corinthians 9:6-11; 1Peter 4:10; Luke 42-48; Matthew 25:14-30;]

BEING A FOLLOWER OF CHRIST

Being a true follower of Jesus Christ requires your complete and total surrender to the truth and will of God in your life. In doing so, a covenant is made that, indeed, will strengthen your relationship, in truth, with the Word of God. Through devout submission, trust is established, causing more frequent and close communication with the Heavenly Father. Through these acts of obedience, understanding, and guidance are provided by the Holy Spirit. Causing you to walk in the spirit and not by sight. You now think, see, and live in the spiritual realm, which is supernatural. You follow the teachings of our Blessed Savior Jesus Christ, who was sent to you, leading you to be a witness, ambassador of God, and disciple of Christ.

You have heard God trying to reach you at various times in your life. Yet you refuse to hear, listen, and follow Him.

Don't be a grasshopper like the one in the fable of the "Ant and the Grasshopper. Tomorrow may be too late. Do it now, turn, and follow Jesus. Only goodness and mercy shall be at your beck and call, in Jesus' name. Being a follower of Jesus Christ means that you are to listen for God's calling through the holy spirit; it's as if your creator, Jehovah, put a homing device inside of you so that wherever or whenever you call out to the heavens. Jesus is your intercessor and advocate before Him. You know how your phone has the ability to track your loved ones? Is anyone's location divulging their whereabouts around the world? Well, this is the magnetism that you have in you. It is called a conscience. God placed that inside you, including all humanity.

Take, for instance, you borrowed [$10.34] ten dollars and thirty-four cents, establishing a verbal contract or agreement with someone, let's say, Bill. Time passes, and you haven't seen Bill for some time. Then, one day, you are walking down the street, and who do you see walking straight toward you is the person? Bill, the one who lent you $10.34, through the unique, wonderful, fearlessly, and divine design of your creator, you are immediately prompted by your inner Spirit that you owe him $10.34, and the same actions take place in Bill, reminding him that you owe him, $10.34. This gifted attribute is from your creator, Jehovah, who has been instilled in you, causing you to have a conscience through the Holy Spirit, nudging you to remember the agreement. How awesome is that? It's as if God has for you a "hot line', to keep you safe and protected.

As a servant of Jesus, you use the "hot Line" for it works both ways; Jesus calls you, offering you the "Fruit of the Spirit," the 1-800 connection, along with the GPS to heaven calling you, to come to the altar, where His arms are open wide, welcoming you home to your Father. As a follower of Christ, you know that you can never repay Jesus for what He has done for you. All the apostles were chosen by God for Jesus. In being a follower of Christ, you are continually prepared to answer questions related to how and why you love God. Questions about His Son, Jesus Christ, and the Holy Spirit.

Daily, your walk is challenged to either trip you up, to fall in the snare of the devil, or be delayed and harmed by the fiery arrows of the devil, one way or another. If you look closely at the word lived, you will see an anadrome. When you remove the last two letters, E and D, in the word lived, reverse the word, it spells devil, including the word evil. It appears that living has a lot to do with evil and the devil. Being a follower of Christ consists of several characteristics that are needed to honor this vow.

Tenacity, having the determination to be obedient to God and to follow the 10 Commandments. As a follower of Christ, you are to be reflective of Jesus in every area of your life. Bearing your own cross in self-denial of worldly lust, staying faithful through discipline, and obedience to the Word of God. You display characteristics of patience, kindness, love, gentleness, truthfulness, and humility. Your life is that of total submission to God's will, working tirelessly to promote love to others through the Ways of Christ. You worship and praise the Lord daily, having a strong personal relationship with God while being taught how to be forgiving, understanding, generous, faithful, and righteous.

Having a hunger for the Word of God, you relish the opportunities to be of service to others, not being judgmental nor boastful, always bringing hope to any situation and the recipients of it. You are embarking on discipleship, encouraged by the Holy Spirit, helping others embark on seeking the "Kingdom of God for it is at hand, as close as your hand can reach, and pick up the Bible. Jesus embraces you, wanting you to know all the knowledge that is in the Bible, being the Best Information Before Life Eternal. Being a follower of Christ, you go out into the world, spreading to everyone the "Good News of the Gospel" in faith, truth, obedience, and honor, helping a community of followers to grow in the wisdom of the Lord. Through the various circumstances that you have encountered on your Life Journey, you have become an eyewitness to doing what is right. Following the Spirit of Christ, making choices which are honorable, pure, moral, non-biased, and with integrity, honoring the Lord God. You recognize the power and the authority of the Lord who is over your life. God.

As a follower of Christ, you obey Jesus' commands in gladness and excitement, eager to save souls for the Lord. Winning souls, leading others to the Good News of the Gospel. You have a forgiving heart, willing to forgive any wrong or offense done to you, obeying the command of Jesus. Putting God first is the way of discipleship, by accepting Jesus as your Lord and Savior and admitting that sin causes separation from God. As a follower of Christ, the only agenda you follow is the Lord's, realizing that you have a purpose, which includes living in peace, gaining eternal life, and not making a move without first conferring with the Father. You implement the wisdom, patience, and strength of the Lord, trusting Him in every storm and battle, knowing that you have the victory.

Being a follower of Jesus places you in a position in which you are under the power and authority of Christ Jesus. Discipleship builds a community of other followers of Christ, which is the body of Christ, a holy organization of God. As a follower of Christ, you share how you can be separated from God by sin, needing to repent, coming to God, asking for forgiveness, and showing accountability for what hurt the sins (s) you have committed. Showing the way of being transformed, from being in the world, being rebellious, to receiving forgiveness of sins can be found, freeing you from sin, guilt, and condemnation.

Releasing you from guilt, sin, and condemnation through repentance, gaining purification, and being righteous with God. In the Lord's favor, finding forgiveness, salvation, wiping away all your sin(s), being redeemed by the grace, mercy, and love of Jesus Christ. Discipleship and ministry are the inductions to becoming any of the following: apostle, minister, teacher, prophet, or evangelist, which are all under the tutelage of Jesus Christ's doctrine. Everyone has an office of ministry. No matter your worldly title of employment, you are a representative of God on a mission.

As a follower, you are rooted and grounded in love. Although you may fall into sin again, by the Holy Spirit, you will be reminded of all you know about Jesus, being the "Way," the "Truth," and the Life to surrender to. Being a follower of Christ, you no longer think of yourself but now trust and believe in God for all your needs, protection, and unconditional love. God. There are different ways people are called to serve God. As an ambassador and fisherman of men for Jesus, you minister to the mentally ill, those in financial dismay, the physically sick, and all issues of life. Clergymen are to be a bridge between God and humanity, for they are responsible for speaking the truth of the Bible, sharing it with everyone, accurately, no modifications, corrupting the Word of God.

You walk in discretion and obedience, loving your enemies as you love yourself. You do good to those who hate you, bless those who curse you, and pray for those who mistreat you. As a follower of Jesus, you are to be reflective in your walk, talk, behavior, mannerisms, and worship of Him. Stay focused, surrender everything to Jesus, and voluntarily submit to following the ways of Jesus. It is the beginning of your sanctification and growth in righteousness, looking to Jesus as your solution to all your needs in faithfulness. As a follower of Christ, you make disciples of others to spread the word about Jesus' teachings.

Encouraging others to seek the Kingdom of Heaven is at Hand", for it really is wherever your arm reaches, is for your Bible, the Best Instructions Before Life Eternal. They are to encourage others by sharing the Good News of the Gospel, building trust between them and God. Discipleship requires honesty, humility, and devoutness to God and His word, wavering. The devil seeks to put problems in your life, but fear not. **GPS>**"Resist the devil, and he will flee from you" **[James 4:7]**. The experiences that you encountered and got through victoriously can help others when they encounter worldly troubles in life.

Jesus told the disciples that they must deny themselves and follow Him. In being a follower of Christ, you are to be able to project peace to those who are looking at you. Being a Follower of Christ means that you are walking by the Holy

Spirit, and in your lifestyle, you follow the path journey, allowing you to grow in the precious words of God sent down to earth with Jesus, for God knew that the world needed a Savior to follow, as you were blinded by worldly issues, walking lost in sin and death. There is a reason why being a follower of Christ is important: it allows you to feed others the Word of God and spiritual nourishment for the spirit, mind, and soul.

The ultimate reason was that you needed a Savior. Jesus was your only human blessed sacrifice; that was the only way for you to be saved from damnation. Jesus was the only sacrifice that God the Father found acceptable for the redemption of your sins. Being a follower of Christ, you were told to heal the sick, raise, cause the lame to walk, cast out demons, cause the blind to see, raise the dead, cause the lame to walk, and free those oppressed. Drink anything, it shall not harm you through the power and authority of God.

As followers of Christ, you are encouraged in faithfulness and committed and motivated to be kind, good, and God-fearing. Willing to turn your back on worldly vices and sins that can entice you into darkness, bringing death, destruction, pain, and loss. Satan came here to steal, kill, and destroy. If you're following Christ Jesus, this makes him very angry because he wants to hurt you. Why? Because God loves you, and you are imitating Jesus, spreading the Word, witness of the omnipotent, miraculous, limitless power and authority that God has. In being a follower of Christ, you are light, shining for others to see and feel the warmth through the love of God and His Word. Giving Him glory for all that He is, for all that He does, and for what He did for you at Calvary, be that light that draws others' lights who are a bit dim to become bright in God's promises.

GPS>[John 15:9-1; Matthew 16:24-26; Luke 9:23; John 8:31-38; 2 Timothy 2:1-2]

BEING UNSELFISH AND OBEDIENT

Being unselfish means to put the needs or wishes of others before your own. You are to be unselfish, being generous, volunteering your time, having empathy giving emotional support. You are humble and not prideful, having an ego that wants feeding; you instead admit when you are not correct. Treating others with dignity, even if you do not agree, you are willing to compromise. You give and edify, encouraging others as you rejoice with them in their accomplishments.

You put others first, thinking about what is best for them. You have ethics and morals that you follow as you evaluate yourself in order to stay in the good graces of the Lord, being an example to others. Having heartfelt sentiments of being kind helps to increase good health, both mentally and physically, as love is all you need. In unselfishness, you do not seek attention or limelight for anything that you do.

In being unselfish, you promote unity in your surroundings, causing others to have a feeling of belonging, creating a positive atmosphere. God loves you; He sent His only begotten Son, Jesus, from heaven, to walk and live as a man on earth, among the people. Bring His Word, with Jesus being the example for humanity to follow. **GPS>**"For God so loved the world, that He gave His only begotten Son, that whosoever believeth in Him should not perish, but have Everlasting Life." **[John 3:16]**

GPS>[Luke 6:32-34; 2 Corinthians 8:9; Proverb 11:25; Galatians 5:13; James 4:10]

OBEDIENCE

Obedience is hearing the Word of God and acting on it. It means that you are willing to do God's will. Surrendering to His authority, living righteously, and making choices that are of good report. Obedience shows respect in following the rules and guidelines set up to keep you safe. Assisting you to accomplish your calling(s), which God has for you to do. Not engaging in your own understanding, but dutifully remaining in compliance with the ways of God. **GPS>**"Trust in the Lord with all thine heart; and lean not unto thine own understanding. In all, thy ways acknowledge him and shall direct thy paths" **[Proverbs 3:5-6].** Which, indeed, is very important in your Life's Journey, both spiritually and physically.

Being obedient brings many blessings as you live in humility and righteousness, following the ways of Christ. Obedience will deliver you from the snares of Satan. Through prayer and keeping the Ten Commandments, you find favor. As you further reveal your faithfulness and belief in Jehovah. You being obedient causes you to see prosperity and miracles in your life affairs. **GPS>**"If you are willing and obedient, You shall eat the good of the land; But if you refuse and rebel, You shall be devoured by the sword," for the mouth of the Lord has spoken." [1:19-20 **[Isaiah 1;19-20]**

In obedience, you are meek yet bold in declaring your devotion, belief, and trust in God. Finding healing, redemption, and manifestation(s) of your needs and desires. As you live in love, studying the Word diligently, causing you to no longer be weak, obeying man, but finding the strength to be strong and brave, having no fear of what it is that God has chosen for you to do. You worry not, knowing that God is your provider, and that it is He whom you are to obey, and what He wants done, it will be as He wills it. Disobedience comes from a heart and mind that is either rebellious, stubborn, or self-centered.

GPS>[Isaiah 55:11; John 14:15; Ephesians 6:1-3; Romans 1:5; Hebrews 13:17]

CHAPTER 17

You Are To Thank, Love, Praise, Worship, And Honor God

God is worthy of all praise, the reasons being He is God, "THE GREAT I AM"; He is the creator of heaven, earth, and all life forms. He is your provider; He is your protector; He is your guide; He is faithful; He is your help; He is your life source; He is the air that you breathe; He is the author and finisher of your faith and fate; He is your chastiser; He is the powerful answer to all your prayer; He is malevolent; He is omnipresence, He is omniscience; He is a spirit; He is in the heavens having all authority; power which is for eternity; He is above all; He is always available; He is your caretaker because He cares for you, loving you unconditional endlessly.

You have your own list of what God is. God the Father deserves your **praises**, just as you do when you give or receive accolades for something that was relatively difficult, yet you succeeded. You are to **worship** God and His Holy name, celebrating His awe-inspiring power. God is to be given **thanks**, expressing sincere **gratitude**, for all the great things that he has done, is doing, and is going to do for you and those who believe in Him.

You are to show **respect, honor, and obedience** to Him as He controls and rules. The entire universe is His Kingdom, and he is King also, over all earthly, Spiritual, and celestial entities. Jehovah should be revered for his holiness and the wondrous mysteries of life, existence, and time. You are to walk circumspectively in His presence. Showing humility while expressing your **love** for Him. Understanding that He is was and will be forever knowing all, to lead you to Eternal Life.

You are to love God for who He is, realize what he is, giving goodness, grace, mercy, compassion, love, and wisdom to you. By giving Yeshua praise, you are first acknowledging that you believe that God is real. When you honor God, you are causing Him to come closer to you and be in your presence. When you praise God, you are saying that you appreciate what He has done for you and all that He is doing, which is truly tremendous. God deserves praise, worship, and honor. When you express your love, trust, belief, thanks, and respect in obedience to God, there will be blessings to follow in the forms of manifestations of your prayer request, needs, wisdom, and the renewal of your Spirit.

Making all challenges that you are experiencing, no longer have you in the grip of despair, fear, hopelessness, alone, in bondage with doubt. Jesus, being the way, is the solution through God. All the help you need in any situation. Jesus has paved the way and provided a formula to have victory over any and all temptations. There is not one temptation that cannot be overcome because Jesus loved you so much that He experienced them all for you. He then showed you how to overcome them through His examples, and through the Word of God, which He brought from heaven, given to Him by His Father God. God deserves your praise and honor, for He is worthy. God deserves all of the above tributes, just as you do for your earthly parents, friends, associates, strangers, relatives, acquaintances, including your dependable pet. You effortlessly express love, respect, understanding, and admiration, giving time, services, gifts, and treats in recognizing their trivial earthly performances through achievements or appeasing actions.

God deserves so much more for all the powerful miracles, mysteries, and grandeur of his authority in Omnipotence. God helps those who are his children. He is with you forever and will never forsake you. God's love is freely given to you, and you are to freely receive and share it with others. The best way of showing Honor, Love, worship, Thanks, Praise, and Obedience to Yahweh is by obeying the "Ten Commandments" and the Word of God. Following the behavior of Jesus Christ, who is The Way, The Truth, and The Life, leading you to Eternal Life. God is your refuge and strength, a very present help in trouble. There are so many reasons why you are to praise, worship, believe, trust, and honor God.

In such a fallen and bleak world, where nothing is for certain. God's Word and Love, brought to you by His Son Jesus Christ, is your only life vest. The Word of God in the Bible has been proven to be true and has not changed. It provides you with instructions on how to survive in this cursed world. Through communicating with God and giving Him praise, you are inviting the Lord into your presence. Praise facilitates access to God by seeking to gain closeness with Him through following Jesus, "The Living Word." Praise ye the Lord, Sing unto the Lord a new Song, in the congregations.

When you praise, worship, and honor God. You are showing the most demonstrative act of love. It is terrible that mankind is so selfish, ignorant, and arrogant, quickly acknowledging athletic, crooked politician(s), television chefs, and various entertainers for their performances in what they specialize in. Yet, not God, and His Son Jesus, your Good Shepherd and the way. So why not give praise, honor, accolades, thanksgiving, acknowledgments, and worship to the one who has created everything that you see with your natural eyes and don't see, being that things are in another dimension? God is the same today, yesterday, tomorrow, and forever.

What about those special talents and gifts that have been given to you by God that have caused you to be wealthy, famous, and successful? **GPS>**"Let them praise His name in the dance; let them sing praises unto him with the timbrel and harp." **[Psalms 149:3]** God is your creator. You give your earthly parents praise, respect, obedience, and honor. In the form of thank you, right? So why not give praise and show honor to your creator?

GPS>[Psalms 46:1-4, 69:30,79:13, 149:1; John 14:6; Romans 12:1; Revelation4:11; Hebrews 12:28-29]

CHAPTER 18

Being Beautifully Broken

In the world, beauty is determined by the majority's opinion of what is defined as beauty. Often, the characteristics are physical, being seen in natural, with the eyes of mankind. Causing anything that is not of the world's description of beauty to be looked down on, frowned upon, considered less than, unacceptable, ugly, and undesirable. Having this type of worldliness mindset hurts so many, affecting their quality of life and mental stability. Setting standards of what should be, and not leading to your being judgmental of others. Which frequently initiate suicides, drug addictions, and loss.

Though there have been times when worldly ways have made you feel damaged, like a broken teacup in pieces, needing something to put you back together, there is a method of mending broken items with gold. It is called Kintsugi (Kin to Sue gee- "golden joinery" or "golden repair"), which is the Japanese art of repairing broken pottery by mending the areas of breakage, with lacquer dusted or mixed with powdered gold, silver, or platinum, a method similar to the maki-e technique. When you think that you are broken, though you are in pieces, in total submission, present them to God.

Allowing Him, the greatest artist of all, to put you back together, using his golden Resurrection power and pure love. God is the only one who can restore you from the broken state you are in through the life-changing gift of embodiment, making you whole, spiritually and naturally, in the rebirth of righteousness, in luminous beauty.

GPS>"He heals the brokenhearted and binds up their wounds." **[Psalm 147:3]** Learn to embrace the cracks and imperfections that you have. Yes, you are beautifully broken from all the battles on earth you've encountered due to your having a worldly mindset. Because of a lack of knowledge, you've tried to fight your battles alone. God says to let Him fight your battles, and that he is El Elyon is the only judge. **GPS>**"The LORD will fight for you, and you have only to be silent." **[Exodus 14:14]**

Nevertheless, after submitting yourself and your mindset to following the Holy Spirit. You have found the way, now having priceless wisdom, filling your cracks in gold, causing your unique imperfections to shine beautifully, and becoming more valuable than before, which was due to your having a lack of knowledge, in disobedience, toward God and His Word. Kintsugi teaches you that the brokenness in your heart, mind, body, and soul, having faith in God, these breaks will make you better, stronger, and more valuable than you were before. Living in righteousness through renewal and salvation.

GPS>[Psalms 34:18, 51:10; Luke 4:18; Joel 2:13; Matthew 5:4; Isaiah 53:5]2 Corinthians 4:7-9; 2 Chronicles 20:17]

RESURRECTION POWER

Resurrection Power is what God used to bring Jesus Christ back from the dead. It is through this Supernatural power that we have authority over all. Making miracles occur is what God used to resurrect Jesus. After his being crucified, he died and was placed in the tomb. Through this miraculous power, the resurrecting of Jesus is evidence confirming that your Almighty Heavenly Father, indeed, has authority and power over death and life. When you remember God's miraculous Resurrection Power, you are acknowledging His Omnipotence. When you remember Jesus' Resurrection, you are celebrating the power of God that raised Him from the dead. This Celestial event addresses and confirms all prophecies foretelling the coming of Jesus. God's only begotten Son, coming from heaven to live among the people, spreading the Word of His Father God in obedience, bringing salvation to the world, freeing you from sin and death. Through Jesus' birth, life, crucifixion, death, and resurrection, Jesus' purpose was fulfilled.

GPS>"But Jesus uttered a loud cry, and breathed out His last [voluntarily, sovereignty dismissing and releasing His spirit from His body in submission to His Father's plan]." **[Mark 15:37]** When the curtain in the temple ripped, which separated the high priests, priestesses, Pharisees, and Sadducees from the people. This was a sign from God that He accepted Jesus Christ's body and blood as a living sacrifice, in atonement for all of mankind's sins, becoming the ultimate sacrifice to God.

No longer were they to offer or sacrifice anything to God. Jesus' Crucifixion was the ultimate sacrifice. Guiding the way for all to be free to seek God and have an intimate relationship with Him, as He was now approachable to each individual. God says to bring all your sins and concerns, no matter what they are, come, and He will show you love and forgiveness. The resurrection of Jesus and his ascension back to heaven made HIM your intercessor, causing God to see Jesus as Christ Jesus. No longer was He Jesus Christ. He had done the ultimate, changing back to the original form he was before leaving heaven.

Now, being seated on the right hand of His Father. That is why you call your heavenly Father Abba Father, meaning that you have now been adopted into Jesus' family; through His suffering and death, you are now His child. Whenever you pray to the Father, regardless of your state, He sees Jesus when He looks at you and how you have accepted Christ Jesus as your Lord and Savior. None of your ugliness is seen, only Jesus, who died for you. Causing you to also be dead in the worldliness, yet alive in Christ Jesus. Being revived from the dead, being resurrected into a new creature in Christ Jesus. Believing in His death and miraculous resurrection, you are very precious in His sight, for you are Jesus' disciple. Whenever you change your mindset to righteousness and repent, you, too, are resurrected as a new creature in Christ. Being resurrected by the same power that raised Jesus from the dead.

The power of Resurrection differs from having authority. It is a miraculous Power. It achieves for us supernatural strength. The word Resurrection is Greek, with several meanings. One meaning is to "stand," "again," and "to stand up." Visualize a dead body standing up. It is quite a visual, right? This is one way a resurrection looks. It also means standing up to your problems. God's Resurrection Power will cause you to stand up and face all your problems, following

Jesus' way. Resurrection Power makes you a victor, overcoming all circumstances. Be it mental, be it emotional, be it physical, and, of course, Spiritual.

Resurrection Power will cause you to overcome your situations; it also gives way to breakthroughs of stubborn strongholds over you. If you are depressed, then call out to God, using the authority and Resurrection power over depression. That God has given you. Just like in everything, there is another to follow. First, in order for Resurrection power to manifest, you have to be Spiritual Resurrection. You must be pure in heart, accepting Jesus Christ as your Lord and Savior. His power will benefit us now and eternally. You must believe in the one true living God, even if you don't do it in the right order. God is a good God and merciful. He will find ways to accommodate you when your heart is true. Granting you Resurrection power. To allow you to accomplish that which you are meant to do while you follow His will.

Once you receive the power, use it to accomplish what it was meant for. It then returns to God as a job well done in obedience, **GPS>**"So shall my word be that goes forth from My mouth; it shall not return to Me void, but it shall accomplish what I please, and it shall prosper in the thing for which I sent it." **[Isaiah 55:11]** The power of Resurrection differs from having authority; it is a miraculous Power. It achieves for us supernatural strength. The word Resurrection is Greek, with several meanings. One meaning is to "stand," "again," and "to stand up." Visualize a dead body standing up, and you'll get the idea of what a resurrection is. It also means standing up to your problems. God's Resurrection Power will cause you to stand up to and face your problems Jesus' way.

Resurrection Power makes you a victor, overcoming all circumstances. Be it mental, be it emotional, be it physical, and, of course, Spiritual. Resurrection Power will cause you to overcome your situations; it also gives way to breakthroughs of stubborn strongholds over you. If you are depressed, then call out to God, using the authority and Resurrection power over depression. That He has given you. But know that first, in order for Resurrection power to manifest, you must have Spiritual Resurrection must precede any Resurrection. You must be pure in heart, accepting Jesus Christ as your Lord and Savior. His power will benefit you now and eternally.

You must believe in the one true living God, even if you don't do it in the right order. God is a good God and merciful. He will find ways to accommodate you when your heart is true. Accomplishing that which you are meant to follow His will. Once you receive the power, use it to accomplish what it was meant for. It then returns to God as a job well done in obedience. The key to unlocking resurrection power is your willingness to cooperate with the Holy Spirit. Cooperation is critical in every endeavor a person may attempt. If you are to live successfully in resurrection power, you must follow Jesus' example of how he walked in obedience and humility. You must learn to cooperate with the Holy Spirit. Look around and reflect on the state of your world; it is more obvious than ever that "you need supernatural power" to defeat your challenges. Mankind's needs of the world are more evident than ever.

It is evident that restoration through repentance, belief, and love of Christ is the key to having peace both inside and out. So many are still in need today of guidance from your Savior, Jesus Christ. Let Jehovah know you are giving back to Him because of what He did for you. Not because of what you've done! Let God always be first in your life, surrendering all to Him. Spiritual blind with no love in their hearts. This can be reversed; you must have no Fear, and you must trust Jesus. When you accept Jesus as your Lord and Savior, His power will benefit you now and eternally. If Christ is in you, although the body is dead because of sin, the Spirit is life because of righteousness. If the Spirit of him who raised Jesus from the dead dwells in you, he who raised Christ Jesus from the dead will also give life to your mortal bodies through his Spirit who dwells in you.

GPS>"Let not sin therefore reign in your mortal body, to make you obey its passions. Do not present your members to sin as instruments for unrighteousness, but present yourselves to God as those who have been brought from death to life, and your members to God as instruments for righteousness." **[Romans 6:12-13]** Sin keeps you in our brokenness and our bondage. It manifested itself in our lives as guilt, shame, and misery. These lead you to dark paths of despair, depression, and feelings of hopelessness. However, as new creatures in Christ, you have access to the same resurrection power that raised Jesus from the grave, which is also known as being resurrected or restored. Jesus never knew separation from Almighty God.

When Jesus cried out on the cross, "Father, why hast thou forsaken me? He was expressing the hurt of being separated from His Father. You know how to walk in Resurrection Power. You must not be afraid; this Resurrection Power is an anointed Power. The 39 whip strips that Jesus endured on his body for you. It is for your healing. That is why He took them without complaint. Every door of healing should be open to you. You are in Christ, and His victory is your victory. Satan's head is crushed at the cross by Christ, and by all who are Christ's throughout all time in redemption; you are free. You have been sealed with the Holy Spirit until you arrive in heaven, living in the power of the Resurrection.

Through resurrection power, you, being a 21st-century disciple, can gain the same strength to accomplish God's purpose. In addition, it is through this power that you can find personal forgiveness, acceptance, and wholeness. The work that has been entrusted to you is destined for success because of the Holy Spirit working within you so that you can understand the truths that God's word provides, which are in the forms of love, patience, and forgiveness. The following of the Holy Spirit is wisdom, trust, renewal, and Spiritual growth in the truth of God's Word. Although you were once an enemy of God, through the precious blood and body of His Son, Jesus Christ, you have been reconciled back to God. Being both a witness in testimonies of the Resurrection Power of the LORD and a light for the paths of others, seeing you as an ambassador of God.

GPS>[Matthew 11:28-29; 2 Corinthians 5:17; John 11:28; Philippians 3:10; 1 Corinthians 15:1-8; Romans 1:4, 6:4]

WHAT IS RESURRECTION POWER?

Here is the truth about Easter Sunday, which all along was and is a lie. It is not for Christians. We need to separate lies from the truth. When you say, "Sunday is Easter Sunday," it is much more than that. It is because of the death of Jesus on that Friday. Death thought that he had won by the death of

Jesus. When Sunday came, Death came to realize that there was a power that Death could not stop called "RESURRECTION POWER." That Resurrection Power is what brought Jesus back to life from the dead.

WHAT IS RESURRECTION SUNDAY?

Though the world uses Jesus' Resurrection as "Easter Sunday." You, as Christians, are not to call it "Easter Sunday." Easter Sunday is truly "The Resurrection Sunday" because that is actually the day when Jesus rose from the dead. Called "The Resurrection," as it should be.

The name Easter originated from the word "Easter," meaning Spring goddess, Rebirth. The name of a pagan goddess. She is the goddess of fertility; her trademark is the bunny rabbit. The importance of her and the bunny is that the bunny rabbit is known for giving birth rapidly.

Another trademark was the eggs for the Goddess during the Spring Equinox, meaning life, birth, and fertility. The Lenten season begins on the first Sunday, ending after 40 days of fasting. It is also the First Sunday on which Jesus was tempted in the desert. While He began His fast of 40 days and 40 nights. The eggs are supposed to show the trademark of Easter.

Easter has the rabbit laying eggs to produce life. Jesus is the God of All. Jesus came to do the same thing: bring life. Yet they practiced the tradition of Easter and boiled the eggs, which did not create life. In fact, it killed the life that was inside the egg.

In England, the name took on a different tone. In Britain, Easter occurs at a different time each year. It is observed on the first Sunday after the full moon following the first day of spring in the Northern Hemisphere, where festivals may occur anytime during those time periods. The Bunny rabbit has many names, bringing eggs, chocolates, gifts, and treats depending on which country he hopped up in. Germany's celebration of the arrival of the Easter Bunny is called "Easter Monday" (Ostermontag). This tradition consists of an Easter Bunny who delivers eggs, candy, and toys to children. Originated among German Lutherans. Stating that "It was first a Santa-like figure who judged whether children had behaved well." It is an annual public holiday that follows Easter Sunday, remembering Jesus Christ's resurrection, according to Christian belief, which was originally shunned by Christians.

Including, in the beginning, also by the Quakers, Episcopalians, Catholics, and Presbyterians. The Pennsylvania Dutch began the custom of supplying children with colored eggs on Easter day. The Easter celebration caught on, with the start of using different animals and things depending on where you lived. It was then said that the Easter Bunny went all over, going from place to place, delivering wonderful goodies by the 17th century in Europe. There was a connection between Easter and the bunny. Some believe the tale that the Easter Bunny came from England.

Now, it was said to travel all around the world. People were told that the bunny lived on Easter Island. Curious followers hearing this had to go to Easter Island to find where the bunny lived. So, they boarded a ship traveling some 8,468 miles, in kilometers of 13,627. Motivated to search for that infamous Easter bunny, with those delectable chocolates, colored eggs, gifts, and other yummy treats. Upon their arrival, they found a giant carved stone of pagan gods called Moai, which were estimated by archeologists to have been made between roughly 100 and 1650. Rapa Nui Polynesian descendants. Carvers created some 900 of these sculptures.

The Moai represent ancestral chiefs who were believed to have been descended directly from the gods and whose supernatural powers could be harnessed for the benefit of humanity, but no Easter bunny. While the fable of the Easter bunny circulated around the globe. Now, in Australia, the bunny is called the Easter Bilby, also known as the rabbit-eared Bandicoot. Which description is of a small marsupial with long ears, a pointy snout, a black and white tail, and greyish fur? In Switzerland, they changed the bunny to Easter Cuckoo; it is no longer called Easter Bunny. It was now replaced by the Cuckoo, which is a medium-sized long-tailed bird, typically with a gray or brown back with bared to pale underparts.

Many Cuckoos lay their egg in the nests of small songbirds. They are called the Easter Cuckoos. In Switzerland, Easter means Chocolate Hares are given (aka Murder Bunnies) instead of Eggs. Here, only chocolate bunnies are given. The egg-laying rabbit with bright-colored eggs is hidden with chocolates so that kids can find them. Now, the parents have become the rabbit. Telling the children in the morning that the rabbit came and left the brightly colored eggs with other yummy goodies. They were now part of this farce. Children, being children in innocence, saw those eggs and treats where actually in the nests of (real) birds. Asked their parents if they could or should leave carrots for the Easter Bunny. Also, many Catholic religions use statues of pagan gods and goddesses in their churches. The reason is that the early Church had to merge with pagan practices and beliefs in order to blend into Roman society. In the rites and symbols of the Roman Catholic Church, you can find surviving, though re-branded, pre-Christianity myths, deities, festivals, and rituals.

I am not trying to take away the wonderful treats for all of you who have a sweet tooth, with Easter as one of your best days for indulging. It is understandable because I myself have a sweet mouth, I've said. So much so that there are times when I actually order my dessert first before I receive my meal; those at the table with me look amazed sometimes, wondering why I did that. I just say, "Because I'm grown now." :-) Then, hearing chuckles shared by all while the festivities continue, I dig into my sweet treat.

Nor am I picking on the Catholic religion. I myself attended Parochial schools. In fact, I wanted to be a nun until I turned 15 years old. The truth is that I used to pray to the statues, burn candles, bless myself with holy water all the rites. I followed, but wisdom is power, and so is truth. I believe you want to know the truth, so I have presented you with it. The world is full of danger and deceit. As Christians, we have spiritual enemies who lie in wait, ready to poison our lives with their lies. But where Jesus sends us, He also equips us. As you walk in His truth, by His power, He protects you from the lies of the world and the schemes of the enemy so that through you. His truth may bring Him glory. You should thank the Father for guiding your steps as you walk so that you may remain in His truth. Thank Him for giving you eyes to see the danger that awaits and the power to stomp any lie that might lead you astray, causing you to be a stumbling block for others.

Christianity has nothing to do with the bunny, the eggs, or their coloring. Easter Sunday is **"The Resurrection Sunday."** Your focus is on celebrating the Resurrection of Jesus. Resurrection Power works miracles; it is Dunamis Power. In it, you have authority and are anointed to do what God wants you to do; it is for His will. This power is like dynamite. Example: As a police officer, you have a gun, a taser, handcuffs, badge with the authority to use them whenever a situation requires the use of them, by following laws and regulations associated with this authoritative power. This is the same for you as a Christian with resurrection power; you are armed with the Authority and Power of God by His rules and regulations.

GPS>[Isaiah 55:11, 53:4-5; Luke 10:19; Mark 1:12; Ephesians 1:19-22; Colossians 2:15; John 14:12, 16:13-15; Philippians 2:8, 3:10]

CHAPTER 19

Forgiveness

What is Forgiveness? The definition of forgiveness is essentially the act of pardoning an offender. In the Bible, the Greek word translated as "forgiveness" literally means "to let go," as when a person does not demand payment for a debt. The Bible says that you are to **GPS>**"Be kind and compassionate to one another, forgiving each other, just as Christ forgave you." **[Ephesians 4:32]** You must admit, sometimes it is not easy to forgive someone for something that they have said or done that has caused pain to you or loved ones. In situations where you may find it difficult to forgive someone for an offense, ask God to teach you how to forgive and to take your bitterness away regarding the hurt you have incurred.

Jesus said, **GPS>**"For if you forgive other people when they sin against you, your heavenly Father will also forgive you. But if you do not forgive others their sins. Your Father will not forgive your sins." **[Matthew 6:14-15]** You are to tolerate the weaknesses of others, including those who are of the family of faith, forgiving one another in the same way you have been graciously forgiven by Jesus Christ. If you find fault with someone, release this same gift of forgiveness to them. When you don't forgive, it is as if you are drinking the poison you wanted the person who hurt you to drink.

Have you ever noticed that the one(s) that has offended you seem to be as happy as a lark, living their best life, with a smile on their face? While you are about to pop a vein in your head, think about how you dislike or hate them. You don't realize it, but you are actually empowering that individual to control how you feel and live. Wow, that is indeed too much power for one human being to have over you! Wouldn't you agree?

When there is no forgiveness, the hurt that you have begins to fester into a sore inside your heart, oozing bitterness. The entire issue of being offended really is an emotion that awakens harmful chemicals in your body that can lead to physical illnesses, such as Cancer, high blood pressure, heart issues leading to stroke, mental health conditions, and other medical problems, which frequently lead to death. Have you ever thought to yourself or said out loud, "I feel sick?" Often, this is true because what you are harboring inside is causing you to feel nauseous, and making the statement, "You make me sick," is true. Holding the seed of unforgiveness does that.

In fact, you must not go about life acting as if nothing has happened. If you've ever been deeply wounded or wronged by someone, the Lord knows how you feel all too well. He addresses it in scripture. **GPS>**"Be angry and do not sin; do not let the sun go down on your anger, and give no opportunity to the devil." **[Ephesians 4:26-27]** Many times in the Bible, people said and did awful things to Jesus, yet he remained walking in the Holy Spirit and refused to allow himself to become hardened.

You must address your issue of offense and hurt with the individual. If this is not an opinion, then seek experienced counsel. If that doesn't render the situation, remember that God is your avenger, and he will handle it. When you let go and let God, you are not condoning or excusing what happened; you have made the righteous choice to release the resentment and allow the Lord to heal you of any damages caused. Your way and thoughts of revenge are not at all like God's revenge. As difficult as it may be, strive to be kind and compassionate, forgiving others of their trespasses.

With all the noise in the world and melting pots of opinions on how to deal with hurt, the act of forgiveness is often drowned out. However, you are seeing a fallen world, which often resembles the "New Babylon" of today, full of mayhem, chaos, wickedness, and pain. Thankfully, as a Christian, you don't have to live by the ways of the world because Jesus has already overcome it.

Forgiveness is difficult for your flesh to grasp, which is why it's so vital that you draw close to God. Desiring in prayer to hear the Lord speak to you, bringing peace to your heart wherever it is needed. Another reason why you should forgive others, including yourself, is that God forgave you first.

Clemency frees you from allowing a means for the enemy to have your blessings blocked because your heart is not free to receive them and the loving forgiveness that God has for you. Instead of receiving these gifts, they are lost because of your heart being stony, filled with rocks of unforgiveness. Show mercy toward others in forgiveness. It is good for the soul and others around you. Forgiveness causes you to be like a beautiful vine, graciously growing stronger with exquisite blossoms of sweet, fragrant flowers, bringing pleasure to others, igniting all senses of goodness, compassion, kindness, grace, and understanding in love.

When you choose to forgive, it's not the same as choosing to condone or excuse what has happened. It's choosing to release the resentment, hurt and allowing the Lord to heal you of any damage it may have caused. Whenever someone says or does something that offends you, it's much easier, in the long run, to do yourself a favor and forgive as quickly as possible. God does not want you to hurt; He wants you to be at peace and happy. Forgiveness is not just for the person that you are forgiving; it is also for you, to help you spiritually, to be merciful in empathy, learning to grow, in compassion, and charity.

Forgiveness is so very powerful for you, for as you forgive, so are you forgiven. There are two types of forgiveness: one is the forgiveness of your sin(s), and the other is the forgiveness of others. Both require prayer, confession, and true repentance, followed by acceptance of being forgiven. The forgiveness of self requires an honest evaluation of yourself. It means that you have to acknowledge what you've done. This type of forgiveness can be delayed due to feelings of guilt, shame, denial, and feelings of less than. It is the devil's plan to have you in such a state of torment and in anger with others, causing you to turn away from your belief in the Word. Forgiveness of others requires you to let go and let God see Him as your help. He is your rescuer, way-maker, and avenger. Through prayer, calling out to Him, and following His Word, you will find peace in forgiveness, leading to Eternal Life.

GPS>[Colossians 2:10-11, 3:13; Ephesians 4:32; Matthew 6:14-15, 18:21-22; Mark 11:25; 1 John 1:9; Luke 6:37]

RIGHTEOUSNESS

What is Righteousness? Righteousness is having a standard in your behavior, regarding beliefs, concerning what is and is not acceptable for you to do. Your behavior is found by most people to be good in heart and prudent. You are just in your actions and affairs. You are honorable, have integrity, with an irreproachable mindset. You have a pure heart and good intentions, along with being pious, decency, and having an upright mannerism are all traits of what righteousness consists of. Being virtuous, with a pure heart and intentions, are some of the characteristics of you as a Righteous person. Your life is in integrity, walking in the Spirit, living a life that imitates the Ways of Christ, in standards, relationship, faithfulness, and growing in godliness.

You do righteous things secretly; you do not do good deeds to have people give you praise. You keep your acts of mercy and kindness to yourself, for you know that God sees you, and you are confident that He is pleased with your obedience, righteousness, and love of your neighbor. You give gladly without begrudging, giving generously, having a willingness to give happily, in your love of God, and walking in righteousness. You have found a secret place where you are able to pray on your knees to God, uninterrupted or distracted. Having a loving personal fellowship with the Father in secret. Your hiding place is where you get on your knees, seeking the glorious presence of God. It is the place where you can run to find refuge, help, peace, love, grace, mercy, and anything and all that you need. Your faith in God's Word, by following the Holy Spirit, establishes a more intimate relationship with God.

You pray in secret, and God rewards you openly, causing you to have a testimony, witnessing of the Truth, the Power, and Might of God. You speak using words from your heart, which the Holy Spirit has given you to speak. Never make it a chore, and in wisdom, always receive the Spirit's guidance as a blessing, which is as refreshing as a drink from a clean stream of living water. Refreshing your soul, spirit, mind, and heart. You are creative in speaking with the Father; you don't just repeat the same thing over and over. You know that when you speak something to God, if it is in His will, it will manifest. You know that the Lord is your helper, and there is nothing to fear. For you are with Jesus, what can man do to you? You believe that if God is for you, who can be against you?

As you are walking in righteousness, in wisdom, you understand that the Lord is your helper, and by His grace, you live a righteous life. You truly believe that the promises of God are all true, and thank God for not being at all like mankind, wishy-washy, fickle, maybe, maybe not, I don't think so, will see, and I don't know ways of the world. God is the same today, yesterday, and tomorrow. He is faithful, so is His Word, which has been proven over centuries, with no change, nor mistakes spoken by Jesus, from God the Father. **GPS>**"But thou, when thou pray, enter into thy closet, and when thou hast shut thy door, pray to thy father who is in secret; and thy Father who sees in secret shall reward thee openly." **[Matthew 6-7]** You have made a habit of fasting, denying yourself willingly in humility and praise, to be a living sacrifice for God.

Understanding that when you do your fast, it is not for men to know. Your fast is a personal promise from you to God. Fasting helps you with the Spiritual needs of breakthroughs, with stubborn attitudes and mindsets, in diminishing such strongholds. Fasting has often been used in the Bible by people who were in dire situations(s), bringing victory and deliverance to those who are believers in Christ Jesus.

GPS>[Judges 20:26; a Corinthians 1:30; Genesis 15:6; 1 Samuel 26:23; Job 27:6; Esther 4:15-16]

CHAPTER 20

Worry And Fear of Worldly Situations and Issues

Worry is a sin, says the Lord. When you worry about challenges in your life journey, basically saying to God, "I don't trust you for help, which is a sin. You may think that friends and family members may come to your aid.

Even if someone does help you, it is because it is the Will of God! As mere humans, there are only two things that you are sure of here on earth: #1, You have to pay taxes, and #2, You are going to die. Anything else, no human can give the true help that you are in need of ever. Jesus is the solution to all of your issues in life, no matter how dire they are. As humans, your capabilities are limited; you honestly don't know what tomorrow will bring.

"Instead, you ought to say, 'If the Lord wills,' we shall live and do this or that." **[James 4:15]** Really, there is only about 10% of what you have control over, and that is how you face the chaos, tests, trials, circumstances, and dramas in your life. Are you going to curse it? Are you going to face it in a peaceful manner, learning from it? Will you address it in pieces? To ensure victory in your life journey battles, you need to have an intimate relationship with God through Jesus Christ. It is never too late to claim Jesus as your Lord and Savior. Seek ye first the Kingdom of God, for Heaven is at hand. Prayer is the best way to get help from your heavenly Father through Jesus, your intercessor, and the solution for everything.

GPS>His Words are Spirit, Truth, and Life. As an adult, throughout my life, I noticed that whenever someone says that someone has Cancer or died from Cancer. I immediately say a prayer for their family members to be strengthened by God in every area of their lives. I have an elimination method I use to discover what caused the Cancer. Usually, it is 1. From stress, 2. Financial Issues, 3. Family problems 4. Relationship issues 5. Work or 6. Hereditary. When you worry, chemicals that are not good for the body emerge and cause havoc in your system. Often, fear plays an enormous part in illnesses, releasing similar chemicals in your body that are also not good for your health physically, mentally, emotionally, and spiritually.

God is your source for everything. Yahweh is the solution for all of your needs and concerns; God has not given you a Spirit of fear but of a sound mind. Also, why worry? You can't change anything that happens. This is why GPS is needed to guide you in making decisions and choices that can and do affect your health and life journey. **GPS>**"Who of you, by worrying, can add a single hour to your life? "Since you cannot do this very little thing, why do you worry about the rest? Whereas ye know not what shall be on the morrow. For what is your life? It is even a vapor that appeareth for a little time, and then vanisheth away. Yet you do not know what tomorrow will bring." **[James 4:14]** You are a servant of the LORD; you are to follow Jesus. Even when you feel that you lack knowledge, you must first seek the Kingdom of God and find the door that leads to where Jesus is knocking, waiting for you to open your heart and let Him in.

After gaining knowledge, you are to come boldly to the throne of God, for Heaven is at hand. You are more than a conqueror through the love of Christ, which is the jurisdiction you are in. You must make a choice about who you will serve, man or God; you cannot serve both. When you walk in the flesh, you are in a worldly mindset, where material things are more important than God. El Shaddai is your heavenly Father. He knows your needs better than you do and wants to bless you with more.

GPS>"So do not worry, saying, 'What shall we eat?' or 'What shall we drink?' or 'What shall we wear?' For the pagans run after all these things, and your heavenly Father knows that you are in need of them. But seek first his kingdom and his righteousness, and all these things will be given to you as well. Therefore, do not worry about tomorrow, for tomorrow, for tomorrow, worry about itself. Each day has enough trouble of its own." [Matthew 6:31-34] Except, you are saying that you are a Christian, yet you are doing earthly things, which are sinful, being a stumbling block, and an abomination to God.

You cannot be a double-minded person. Whether you choose life or death, walking either in the Spirit or in the flesh, the choice is yours. Think about things that are above, occupying your mind with things that are true, honest, just, pure, lovely, and of good report, not on things that are worldly. In any situation you encounter, in the name of Jesus, speak to those mountains, while on the paths in your life journey. You follow what you see, which is only temporal props. Experiencing corruption of the soul, spirit, mind, and body, along with all sorts of ungodliness and loss. This is what the devil came to do: steal, kill, and destroy. You must live in faith and truth, trusting God for all your needs.

You need Jesus as an example to help you attain this level of following this Supernatural frame of mind. If not, you may get swept up in the chaotic world of events on every level, leading you to a dark place, melting away in doubt. In the world, there are different things that can take you to a place of hopelessness and less than. News is a strong clutch that carries exposure to so much pain, hatred, racism, corruption, murders, infectious opinions, and not seeing the wrath of God addressing these things. It can cause you to become quite annoyed and disappointed.

Don't fall into the trap of worldliness and doubt; God is REAL and ALIVE. Frustration is a worry, and it takes away so much. Relinquish it to Jesus, humble yourself in the sight of the LORD, and HE will lift you up! The LORD has made everything for its purpose, even the wicked, for the day of trouble. Let tomorrow take care of itself. Yesterday is long gone, while you continue to grow in wisdom and righteousness. Within this newness of life, you find many hurdles, but through Jesus, you have the victory to overcome them all. Let this be a statement of your own personal eyewitness experience, causing others to be restored in having hope and trust in Jehovah.

GPS>[John 15:5; Psalms 55:22,118:8; 1 Peter 5:6-8; Jeremiah 17:5; Luke 12:25-31; 2 Timothy 1:6-7; Roman 8:37]

SINS OF COMPLAINING AND MURMURING

Murmurings and complaining are sins. Murmuring is being rebellious against God. The definition of murmuring is a soft, low, or indistinct sound produced by a person or group of people speaking quietly or at a distance.

The definition for complaining is the act by which someone expresses discontent, dissatisfaction, or an insinuation by speaking. In the Bible, murmuring means to grumble or whine. These sins are not physically seen, but they do carry consequences with them. The Lord God, on several occasions, through scriptures, showed his discontent toward those who murmured or complained.

GPS>"The LORD spoke to Moses and Aaron, saying. "How long shall I put up with this evil congregation, who murmur in discontent against Me? I have heard the complaints of the Israelites, which they are making against Me." **[Numbers 13, 14:26-45]** The Israelites were so disrespectful, murmuring and complaining so that God led them in circles for 40 years, allowing those of the old corruptible mindset to all die off, never to live in the promised land, mainly due to their own fault, of not trusting God, who had given them the land to take.

But they, in fear, declined to take the land promised to them. Causing others to cry in the night because of their erroneous decision. [Read Book of Numbers 13, 14:1-19] All murmuring is rebellion toward God, which most of you don't realize. When you were growing up, you received a few of those, "What for? How come?" Licks or smacks on the bottom, whenever you were heard murmuring, which was called back talking, or sassing, an elder [senior] person who was in authority, showing no respect. Do you remember how your misbehaving was soon broken, being disciplined one way or another? There was no such thing as "time out." This disrespect was addressed immediately. Grumbling and complaining is saying to God that you don't like his way of doing something. It says you think you know better than he does. Murmuring and complaining are blatant disregard for authority, displaying arrogance, ignorance, and sinfulness. This disposition toward the Lord is a dangerous tool to toy with.

Often bringing about more devastation than what you were complaining about in the first place. While in difficulties, as you murmur and complain, you bring more misery and calamities to your situation. The reason is that you have placed yourself under a curse, inviting greater adversities and catastrophe occurrences to manifest. This type of attitude does, in fact, lead to consequences that you encounter, which result in more tests, trials, and tribulations. These supernatural reactions are the same as when you were younger and told to "stop whining before you were given something to really cry about." Well, that is what you bring upon yourself when you complain and murmur against the Lord's divine actions and directions.

Challenging the Lord God to the point that he answers you with this question? "You didn't like what I did or what I am doing?" "Well, now, here is a reason to cry!" Then, a big whammy drops down on you in the form of more damaging responses to your grumble and murmuring against what Jehovah, your Creator, is doing or has done for you. Any rebellion against God is very serious, as it shows that you think that God doesn't know what he is doing and that you think you could do better. You are saying and showing that you disregard Yahweh's faithfulness and love. Treating the Lord God as a mere human, capable of making mistakes, selfish, walking in the flesh. Not worthy of respect, nor trusting Him enough to love and obey Him.

Instead of sitting still, waiting on the Lord to rescue you from the wicked hold that worldly ways have on you. Instead of complaining, get into the practice of taking a step back and looking at the whole picture. Look for the positives and blessings in your situations. Search within to find the strength that the Lord has given you through belief and trust in His Word. Be thankful for whatever is taking place while on your life journey, remembering that nothing last forever. God has plans already made for your life journey, with the GPS already set to keep you, grow you, bless you, and train you in following the Holy Spirit of God and not of the world. In your ignorance and blindness, you dare to question your Creator, your Heavenly Father.

Sometimes it is because of what you have said or done. God sees it all and knows all. You must not doubt God ever. You are to keep your mouth shut and your heart open for the Words of God, reminding you through the Holy Spirit. Everything that God does is for your good. God says, **GPS>**"Do all things without murmurings and disputing: That ye may be blameless and harmless, the sons of God, without rebuke, in the midst of a crooked and perverse nation, among whom ye shine as lights in the world." **[Philippians 2:14-15]**

GPS>[Jude 1:3-18,4; Jeremiah 29:11; Numbers 12:1-16] Romans 8:28]

CHAPTER 21

The Power Of The Tongue

The power of the tongue is very strong, for there is both life and death in the tongue. You can speak nice things with it, and you can speak words that can bring harm. **GPS>**"No man can tame the tongue-it is an unruly evil, full of poison." **[James 3:6-8]** The tongue is like a tiny flame from hell. Uncontrolled speech can set aflame an entire forest worth of sin and set your own body on fire as well. How can you control the tongue is by practicing discipline, using techniques to think before you speak.

If you can't say something kind or true that edifies a person, keep it to yourself and pray for help in bridling your tongue, using your Holy Spirit's guidance. There is a saying that was popular when I was growing up. There was a saying, "Sticks and stones may break my bones, but words will never hurt me!" Well, at age 72, I now realize that was a lie. How many times have I cried from what someone has said to me, while on my life journey? How many people have actually died in altercations stemming from the words that came out of an unconstrained mouth? How many divorces and broken relations have happened because of the tongue? I can tell you a lot!

Words do hurt, and death is a prime example of what the effects of your tongue and mouth spew out. It is easy to slip and say something that you regret later. The effects that come from words are so crucial in everyday living when surrounded by unrestrained tongues. It does take prayer, discipline, and practice to train your mindset, heart, and mouth in the effort to keep speaking in what is righteousness, holy, true, and edifying. That is what you are to do. You are to uplift one another with your words, speaking in wisdom, understanding, and forgiveness.

In continual prayer, ask God to bridle your mouth, removing all stubborn and rampant words and purifying your mouth and Spirit so that improvement may be accomplished, causing you to have a testimonial of your growth in the newness of Christ. I used to cuss like a sailor, so bad that I made men cry; I was on a roll. In my ignorance and sinfulness while in school, I couldn't wait to grow up just so I could curse.

After getting older and reading the Word, I started to apply what I read in the bible to my worldly walk, which eventually changed to walking, listening, and walking in the Holy Spirit; I not only became older, I became wiser. My motto was, "Don't sweat the small stuff!" In fact, everything that happened became small stuff to me because I realized that God is bigger than anything I encounter. I learned to let go, trust, and let God! You are more powerful than you know. God made you marvelous, a powerful species, being a little less than the angels, crowned in glory and honor. Giving you dominion over the works of His hands. Along with power and authority to tread on serpents, scorpions, and over all the power of the enemy, in safety, Hallelujah!

Yet, there is a vile member of your body that is as deadly as the poison of scorpions dwelling inside of you. It is one of the deadliest and most destructive parts of your tongue. Your tongue is, at times, your own enemy, being (in me), starting from your heart and mind to your tongue. It is not what you put inside your mouth that defiles you; it is what comes out of your mouth. An angry tongue does not produce the righteousness which God desires. You are to preach the Good News of the Gospel boldly proclaiming that both the Kingdom of God and Heaven are at hand, for you have been freely given this blessing, and freely you are to give to others. The power of the tongue is very powerful, for "out of the same mouth, come blessings and cursing, my brothers and sisters, this is not right."

This little part of the body has caused so many battles, divisions, pain, sickness, loss, and deaths. What you say has power, your words, though they may not be seen by the natural eye. They are flames that, when spoken, release a power source that can bring about what has been spoken. When you speak, the trees, rocks, wind, the universe, beings in other realms, including all of nature, hear and do understand, as your words yield power to enact whatever it is sent to do. This same principle is proven: reflect on something you've said that would happen that wasn't so nice, then actually see that it did happen. It was a, wow, moment, right? This same concept works on speaking good things, causing those things to manifest, too. Power in the tongue, if you are not careful, can cause you to be sick, be hurt, be in poverty, have a loss, and the list goes on. It is all by the tongue and also by your heart, mind, spirit, and soul.

When you say, "I am not going to get that job." Usually, you don't get it. Some say this is considered positive thinking and speaking. Regardless of what names this power is called. It still has to do with the power of your tongue.

You say you feel sick, or she is going to die. Realize that you are sending those words and energy out into the universe. Being able to speak doesn't mean that you can say anything and not have consequences. Everything you have has been blessed; tho it is not free, there is some type of payment for these benefits. Remember, you, being part of humanity, were cursed by God in the Garden of Eden. Jesus died for your sins, but you still must follow the laws of God, which are listed in the "Ten Commandments and in the Words of the Bible, brought down from heaven through Jesus Christ. The tongue is so powerful that God actually instructs you to speak to your mountains, things that are troubling you.

Jehovah has given you the power to raise the dead, cast out devils, cause the dead to hear, the mute to speak, prisoners to be set free, and give liberty to the oppressed by speaking life and blessings. See how powerful the tongue is; as small as it is, it can raise the dead and cast out devils; this is so amazing. In the book of Job, scripture confirms how he cursed himself, saying, **GPS>**"For the thing which I greatly feared is come upon me, and that which I was afraid of is come unto me." **[Job 3:25]**

There is another major part regarding the tongue, it is that whenever someone speaks, you are to give 100% attention, listening to every word spoken, for this is your portion in being a Christian. The Word says, "You are to be quick to listen and slow to speak. Often, many verbal confrontations arise from someone saying something, resulting in an argument where neither one can hear nor understand what the other is saying because no one is able to actually hear by taking time to stop and listen, making the entire incident pointless, ignorant, and rude.

You are to edify others, lifting them up in compassion, praise, kindness, wisdom, patience, truth, and love. In other words, if you can't say anything nice, don't say anything. Often, ignorance is made known when you speak. It is alright if someone thinks you're not the brightest light on the tree. It's when you open your mouth and speak, confirming your thoughts. Often, sitting still, listening, and focusing on God and the ways of Jesus in the effort of being obedient to his purpose. You may not realize it, but your tongue can bring trouble, destruction, and death to yourself, associates, others, and family members.

GPS>"Let Him be crucified." The governor of the Roman province of Judaea, Pontius Pilate, asked for a basin of water; walking over to it, he washed his hands before the multitude, saying. I am innocent of the blood of this just person; see ye to it." Then answered all the people and said, "His blood be on us and on our children." **[Matthew 27:23-25]** These people cursed their generations and family bloodlines. Today in the Middle East, there has been wearing ever since, before and after the death of Jesus. Warring about land, which Jehovah created, belonging to none of mankind.

GPS>[Psalm 8:4-8; Luke 9:40, 10:19; James 1:19-20, 3:10; Entire book of Job 1-42; Matthew 10:7-9, 15:11-20]

THE NAME OF JESUS

Before the birth of Jesus, the angel Gabriel visited his to be, birth mother, Mary, informing her that she would become pregnant and name the child Jesus. **GPS>**"Behold, the angel of the Lord appeared unto him in a dream, saying. Joseph, thou son of David, fear not to take them to Mary, by wife; for that which is conceived in her is of the Holy Ghost. And she shall bring forth our son, and thou shalt call his name Jesus: for he shall save his people from their sins." **[Matthew 1:20-21]** This was the name selected by God, the father of Jesus. Using the same authority that earth fathers administered during that time period, where the father of the child chose the name. God has given Jesus a name that is above all names.

Jesus is the direct heir of the King of all things. He is royalty, in his name, being the Son of God, carrying transcendental power, incomprehensible authority, supernatural purpose, bringing celestial salvation, and the Word of God. Accomplishing miraculous, prophetic declarations of the arrival of a King, an anointed Savior, the Messiah to earth, which no one had or has ever done. Coming from heaven, living among you in the flesh, being crucified, died, was buried, resurrected, then, in view of eyewitnesses, ascended into the heavens, returning to his Heavenly Father on the throne, to sit beside him, as His heir. Angels who were physically present, verbally interacting, spoke to those witnessing the event. Jesus is divinity in perfection, a light so bright that not even the sun can be compared to his glory.

GPS>"that at the name of Jesus every name knee should bow, of those in heaven, and of those on earth, and of those under the earth, and that every tongue should confess that Jesus Christ is Lord, to the glory of God the Father." **[Philippians 2:10-11]** This blessed and holy name is the epitome of God's love for humanity, sending his only begotten son to bring his Word and to save mankind from damnation. Giving his body willing, becoming the ultimate sacrifice, as the

Lamb of God, full of grace and truth. This is why the name of Jesus is so powerful; it carries healing, deliverance, breakthroughs, being a weapon, taking you out of the snares of the devil's pitfalls.

This name can break all chains of bondage and wickedness. It is a refuge and shelter in times of need. The name of Jesus shows the power that Jesus Christ has over demons, devils, and all evil. **GPS>**Scripture tells that on one occasion, Jesus and his followers encountered two men, who were exceedingly fierce, coming out of the tombs, forbidding anyone to pass, as they were demon-possessed. This causes the people to be afraid of them. Jesus approached the demon-possessed men and asked the demon's name; it replied, "My name is many, for there are many of us." The demon responded to Jesus and asked Him if it could leave the man and go into the pigs that were nearby. Jesus let them do what they wanted to do. So, they went into the pigs and ran fast down the side of the mountain and into the sea, and died. There were about 2000." **[Mark 5:1-20]**

This is so powerful, just knowing that Jesus has Authority that demons ask HIM what they can do and not do, proving that there are rules and jurisdictions at play. That must be obeyed, and the spirits, demons, Satan, and his helpers are well aware of the Dunamis power of this Holy blessed man, named Jesus, the Son of God, in all His Glory and authority. The name of Jesus also has power over the tongue, winning battles for you. The name of Jesus can save you, can restore, renew you, bless you, and free you. Just call and shout out the name of Jesus; believe, feel, see, and behold! In the name of Jesus, there is a place to hide. There is shelter, a strong tower, refuge, and peace. Having the ability to break chains of bondage, stop the devil, destroy evil, resurrect the dead, strengthen your faith, and cause the devil to flee.

The name of Jesus holds incredible power, causing troublesome situations to cease and giving you victory. **GPS>**"If you ask the Father in my name, he will give it to you." **[John 16:23]** The name of Jesus brings, calms storms, causes things to grow, including finances, and moves mountains. If you will only believe, all things are possible to those who believe. Jesus Christ means the power of God and the wisdom of God. Through the usage of Jesus' name, their miracles manifest, along with the Holy Spirit glorifying His name. The name of Jesus gives you the Spirit, not to fear, to be strengthened in power, love, and self-control. Learn to call out the name, whispering the name Jesus, and be renewed in faith, for he is faithful.

GPS>6-38; Acts 1:10-11; John 14:12-15; 1 Corinthians 1:24; John 14:13-16, John 15:16; Isaiah 9:6; Hebrew 1:3; 2 Timothy 1:7]

REBUKE, BIND, AND LOSE

Rebuking, Binding, and loosening are the authorities that have been given to you by Jesus. This authority instructs you to rebuke and bind the temptations of the devil and to lose goodness and mercy upon your life, all in the name of Jesus. Rebuking is a way to keep someone from a destructive path, either in speaking or by physical behavior and choices, which may lead to dire consequences. In patience, you teach them to learn and grow, teaching them in patience, correcting in errors, and warning them to stop so that they will not have to face the consequences. He goal of rebuking is to help them learn and grow. **Here is an example of **Rebuking**: "I rebuke that in the name of Jesus. I rebuke you in the name of Jesus. **GPS>**"All Scriptures are spoken words of God directed, may be used for teaching, rebuking, correcting, and training in righteousness, so that the man[you]of God may be thoroughly equipped for every good work. **[2 Timothy 3:16-17]**

When you bind anything, scriptures, along with your decree and declaration, are weapons and ammunition against any circumstance, temptation, situation, or issues of the world that come upon you. Those who are attempting to place you in bondage, and if it has you in bondage, you have the authority to bind it and remove it from your life. Anything that places you in a snare, causing you to lose your peace, causing you to fear, or doubt, causing you to lose faith. In these situations, take authority and lose victory in those areas of your life.

Here are examples of **Binding and Loosing declarations: "In the mighty name of Jesus, in knowing who I am, a child of the Most High God, by the authority of Christ Jesus given to me. "I bind you up [i.e., illness, deceit, confusion, finances, sinfulness]in the name of the Lord Jesus, I bind you up, and with the same authority, I lose [i.e., complete healing, success, blessing, peace, righteousness] in the name of Jesus.

Thank you, Lord, you will be done. Rebuking, binding up, and losing include you daily under the "Kingdom of Authority of God. Empowering you in the name of the Lord, with this blessed Holy gift to you, giving you permission to speak against Satan and evil anytime, anywhere. Every day, you are under the authority of God, so I bless you under the authority of God so that when you move in the Authority of the Lord, you have victory. The enemy cannot do anything when you stand up to him. Scriptures say, "To resist the devil, and he will flee."

Tell the temptations, unrighteousness, sinful behavior, and thoughts that they have to go now! In Jesus's name, tell the devil, his imps, and demons they have to go! Take your life back and place Satan under your feet, along with sinfulness, in the name of Jesus. Demand that the devil get off your back, in the name of Jesus, binding all under the authority of God! Jesus Himself rebuked and gave one of His disciples, Simon Barjona, the keys to the "Kingdom of Heaven," along with the authority to bind and loosen anything on earth, and it will be done in heaven during His ministry.

GPS>"And whatsoever thou shalt Bind on Earth Shall Be Bound in Heaven, and whatsoever thou shalt loose on Earth shall be loosed in Heaven." **[Matthew 16 18-19]** Having the authority to Rebuke, Bind, and Lose has been given to followers of Christ. This absolute authority means to forbid by an indisputable authority, and to permit by an indisputable authority.

Authority to Bind and Loosen was given to Simon Barjona by Jesus, when he received truth from the Heavenly Father of whom Jesus really was. Jesus presented a question to his disciples. **GPS>**"Behold, I give unto you the power to tread on serpents and scorpions, and over all the power of the enemy: and nothing shall by any means hurt you." **[Luke 10:19]** The power that Jesus has given you allows you to have the authority to bind, which means restraining any situation. Authority to loosen means that when any type of bondage, be it a spiritual or earthly situation, emerges from your life journey. This God-given authority allows you to, at any time, lose goodness, blessings, peace, righteousness, healing, debt-free, success, and the list goes on, as does life. Don't hesitate to use your God-given power and authority against evil temptations and worldly issues. Praying always brings solutions to any type of situation or circumstance, strengthening a genuine relationship with God; it is a weapon to break chains of bondage.

GPS>[Peter 5:8; Acts 5; 1 Corinthians 5:1-13; 2 Corinthians 2:4-8; Proverbs 1:23]

CHAPTER 22

God Controls the Issuance of Challenges and circumstances, and "Jesus Is the Solution."

Does God control what happens in your life, the good and the bad? This is a question all of you have asked at one time or another. Seeing so much pain, loss, and confusion, existing not just in one country but all over the world.

Although these exist, they are not new to your world. There have been times when you have read the Bible and often wondered if this is the Babylon that the Lord speaks of and refers to in the Bible. The same scenarios are sadly replaying themselves. Yet many ask why God let these things happen. You realized through the revelation of Christ's knowledge that you need to realize that Your Father God (Other names of God are known as Jehovah, El Elyon, Yahweh, Jah, Yashuda, I AM, Adoni Zedek) is the solution, no matter what name He is called. He is still God of all and is all. God has ultimate power; He is the reason and the solution for all that happens. The Lord states in the Bible that he is the creator of evil for the evil day. **GPS>**"The LORD has made everything for its purpose, even the wicked for the day of trouble." **[Proverbs 16:4]**

Though this truth may sound strange, understand that God allows things to happen so that you will turn around to him, dying yourself of worldly sinfulness. Through Christ's revelation, He understands that He is your source, your solution in everything. Providing help for you to defeat the evil that tempts you. There are some people who are evil and wicked walking the earth daily. God has created beings that are to exercise and inflict pain using whatever weapons/gifts He has authorized, giving them the empowerment to defeat these evil beings. These beings are like the heavies or the hit man on earth and in the heavenly realms, battling in spiritual warfare for you.

Throughout the universe, God fights evil with evil. Like Gargoyles, pictures of them are not very attractive; in fact, they are quite intimidating. This is a good thing because they are fighting ugly with ugly. What gargoyles have been credited with is having the power to keep evil spirits away. Guarding buildings they occupy, protecting those inside. You see them as doing God's will for his purposes. If they can protect the people inside, why can't they help people on their life journeys if it is God's will? Metaphorically, dying yourself of fleshly lust, worldly passions, desires, living in disciplined righteousness and Godliness. God is your creator, your Abba Father, and he wants your attention in order to teach you how to survive on this earth having unlimited peace.

You believe the earth is an introduction to hell, and the Bible gives you instructions on how to survive this journey on earth. You are saved and called by God. You are to be different, being led by God's word through Jesus Christ. You have been tested, fallen in sin, repented, and saved by God's Grace and Mercy. These tests are needed in order to strengthen you spiritually, which will be a help in overcoming worldly issues of life. Repetitions are not spared because it is a necessity that helps you mature in spirit. Strengthening you so that you are able to face the next challenge until you reach the heavenly Kingdom of God. All that God does is for Good. **GPS>**"And we know that all things work together for good to them that love God. To them who are the called according to His purpose." **[Romans 8:28]** Your journey is not easy, and you are an ambassador of Christ who must be armed with weapons that will defeat the enemy, both spiritually and physically, after you have been stung by the cross that you must bear.

Through the Kingdom of Heaven being at hand, the weight, piercing pain, and anguish are lessened with each step you take toward learning to walk in righteousness through the Holy Spirit. There, you are to be given time to let that experience set in, just like any lesson you have been taught. You need time to contemplate and study the Spiritual wisdom of the information you have been given objectively. After that period, it is then confirmed that the time you went through was a time in which you were tested. Tried, purified, through pain and renewal of your heart and mindset. This testing will show you what your strong points, strengths, and weaknesses are on your journey if you find that you haven't met the test by not using the Christ-like manner.

Then, there will, at some time, be another similar test, hoping that in time, you have matured in wisdom, strength, and commitment to God. God allows for all these transgressions and painful experiences to take place, giving permission to Satan to do so. Though this is so, there are two jurisdictions working in this organized design. When you are in the jurisdiction of God, walking in the Spirit and in

Righteousness. This is the Jurisdiction of Christ, in which you are able to speak to Satan and all evil, telling it to shut up go reminding it that they have no power; in the Jurisdiction of the Power and light of God. Now, when you are in the Jurisdiction of Satan's domain, which is in sinfulness and unrighteousness.

In this jurisdiction, Satan and his cohorts may inflict upon you whatever evil and pain the devil says is alright, of course, within the scope that God has allowed him to have. Walking by faith and not by sight, trusting God completely, surrendering all of you to Him. You will be a teacher and now an eyewitness to all that has endured. Coming out of it victoriously, by the Words of God. Enabling your ability as an agent for God to help others by your faith, experiences, solutions, and love. Testings, along with trials of your spirit, are promotions you should strive to pass, furthering your Spiritual ascension. Making you become more conscious of your right senses and your non-connection with the world around you. Having the ability to walk by faith and not by sight. Not succumbing to any worldliness, be it physical or mental, when you pass over to the other side with Jesus.

Your life journey will be less stressful when you learn to enjoy the journey. Laugh at yourself, seeing Life as a game full of tricks and turns that are sure to show you remarkable things. Seeing each encounter as a ticket to Eternal Life. Chasing after money and losing your children, loved ones, and life is not the way. Stay faithful when you are tried and tested, trust God. Through faith and patience, you inherit the promises of God. **GPS>**"Fear not, for I am with you; Be not dismayed, for I am your God. I will strengthen you; yes, I will help you." **[Isaiah 41:10]** When things seem to be out of whack so badly that you feel like you are being picked on.

Well, you are not alone; being on earth, it is inevitable that you will encounter those types of days, weeks, months, and years. Facing challenges and unwanted situations throughout your life, known as seasons. During this vulnerable time which you are in, the devil can and will slip in any time there is a crack that you have left open, allowing for Satan, his demons, imps, and fallen angels. To administer various tests, trials, tribulations, challenges, chaos, and all disruptions of peace, being in the world while living worldly. Different tests you will encounter, but the solution is always God. Trust God, believe, and be patient.

You are on your own pilgrimage; sometimes, you can be your own enemy. Satan knows that the truth has been spoken, but his role is to trip you up and make you a sinner. Remember that Satan has been destroying people from the beginning of time. He has mastered trickery and trained his imps, spawns, and demons as well, in various twisted techniques. **GPS>**"No temptation has overtaken you; this is not common to man. God is faithful, and he will not let you be tempted beyond your ability, but with the temptation, he will also provide a way of escape that you may be able to endure. it." **[1 Corinthians 10:13]**

You must not lose heart; know that as a Christian, you don't nor should you stay on the same level on this life journey; you are a person of change. You must pray, wait, and listen to the Holy Spirit in using the ammunition and weapons to lose and rescue you, which God provides for you to get away through these ordeals of circumstances and challenges.

Never let any circumstance cause you to fear or run from whatever the devil is throwing at you, because fear is **F**alse

Evidence, Appearing Real. Think about it: each time you are faced with a dilemma, there is a tendency to assume negative parts of the situation that you are facing. It is like the fable of "Chicken Little." That started a big mess when she ran about in panic and dread, declaring to other animals that the sky was falling. After a little acorn dropped and fell, it hit her on the head. This is one of the ways Satan operates, having you believe baseless exaggerations of defeat or danger when it's all in the imagination of your mind.

Jesus said to his disciples then, and you are now a disciple and a representative of His. Going through it is victorious; you win! You are a person of change; you are equipped with the ability to transform, just as the butterfly does through metamorphosis. When you become more aware of God's will, you will achieve, having a more intimate relationship with the Father. While you are renewed, resurrected, restored, and transcended into becoming a new being. You are to hold on to your understanding, knowing that you are going through some things, but know you will get through them all; nothing last forever. Jesus is pulling you through the fires of troubles and issues of life on earth. You will emerge victorious, not being burned, not even smelling like smoke; the only fire that will be upon you is the Holy Ghost Fire, resurrecting you to new life in Christ Jesus.

What a magnificent and Glorious God you serve. You are to rise above it! When you focus on the situation natural, it becomes more frightening. **GPS>**"For God hath not given us the spirit of fear; but of power, and of love, and of a sound mind." **[2 Timothy 1:7]** Satan wants to take away the Word because of the power and authority that it has, empowering you with Spiritual ammunition to kill his thwarts of wickedness by your being set free through knowing the truth of the Good News of the Gospel.

Through the goodness of the Gospel, you are aware of the Word of God, and you both believe and know that you are a child of the Most High God, and if God be for you, who can be against you? Christ became the end of the Law, giving you freedom/liberty from any and all bondage; Satan wants to keep you in bondage.

GPS>"Many are the plans in the mind of a man, but it is the purpose of the LORD that will stand. **[Proverbs 19:21]** When you pray and ask God, believe that you have received what you have asked for. Though you must go through trials and tribulations, you are not to let any circumstance defeat you. You are called to rise above them all in Christ Jesus.

GPS>[Philippians 3:21, 4:6-7; John 8:44-47, 16:33; Titus 2:11-15; 2 Timothy 1:7; Exodus 15:23; Matthew 10:26-28; 1 Peter 1:4; Genesis 3:15-18; 1 John 5:4; Isaiah 45:7; Roman 13:1-2; Psalm 115:3]

EACH DAY IS SUPPOSED TO BE BAD

In the book of Genesis, because of the sin of Adam and Eve, God cursed the earth, assigning death to all the inhabitants of it. The curse says that the ground is cursed and that in sorrow and pain, you/mankind shall have all the days of your lives. All your life, you will struggle to scratch a living from it. Decreeing that each day is supposed to be bad." This is why the world is so evil; it is supposed to be like this. Your daily challenges, tests, trials, and chaos in your life are all part of your life journey. God says, **GPS>**"And to the man he said, since you listened to your wife and ate from the tree whose fruit I commanded you not to eat, the ground is cursed because of you. All your life, you will struggle to scratch a living from it." **[Genesis 3:17]**

God does not lie; just as he declared, you see and experience along with others this painful and challenging survival from sunup to sundown, even when you are sleeping. Complexities or ramifications are manifesting to bring you ill will. Not just to you but to all the inhabitants of the world. It is not because people have changed; no, it is because the true nature of man is being disobedient. This is how the world is supposed to be: defiant, contrary, and disorderly. Producing hate, fear, death, destruction, confusion, jealousy, and all types of sinful, wicked, and ungodliness. Enhancing all the evil that on set, when you live on earth, which spells the word evil, when the letters are reversed, spelling live. Helping the earth to be as it is, a beautiful place created by God, yet now being run by Satan, for a period of time, which has been allocated by the Almighty Creator and judge El Elyon. Who will judge you and all of mankind at the end of their lifetime here on earth ends.

No matter what you do or who you are, you still face regrets, mayhem, and troubles each day. Walking in the world, not knowing what is going to happen next. Because your life is meant to be callous, mysterious, and full of surprises, some that seem good, God does not lie; just as he declared, you see experience along with others, this painful and challenging survival from sun up to sun down, even when you are sleeping. Complexities or ramifications are manifesting to bring you ill will. Not just to you but to all, who try to bring hurt when you become too happy about what the day has brought you. Have you ever noticed that when you get something extra, happy about some event or thing in your life?

Soon after, something happens so traumatically that it literally takes your breath away, often leaving you speechless, soon to be in tears, from the anguish and cataclysmic situation that has befallen you. The Bible, within its scriptures, has predicted how life in the world is supposed to be before you are born. Stating that men shall be lovers of their own selves. Covetous boasters, proud blasphemers, who are disobedient to parents. Being ungrateful, unholy, without natural affection. Truce breakers, false accusers, incontinent, and fierce despisers of those that are good. Traitors, heady, high-minded, lovers of pleasures, more than lovers of God.

GPS>"The LORD gave, and the LORD has taken away; blessed be the name of the LORD." **[Job 1:21]** You are to face each day, regardless of what it brings, with joy. That is why you must realize that you are in the world but not in it. The only way to do this is to trust, believe, and depend on God. Jesus said that there would be trials and tribulations; he didn't say there might be trials and tribulations, as this is why the world is evil, which, when you turn the letters around, they do spell live. So, living in the world is evil, and the devil comes to steal, kill, and destroy. When times are good, be happy, but when times are bad, consider this: God has made the one as well as the other. Therefore, no one can discover anything about their future.

There is nothing that the world can give you that is good or beneficial for you. Even the media is part of this Pandora's box. Daily, it is the delivery of the "Bad News of the Day!"

That is why God sent Jesus to bring the "Good News of the Gospel," as it is your hope for survival in this introduction to hell called earth. The book of Ecclesiastes confirms that all life is vanity. There is nothing to look forward to on this earth except doing God's will. However, each day is supposed to be bad. Do not lose hope or faith. This is what the devil wants you to do. He wants you to feel alone, defeated, in hopelessness, abandoned, and fearful. Your power is in the LORD and all His might; he has given you power and authority to defeat any and all things that can be thrown at you.

You have the power to throw it back, putting all its temptations and unwanted circumstances under your feet. Remember, you are never alone; God is faithful. The world does not love you, nor those who have chosen worldly lust and sinfulness. The only way to survive is by having a sincere relationship with your heavenly Father; it is essential in surviving the not using the ways of the world. God is not a liar. Everything that His Son Jesus taught through the Word of God has been tested and proven over centuries to still hold true. He is the same today, yesterday, and tomorrow. He has not lost any battles for you. However, you are promised to have rain in the form of pain and trauma in various circumstances in the life of this journey. Know that no one is exempt from these challenges.

GPS>"God makes his sun rise on the evil and on the good, and sends rain on the just and on the unjust." **[Matthew 5:45]** God loves us more than we can imagine. He always provides a way for us to defeat the enemy, and when it is too much, He is our unwavering help. Though days are lined up with problems, issues, pain, and challenges of all sorts, we can rely on Jesus to get us through them all. By trusting God through Jesus, emulating Him, and you will be able to walk through any storms of life. Tho storms may come to stand firm in their midst, for they soon will pass, nothing stays forever. Grow in wisdom and strength, knowing that God has given you the power and authority to trample on snake scorpions and to overcome all the power of the enemy, and nothing will harm you. This, too, will pass.

Stay in prayer, trusting God in strength, knowing that nothing last forever, and this time and season will pass. Jesus Christ is your intercessor before God. When you pray, God sees His Son, Jesus, standing in place of you. Jesus, the Way, is always the solution to any and all encounters you are faced with. True, you have the choice to follow God or not, still either way, you are going to go through something. When you choose to follow the word of God through Jesus Christ, you have an anchor; you are not fighting these physical and spiritual battles alone, for God is faithful; you have the ONE who knows all and is all.

Remember, now God is continually being bombarded by Satan with complaints against you. It is then that Jesus, your Savior and intercessor, comes to your defense, advocating to the Father on your behalf. These spiritual fights are going on twenty-four-seven. God allows Satan to do things to you; sometimes it is to discipline you. To help you grow spiritually through wisdom and experience. There are times when God wants you to honor him and get your attention. Letting you know that you can hide in his protection from all the troubles that surround you daily. All you need to do is ask and seek the Kingdom of Heaven, for it is at Hand. Through the revelation of Christ's knowledge, this may be part of the method to help you ascend by walking in and following the Holy Spirit.

GPS>"Be very careful, then, how you live -not as unwise but as wise, making the most of every opportunity because the days are evil.

GPS>[Ecclesiastes 1:2-2:26, 3:4, 6:2, 7:14, 8:14; Psalm 9:9, 32:7, 50:15, 121:7; Ephesians 6:13; 2 Timothy 3:15; Job 1:21; Deuteronomy 32:39-41; Genesis 3:16; Romans 5:3, 8:35-39; John 16:33; Matthew 11:28-30; Luke 10:19-37]

GOD CREATED EVIL FOR THE EVIL DAY

This topic itself makes you uncomfortable. Because all of your life, you've been told God is good and does nothing bad. Having the understanding that whenever something is considered to be bad, it is because of evil directed by the devil. Yes, both of those statements are. The only difference is that now, you have access to learn, understand, and gain wisdom on how life journeys operate regarding good and evil. God is a truthful God, and he does acknowledge His interactions with disasters and destruction. Admitting in scriptures that He created calamity and is the author of evil. **GPS>**"Shall a trumpet be blown in a city, and the people are not afraid? Does disaster come to a city unless the Lord has done it?" **[Amos 3:6]**

True God does confer with the adversary Satan, the accuser of the brethren; you can be certain that the All-Knowing God is good, faithful, having ultimate Authority and power over the adversary, the universe, realms, and kingdoms. Almighty God is Omnipotent, and he has given you the solution to facing evil and all challenges you incur through believing in His Son, Jesus Christ, as your Lord and Savior. You may ask why God would create a world full of evil. God says he is the author of evil. **GPS>**"I form the light and create darkness, I make peace and create evil; I, the Lord, do all these things." **[Isaiah 45:7]**

God sees the good that can come out of evil. If evil did not exist, there would be no reason to pray to God and pay him homage for using his miraculous power to save you, thereby giving Glory to Him. God uses acts of moral and functional evil, destroying them, thereby giving Him glory. Don't be misled by the statement that God allows awful things to happen to you just for His Glory. God's glory is a double-edged sword. First, it makes you part of mankind, see with the physical eye, witnessing proof that God does exist and that he is alive now and forever.

Giving you the ability to experience an eyewitness account of His ultimate supernatural Power and supremacy of authority over all evil. Delivering you from your dilemmas, catalytic chaos, along with whatever perilous circumstance(s) you were and are possibly facing now.

God will bring you through it, using His power. There is no way any human could accomplish what transpired in their life when convinced in awe that the resolution of their situation was miraculously done, giving them peace. Leaving no doubt for you or anyone to say that man had something to do with it. That way, it eliminates any man (human) from boasting that he did the unexplainable. God also allows for evil to transpire in your life journey so that you are convinced, and it is proven that His Word, which is the Bible. Following its' uncorrupted guidelines, along with the Ten Commandments, are your keys to salvation, love, grace, mercy, and wisdom. Convicting you to trust God and to walk in the Spirit, applying your renewed mindset to your life journey.

In righteous, through Christ Jesus, leading you to Eternal Life. Realize that the "Kingdom of Heaven" is at hand, available to you, in the scriptures of the Bible. There, again, is your confirmation that God is real. Thereby giving him Glory for his miraculous loving-kindness and mercy that he has demonstrated for you [mankind] to see and believe. He is able to determine all evil for both His purpose and guidance for you. As he brings you victory, according to what his will is for your absolution and blessing(s), guiding you to his Holy Kingdom. God allows evil to exist because he has given you[mankind] free will, which is a loophole of sorts.

There are two sides to freedom in making choices, and the kind of consequences that determine the outcome that they carry. One way of choosing is based on the God-given freedom of free will, in the hope that the choice that you make will be in the likeness of Jesus Christ, denoting a character of morality, spiritually, and wisdom in your character. The other way of making choices may be those that denote the character of worldliness, walking in the flesh, and having a mindset of immorality, materialism, and selfishness. Many believe that you[mankind], even though you were made to do good, often you[mankind] are the initiators of evil, confirming that humanity is evil, but this is due to having a mindset of sinfulness and evil. This may well carry weight, as when you do make a choice that is sinful and worldly. There are, oftentimes, devastating consequences due to the choice(s) you made.

GPS>"Therefore, be careful how you walk, not as unwise men but as wise, making the most of your time, because the days are evil. So then do not be foolish, but understand what the will of the Lord is. **[Ephesians 5:15-17]** The question of where evil comes from? It is often pondered that evil in itself is anything that is the opposite of the Word of God. The Lord is holy. Therefore, anything that comes against His holy essence is evil. Evil has power and life, which is determined by God.

GPS>"I form light and create darkness, I make well-being and create calamity, I am the Lord, who does all these things." **[Isaiah 45:7]** God allows you to suffer for your good, using it to strengthen you in his service. There are times when you encounter tests, trials, and mayhem that seem too much to endure, overwhelming you to feel defeated and alone. You are not alone, neither are you defeated, for when you hit, so does God. He wants you to know that your tears are not wasted; they are kept in his book as he identifies with your pain and suffering.

Restoring you with unending Agape love in compassion, understanding, wisdom, forgiveness, and truth. Although God is the creator of woe, He is also the creator of His Holy and all-powerful protection, "The Armor of God," which is victorious against all warfare you encounter, both spiritually and physically. Which in itself is a reason to rejoice and be grateful when facing anything. God is Omnipotent, the "Great I Am." Just as he is able to create misfortune, he can turn it around for your good and His glory. Keep your mindset and spiritual eyes on Jesus Christ, not on the pitfalls and snares of the world. Never, ever let situations control you and your peace of mind.

Knowing what the devil meant for evil, God made it for Good. The Lord will not permit evil that he will not reign in the end, overruling Satan for your good. Trust God in all that you encounter, knowing that He is the author of your life, faith, and fate, in ultimate power and authority.

God is sovereign and is the greater good for any solution, being that His will is always for your good; though you may not understand His method(s) nor why there are challenges you must face and go through. They are to bless you, help you learn to trust God in obedience, grow in faith, walk in the Holy Spirit, not by flesh, in Jesus' name, receiving Eternal Life.

There must be pain before gain. You are not supposed to have a good day. Or do not be foolish, but understand what the Lord's will is. Bad days are actually normal; the book of Ecclesiastes tells you what life is really like because of that first sin that took place in the Garden of Eden. No one is exempt from these daily curses and ways of life on earth. For humanity, each sunrise brings new mercy from God, and as soon as you open your eyes and inhale while you put your feet on the floor, evil begins. Life's curse of living springs right into action, bringing some type of chaos. Living is not easy, and God made it that way. You have to pay for having a life, and through the hardships and pains of life, you are paying dearly for it. You are being punished for the sins that Adam and Eve committed; nothing is Free, not even life.

God is making you pay for His, allowing you to live and not take your life. True Jesus is your Lord and Savior, removing the curse of damnation for you by giving his flesh and blood as a living sacrifice for all of humanity. Through his blood and dying on the cross, no longer are you doomed to go straight to hell; you now have been reinstated with God, having the ability to have Eternal Life. All your life, you have been told that if you work hard, you will have great success. So you endure a gruesome grind. In your head, you think that living life is not an unhappy sphere. So when an unexpected event happens, you say, "It's just one of those days." You imagine suffering is short-term, and pain is the exception to the rule, seeing any failure as merely the prelude to victory.

God says, **GPS>**"It is an unhappy business that God has given to the children of man to be busy with. "The LORD has made everything for its purpose, even the wicked for the day of trouble." **[Proverbs 16:4]** These specters cause you to walk unprepared for delays, failures, and devastation, causing you to think in confusion by all the mayhem. In disbelief, you say, "I didn't see that coming; that was not at all expected!" You and others discuss your awful, no good, bad day, like things like this occur every blue moon. The book of Ecclesiastes in the Bible explains to you how and why every day is evil. In this world, "Always expect the unexpected, and you won't be disappointed." Nothing happens on the earth, in the earth, universe, realms, and kingdom, without the Lord God knowing.

Satan, the accuser of the brethren, has to get permission from God before he can enact anything in your life journey, be it to you physically or spiritually. Satan has limited power to do evil, even though his name is D evil, D= Do Evil. Whatever the case, "after you have done what you know to do, then you stand in the midst of the happenings, knowing that God is powerfully working in the unseen realm, on your behalf. It is in these times that you are to put on the whole armor of God and "having done all, to stand." In wisdom, you understand the world is what it should be, being that it is the kingdom of Satan.

The more you watch the news on television or whatever type of media you use for information about worldly events. Daily 24/7 providing you with constant "Bad News!" This is correct because the only "Good News is that of the Gospel! Once you realize the truth, there are no good days. You will be calmer, wiser, at peace, and secure. You will no longer fear bad news, not because you **hope** that hope is coming, but because you **know** it is coming. You will no longer be anxious about how you can fix the problems at hand. When you are walking by the Spirit of God, you will not panic about falling into pieces or losing your peace. **GPS>**"Hope deferred makes the heart sick, but a desire fulfilled is a tree of life." **[Proverbs 13:12]** Read the Book of Ecclesiastes in the Bible, and you will learn to meet life's unhappy trials, tribulations, challenges, and surprises with understanding and peace. Being strengthened by learning wisdom, being able to smile, and seeing the humor in various situations, which are trying to help you in one way or another. Seek to understand the reasoning and message you have received from the Spiritual realm of God, teaching you how to accept things, knowing that you can trust God. Finally, having peace in your heart by walking in the Spirit and not in the flesh.

Surrendering all your concerns to God, seeing the miraculous power he has, resolving every situation, in unconditional love for you.

GPS>[Genesis 3:16- 19, 5:15-17; Book of Ecclesiastes 1:13, 12:1; Isaiah 48:10-11; Acts 1:15 19. Psalm 112:7]

CHAPTER 23A

Flowchart Of How and Why Things Happen While in Your Life Journey

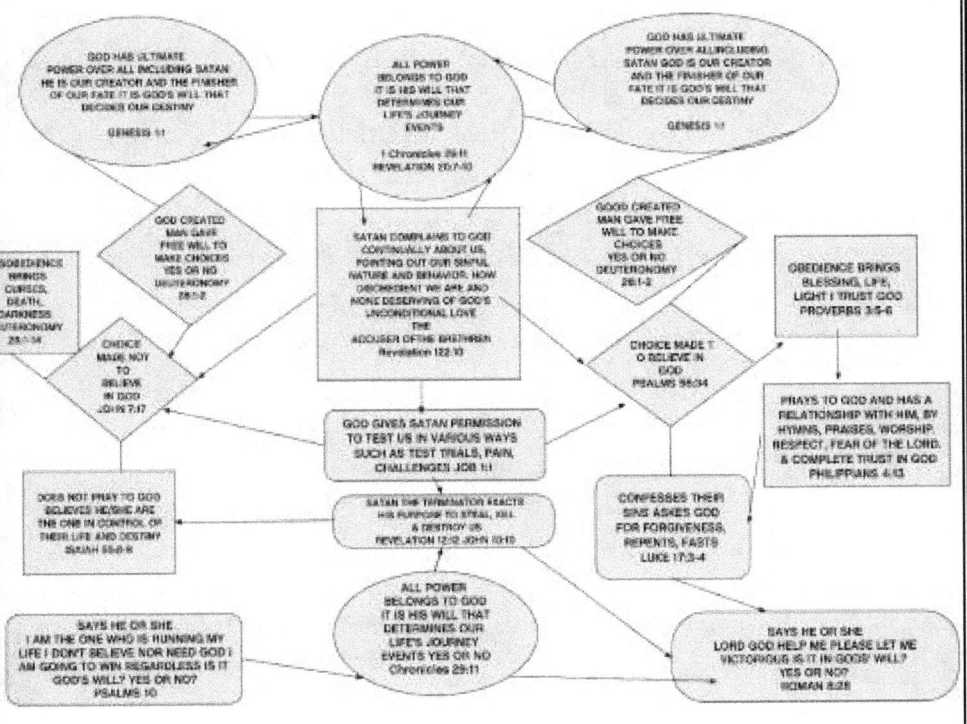

CHAPTER 23B

Interpretation Of Life's Journey Process

[SHOWN ABOVE ON FLOWCHART 23-A]

As you can see from the above flowchart, God controls everything that happens to you, whether you see it as bad or you see it as good. All victories are God's because it is His will that matters, not yours; you are His servants, His ambassadors. The victory or success is all in God's will. God gives you purpose. What your creator deems acceptable is done following His agenda. Think about it: God has never lost a battle, and He never will because He is the beginning and the end. God's Power is Omnipotent. He is Alpha and Omega. **GPS>**"I am the Alpha and the Omega, 'says the Lord God, who is, and who was, and who is to come, the Almighty."

The reason why things happen in your Life Journey is in this order:

#1. All power belongs to God; it is His will that determines your Life Journey. GPS>[Genesis 1:1; Psalm 62:11; John 15:4-5; Job 1:2; 1 Timothy 6:16]

#2 and #3 God is the ultimate power over all, including Satan. He is your creator and the finisher of your fate. It is God's will that decides your destiny. GPS>[Genesis 1:1; Job 1:1; Hebrews 12:2; John 5:19; Acts 26:18]

#4a. God created man and gave free will for the ability to make choices, either yes or no. GPS>[Deuteronomy 28:1-2; 17; Hebrews 3:12; Joshua 24:15; Genesis 1:27]

When you choose **yes**, to believe in God, GPS>Psalm 56:34]:

Making the choice to believe in God gives you Blessings, Life, and the Light of God in your life. GPS>John 15:16; Moses 3:17; Psalm 91; Genesis 1:26-31; Isaiah 1:19]

You trust God and are obedient in following his will. GPS>[Proverbs 3:5-6; Isaiah 1:19; 1 Peter 1:5; Romans 8:37]

You pray to God, having a relationship with Him through hymns, praise, respect, worship, having a fear of the Lord, and complete trust in God. GPS>[Philipians4:13; James 4:7; Luke 10:19; Numbers 22:12, 23:20-21; Matthew 6:6-13]

You confess your sins to God; in repentance, you ask God for forgiveness. GPS>[Luke 17:3-4; James 5:16; 1 John 1:8-9; Psalm 32:5; Acts 2:38]

You ask God to help you become victorious in your battles. Only if it is in God's will will the decision be yes or no. GPS>[1 Corinthians 10:13; Joshua 1:9; Romans 8:28-31; Philippians 4:6-7; Matthew 19:26]

All Power belongs to God. It is His will that determines your life journey events, either yes or no. GPS>[Psalm 62:11, 84:1; Jeremiah 29:11; Proverbs 4:13; Isaiah 60:22]

REGARDLESS OF WHETHER YOU BELIEVE IN GOD OR NOT, YOU STILL GET TESTED

Through your various tests, your faith, trust, belief, and love of God are established. When you recognize obedience is the key to Eternal Life, following Jesus through the Holy Spirit. Causing your mindset to change from walking in worldliness to walking in the Spirit of God, no longer in the flesh** GPS>[2 Corinthians 13:5; Romans 8:18; Isaiah 26:3; 1 Peter 4:12; James 13-6]

Continually, God is being approached by Satan, the Accuser of the Brethren. Complaining to God about how unworthy you are of His carrying and protection. Pointing out your sinful nature and behavior(s).

Saying how you do not deserve his unconditional love. GPS>[Revelation 12:10-12; Matthew 5:25; Ephesians 6:16; John 8:10-11; Peter 5:8]

Satan desires to steal all you have, physically and spiritually, killing and destroying you. GPS>[John 8:44, 10:10-29; 1 John 3:8; 2 Corinthians11:14; Luke 22:31]

Satan is one of God's messengers for implementing His wrath. God gives Satan permission, allowing mankind to be tested in various ways. GPS>[Revelation 12:10-12; Hebrews 2:14-15; Thessalonians 2:7; 1Corinthians 15:56-57; Job 1:12, 21-22]

Through tests, trials, circumstances, challenges, and tribulations. GPS>[Romans 16:20; James 4:7; Isaiah 45:5-7; Proverb 16:4; Exodus 16:4; [Read the Book of Job 1-47:17]

But only within the limitations of the jurisdiction and his specific orders to Satan, which he allows him to enact upon you. GPS>[Acts 26:18; Matthew 12:24-26; Ephesians 2:2, 6:12; John 12:31; Job 1:12]

As a means of testing, discipline, and giving God His Glory. GPS>[Exodus 20:20; Job 23:10; 1 Corinthians 10:13; Genesis 22:1-2; James 1:2-3]

JESUS CHRIST IS THE INTERCESSOR FOR ALL OF MANKIND AND ADVOCATE ON YOUR BEHALF TO THE FATHER GOD

When you choose not to believe in God, [Psalm 56:34]:

Making a choice to believe in God is disobedience in not following God's will for you. GPS>[Matthew 10:33; John 10:10; 2 Thessalonians 2:10-12; Leviticus 26:14-46; Ephesians 2:2]

Curses, darkness, and death are your life. GPS>[Deuteronomy 28:1-15- 68; Galatians 3:10-13; 1 Corinthians 16:22; Malachi 2:2; Proverbs 3:32-33]

You don't pray to God to have a relationship with Him. GPS>[Hebrews 10:25, 12:22-29; John 14:6, 17:3-4; John 15:5]

You believe that you are in control of your life and destiny. GPS>[2 Corinthians 4:4; Revelation 2:4; Isaiah 55:8-9; Proverbs 3:5-6; James 4:8]

Believing that you do not need God and that you will win, regardless. GPS>[John 3:18; Matthew 7:13-14; Philippians 2:21; Ecclesiastes 5:10; Proverbs 3:7-8]

You show no respect to God, have no relationship with God, nor do you fear, worship, or praise the Lord. GPS>[Psalm 28:52, 138:8; Matthew 5:43-44;1 Peter 2:17; Romans 13:1-7]

Only trust yourself, only in your life journey. GPS>[Jeremiah 17:5-9; 1 Samuel 31; Proverbs 11:28, 118:8; Matthew 6:20]

You do not confess your sins to God nor repent; you ask God for nothing because you do not believe in Him. You say that you are running and controlling your own life. GPS>[Psalm 66:18; John 20:23; 1 John 8:8; Isaiah 55:8-9; Revelation 9:20-21]

In ignorance, lack of knowledge, and darkness. GPS>[Psalm 10; Ephesians 4:18-25; Hosea 4; Proverbs 14:18-35; 1 Corinthians 14:38]

Not realizing, nor accepting, that the outcome of your desire(s) is contingent, depending on God's plan for you. Only if your desire is the same as God's will; only then will manifestation take place. You control nothing, except making choices, and how you handle, test, circumstances, and mayhem in your life journey. GPS>[Proverbs 16:4; Psalm 37:4; Luke 8:17; Psalm 66:10; Romans 8:28]

All Power belongs to God. It is His will that determines your life journey events, being yes or no. GPS>[Jeremiah 29:11-13; Acts 9:1-31; Proverbs 16:13, 19:21; Joshua 24:15]

Summation: Once God's will is accomplished. The essence of his will and your obedience return to him. Accomplishing the mission. **GPS>**"So my word that goes out of my mouth will be. It will not return to me without results, but it will certainly accomplish whatever is my delight, and it will have sure success in what I send it to do." **[Isaiah 55:11]** Giving you hope for a future.

CHAPTER 24

Repentance

What is Repentance? Repentance is remorsefully seeking forgiveness of your sin(s) to find salvation. The word "Repent" is interpreted from the Greek word "Metanoia," defining the "change of mind." Repenting means more than just feeling guilty for what you have done. It also means that your mind is to change along with your heartfelt remorse. There are 6 steps in repentance. The first is your believing in the Gospel of Jesus Christ and trusting God's Word. Second, you are to confess your sins(s) to God in order for your Heavenly Father to forgive you. Third, acknowledge your sin(s), expressing sincere regret with heartfelt sorrow for the sinful act(s) that have been committed against God by you. Fourth, have a sincere, remorseful heart, making a covenant with God, in true commitment, to turn away from sinful thoughts and actions. Changing your mindset and behavior to follow the Holy Spirit.

Transforming your heart, leading you to shift your old worldly ways, no longer walking in the flesh. Fifth, ask God for forgiveness. Sixth, you are willing to accept responsibility for any type of restitution that may be warranted for pain or damage that you caused. Repentance requires your self-evaluation, which leads to transforming your heart, evolving in great knowledge, and having a keen understanding of the will of God, causing you in Spiritual reconciliation and wisdom, to be focused on God, thinking on these virtuous things, which are true, honest, just, pure, lovely, and are of good report, including anything, that is excellent, worthy of praise, and the God News of the Gospel of Jesus' life, death, and resurrection.

Throughout the scriptures in the Bible, the call to "repent" is prevalent. It is so powerful that it always avails you the ability to "repent immediately, anywhere, anytime, for Now is the time, for you have a 'Now God,' ready for action. Expressing His faithfulness, through His omnipresence, always there, for you to turn around from sinfulness, to face Him, as he erases your sins in forgiveness, revitalizing you in His unconditional love. Repentance is marvelous, for it allows you to confess your sins to God. Vowing never to repeat the sinful acts you've done, being saved and baptized. Through Jesus Christ, being made clean, leading to Eternal Life. **GPS>**"Repent, for the Kingdom of God is at Hand." **[Matthew 3:2]**

GPS>[Matthew 3:11, 6:15; Philippians 4:8; Acts 3:19; Luke 3:3, 13:5]

WHAT IS SALVATION?

In Christianity, Salvation means the deliverance of the soul from sin and its consequences. The word "Salvation" is from the Latin word salva, which comes from salva, meaning "safe" or "saved."

Salvation is also defined as the state of being saved or protected from harm or dire situations. In order to receive Salvation, being saved from your sin(s), you must have faith and trust God, believing that Jesus Christ is your Lord and Savior, died for your sins, and rose again.

Confession is good for the soul; it is truly a life-saving event. In order to be saved from your sin(s), you must trust God, verbally asking God for forgiveness for them. Willing to turn from your sins and believe that Jesus Christ is your Lord and Savior, died for your sins, and rose again. Confessing with your mouth is the personal way of asking for forgiveness, as speaking with your mouth requires your mind, heart, and soul all be involved in this Miraculous, soul-saving transaction. It is the personal, correct, and respectful way of asking for forgiveness.

Speaking with your mouth requires your mind, heart, and soul to be involved in this Miraculous soul-saving transaction. In fact, speaking to anyone is a personal heart-to-mouth involvement, being that this is the best way of communicating with anyone at any time. The same standards apply when communicating with God; a text just won't do, nor thinking about it in your mind, having it in your head. Anytime you speak, it requires thinking, soul searching, and your heart to be combined in this protocol.

Asking for forgiveness from God and your earthly parent(s) is actually important to speak out loud, using your mouth and voice, to express your sentiments of apologies, or ask for forgiveness. Staying diligent in being found walking righteously, without blemish, in peace. Having the patience of the Lord as salvation, in growing in grace and knowledge of your Lord and Savior, Jesus Christ. When you are forgiven, you have become renewed, being now purified. By God's grace and mercy, we no longer face the consequences, which include death and separation from God due to a sinful mindset.

Causing the transformation of your soul and spirit to be reunited with your Heavenly Abba Father. This is the salvation of God, promises to seek out and save those who are lost, and to bind up the injured. God gave his son Jesus as atonement for your sin(s). Promising to put the Spirit within you and to regenerate your hardened heart. **GPS>**"And I will give you a new heart and put a new spirit within you; I will take the heart of stone out of your flesh and give you a heart of flesh. I will put My Spirit within you and cause you to walk in My statutes, and you will keep My judgments and do them." **[Ezekiel 36:26-27]**

The Lord shows you salvation by fighting your battles; you are not able to defeat the enemy on your own human strength; you need the power of the heavenly Father to bring victory. As being both cherished and called beloved by your heavenly Father, you relish the wait for the return of Christ Jesus.

He is your defender, protector, and all you need whenever you call on him, seeking rescue from the various issues of life's wars, which the world draws you into. **GPS>**"The LORD will fight for you while you only need to keep silent and remain calm." **[Exodus 14:14]**

GPS>[Acts 4:12; Ephesians 2:8-9; Jonah 2:9; Roman 3:21-4:25; Titus 2:11-14]

DELIVERANCE

What is deliverance? In Christianity, Deliverance means to be released from the bondage of sinfulness, freeing you from a sinful heart and mindset. Because of Jesus Christ's ultimate sacrifice, of giving His blood and body, dying on the cross. Through the miraculous Resurrection Power of God the Father, raising Christ from the dead, caused Him to become the Savior and Redeemer for all of humanity, bringing the ability to receive salvation, leading to deliverance from sin and death. No longer is humanity condemned under the laws of Moses and the Old Testament.

Through the ultimate sacrifice of Christ Jesus, "Therefore, there is no longer condemnation, to those who in faith believe that Christ Jesus is their Lord and Savior. Yet, deliverance is needed because of the sinfulness that exists in the forms of temptations through worldly issues of life. Where fear tactics are used by Satan as intimidation schemes, trying to usurp the authority of God, He isn't alone. He has his imps and demons that prowl around, seeking any opening in your heart, soul, mind, and spirit that allows them to enter, bringing corruption in the form of sinfulness. **GPS>**"Resist the devil, and he will flee from you." **[James 4:7]**

Through the miraculous Resurrection power of God and stimulation of your spirit, you are convicted, in your heart, soul, and mind, to seek deliverance through Salvation, and deliverance from sin's penalty, both have been provided through Christ. Deliverance through salvation has been made available to all believers in Christ, translating you into the Kingdom of Heaven. Where the freedom of the Lord is, there is liberty, and this is what deliverance does; it breaks all chains of bondage in the form of sin. God, in all His authority, has declared in the scriptures that you are His child and that He will deliver you from all forms of evil. Providing all your help and means of escape from your circumstances, causing you to become an eyewitness, able to give to others a testimony of His miraculous power, sharing the method(s) in which He used for your deliverance. Freely given in love, forgiveness, and mercy is how Deliverance comes into your spirit after you have received salvation.

Wanting more of the Word of God, this Deliverance is called the "GOSPEL" in the "New Testament." "Gospel" literally means the proclamation of "good news." In surrendering your heart, mind, and soul, gaining faith through prayers, following the True doctrine of Jesus Christ, "The Word, The Way, and The Truth. You've become encouraged by the "Good News of the Gospel." Trusting God to deliver you requires trust, faith, belief, and submission by letting go and letting God be God. Salvation is one thing, and deliverance is another. Deliverance means that you have been lifted to a level of no longer vulnerable to temptations. Being renewed, no longer walking in sinfulness, but now being blameless, through faith.

Take, for example, you really like cheesecake. You have found a way to eat it all day, every day, as you notice your physical health and appearance changing, not for the better. Then, finally, you eat or just look at cheesecake, and you want to regurgitate, causing you to push the dish away from you. You say, "No more, I've had enough!" This is what being delivered is, except it is not cheesecake; you've had enough of it; it is a sin. No longer are you subject to falling back into that weakness that caused you to sin. Finding God's help in perseverance, faith, discipline, obedience, and strength following the Holy Spirit. You have actually been set free from those sins (s), no longer longing for what the flesh wants and its results. You are delivered, tested, and true, now rooted and grounded in uprightness.

In wisdom and obedience, you are following the righteous ways of Jesus, the solution and the answer to every worldly and spiritual problem you encounter. In this delivered state of mind, you are ready to be redeemed, re-accepted, and certified back in good standing with God. **GPS>**"These things I have spoken unto you, that in Me ye might have peace. In the world ye shall have tribulation, but be of good cheer: I have overcome the world." **[John 16:33]**

Your desire is not only to be saved but totally delivered from the temptations that have held you in a stronghold(s). Once this happens, your entire being no longer desires to follow your old ways of living and thinking. You actually know that you have had enough of whatever it was that caused you to fall into the ditches of worldliness. Experiencing His deliverance daily, you increase in faith and in thankfulness for His recessive power, delivering you from all of the worldliness, which leads to sin and death.

The Lord does not want you to be in snares of temptations. He wants you to cast your burdens, cares, and concerns on Him because he cares for you. There are times you may not understand what God is doing, so pray for help. But trust Him, for all that He does is for your good. In the Bible, there are numerous ways that God has delivered others from generation to generation.

GPS>"For you have delivered my soul from death, yes, my feet from falling, that I may walk before God in the light of life." **[Psalm 56:13]** The book of Daniel in the Bible shares the scripture regarding three of Daniel's friends, including himself, who refusal to worship false idols that King Nebuchadnezzar ordered everyone in his kingdom to worship because of their devout faith in the one true living God, Jehovah. These three men, Shadrach, Meshach, and Abednego, were cast into a furnace and delivered unharmed, not even smelling like smoke.

God delivered these three men from death in the furnace, displaying the miraculous power and Glory of God. Changed the mind of King Nebuchadnezzar, causing him to become a believer in Jehovah, the God of Daniel. **[Daniel 3:13-30]** The power of God is so powerful that it can deliver you from the hand of all your enemies. As He did with David, turning his dark desperation into light and hope. **GPS>**"The Lord turns my darkness into light." **[2 Samuel 22:29]** There are scriptures throughout the Bible confirming God's Deliverance power.

GPS>[1 John 4:4; James 4:7; Psalm 34:4, 17; Jeremiah 39:17-18; 1Peter 5:8-9]

REDEMPTION

What is redemption? Redemption is being saved from sin, error, evil, and re-acceptance. It is to be rescued, regaining or gaining possession of something in exchange for payment, or clearing a debt. In order to receive redemption, you must first, after, have shown growth in your renewal of mind, spirit, and soul, walking now in the Holy Spirit. Believing that there is only one true God and that Jesus Christ is your Lord and Savior. Having a repentant heart, seeking forgiveness, you confess your sins, making a covenant with God, promising to make a 360-degree turnaround from your sin(s) and turn to face Jesus following His ways.

Making this reversal of behavior is not easy to do, as it requires a change in your mindset, having faith, and trusting in the promises of God. Being obedient and applying faith, prayer, and fasting are all essential in this Spiritual transformation. The Holy Spirit is your conduit for you and God; in wisdom, you practice listening to hear what guiding steps the Spirit is telling you. Cleansed by the Holy Spirit Fire, in your purification, it allows you to be reinstated by God. This caused the end of a broken relationship, which had become strained once again. To redeem means to buy back. This is what Jesus Christ did; he claimed ownership, bringing salvation for you and the world. Your redemption is all due to Jesus Christ dying on the cross for humanity. By His substitution atoning death, He alone redeems you from hell and gains for your forgiveness of sin, righteousness, and everlasting life. Rekindling a separation between mankind and God due to the sinfulness of living a worldly lifestyle.

Through the ultimate sacrifice of Jesus, through redemption, you have established a reconnection to God, sustaining forgiveness, saving you from being a slave to sin. Salvation leads to deliverance, then deliverance to redemption. Being redeemed does require a lifelong process, as the path to redemption starts from belief, causing faith, leading you to be saved, causing repentance, leading to salvation, and deliverance. In being delivered, you follow the Word of God, reflecting Jesus in your daily walk. You've become a warrior, unable to be swayed by the old sins that once plagued you, meaning you are delivered.

The benefits of receiving redemption are becoming adopted into God's family. Redemption causes you to become righteous, through sanctification, assures you of God's love, and frees you. Through redemption, you can find Eternal Life through the Holy Spirit, guiding you to blessing, protection, and prosperity. Wisdom comes from being redeemed. Renewal of your mind is needed, and scriptures are excellent resources to help you sustain and persevere in your spiritual walk. Scriptures say, **GPS>**"In him, we have the forgiveness of our trespasses, redemption according to the riches of his grace, which he has lavished on us." **[Ephesians 1:7]**

GPS>[Psalm 111:6-9; Hebrews 9:12; Titus 2:14; Ephesians 1:7; Isaiah 44:21-23]

CHAPTER 25

Patience

What is patience? Patience is having the capacity to accept or tolerate delay, trouble, or suffering without getting angry or upset. Patience is a noun; it is a virtue. It is taking no action toward someone or some event that takes a long time to accomplish. It requires self-control and discipline. Patience is a major part of your life journey, as you are daily in an atmosphere of some sort in the world, and patience is needed. Patience is essential in being a genuine Christian. It convicts you to walk in the Spirit, following the ways of Jesus, staying in your peace. Bringing peace to those around you by demonstrating the love of God that you have received in your heart.

Patience is a means of growing in knowledge and understanding, becoming wise in dealing with temptations and the various snares of evil. Patience teaches you how to de-escalate situations of confrontation. Reminding you of the Ten Commandments and the Word of God, commanding you to love your neighbor as yourself. Teaching you how to walk in love, remain calm, and relax when you follow the Spirit, not in the flesh. The flesh is frequently where discord, impatience, selfishness, lack of understanding, and intolerance toward others or experiences. Not falling into the ditch of darkness, wearing dark glasses, seeing only yourself in them, your needs, your wants, and using the timeline that you see as appropriate to appease you.

Patience is gentle, quiet, easy-going, lovely, kind, and joyful, just to list a few of the qualities that it dispels. These qualities are gifts in the form of Supernatural manifestations of the Holy Spirit, prompting you, as a believer in Christ, to walk in them rather than walking in the flesh. These supernatural gifts give way for the "Fruit of the Spirit, to flourish, being made up of nine segments, each holding its own supernatural power within. Consisting of love, joy, peace, patience, kindness, goodness, faithfulness, gentleness, and self-control. All of these Spiritual gifts of the Holy Spirit require that you walk in the Spirit, where you can receive them in your heart, mind, and soul, in the hope that you will apply them in your life journey.

As you see, patience is one of the spiritual gifts, surrounded by all qualities of righteousness. Using this gift will keep you walking and living in the light of God's love. It is patience that causes anything worthy to appear, as God takes his time to provide correct answers to you because He is patient, methodical, in precise. There is no disorganization in anything that God does, has done, or is going to do. Even in the growing of flowers, when you plant a seed, it takes time for it to germinate, and then you have to fertilize it, nourishing it with the rays of the sun's power and water to help the roots grow strong. Then, after time, from the love that you have given, it will bloom, giving you something of beauty that no man can give. This is the same for patience. It is a seed, dying in the dark soil, resurrecting to life through the crap, or manure of the world, consisting of all the trials, traumas, and issues of life.

Strengthening you to break through the filth of the dirt that the world has to offer. Emerging to absorb the sun, which is the Love of God, that also provides you with the living water of life to sustain you into becoming one of the most beautiful, unique flowers ever seen. This is what patience is; it is the maturing of your faith, trust, and love of God's ways that bring life, light, and truth, leading you to Eternal Life. Patience is just one of the many keys to help you be blessed and to bless others. Patience does not mean cruel; it is soothing, bringing comfort to any situation and all involved. Many times, patience is needed when someone understands and needs more help than they do.

Being patient does take self-control, denying yourself, thinking with wisdom, having consideration, and being thoughtful to others. Patience builds character from the various tests, trials, experiences, and issues of life. You encounter overcoming them all with the help of Christ Jesus as your Lord, Savior, and Redeemer. In grace and mercy, your mind is renewed, becoming a new person, no longer angry, arrogant, in a rush, demanding, pushing, and demanding others to jump for your wants and needs. You now wait on the Holy Spirit to guide you into all truths, walking in love and peace, with yourself growing into wisdom, now able to counsel others on how patience works. No longer need anything on the timeline of worldliness. You actually want nothing except to bring only peace to your surroundings and others.

GPS>"Knowing this, that the trying of your faith worketh patience. "But let patience have her perfect work, that ye may be perfect and entire, wanting nothing." Let endurance have its perfect result and do a thorough work so that you may be perfect and completely developed in your faith, lacking in nothing." **[James 1:3-4]**

Patience for you may be difficult due to your mindset. Having an understanding of how to be patient is not hard to do once you surrender your life to Jesus, walking in righteousness and love. One of the gifts from the Holy Spirit is understanding, which is the beginning of wisdom for all things in your life journey. Because patience is having understanding, which indeed is one of the key elements to gaining wisdom. Having an understanding of when you are in a position or situation that could use patience is a blessing both to you and all who are involved in this occurrence.

Giving you an opportunity to show compassion by being tolerant of the events that are playing out in your life at that moment. Asking questions to yourself questions, "What is going on with this person, what's wrong with them? Why are they taking so long? What is the problem or issue? Allow time for the Holy Spirit to guide you in truth, love, and wisdom. Allowing you to ponder that maybe that person or event has something going on in their life, where you can offer in your heart a prayer for that person in the situation. Once you get a grasp of how patience operates, you will soon realize that there really are reasons why there are delays in receiving what you want, regarding service from others, prayers, and all activities in your life journey. Through the use of another key wisdom, you now show leniency toward others regarding their patterns of behavior as they perform their duties to you, a customer.

Many times seen as being weak, but in the Lord, you are strong in the power and the might of the Lord. Bringing love and wisdom through your eye, witnessing what you have seen, and gaining from being both impatience and patient. Even wisdom shows you how to understand that there may be a reason for their actions. Demonstrating patience in a fallen world can be difficult at times, where patience is not often shown, and kindness is considered to be weak. Do you know that sometimes, these delays and events that require patience are tested? Everything you do is all for a purpose; you truly are not alone. Maybe in the natural eye, it seems so, but having Spiritual eyes, you know the truth, seeing God's love, help, even the ability to discern when Lucifer's imps and posse are amidst.

There is a continual Spiritual battle happening in the heavens, on the earth, in the earth, and below the earth. All battling for your soul, one to save it and one to take it. Remember that God has given you choices, which can be life or death; it's up to you. Don't forget about the consequences that follow your choices. Taking your time to pray, waiting on the wisdom and guidance from the Holy Spirit, not making any decisions in the form of choices, rashly. This is the way of Satan; he knows that when you have a situation, you react. When you are walking in the Spirit, you will hesitate, pray, and wait for spiritual guidance. When you are walking in the flesh, thinking worldly, you immediately panic, seeking relief from earthy methods, which have no avail to rescue you from the drama you are facing.

Satan pressures you by using your mindset to control your responses toward making choices. He wants you to act in haste, being caught up in foolishness, deceit, confusion, fear, and bondage. Leading to destruction, loss, and defeat due to ignorance of the Ways of God. You, in fear, rush to make a choice, not realizing that fear is nothing but **False Evidence**

Appearing Real. Making way for your issue to balloon into something worse than before.

In these irritating situations that are getting on your last nerve, you can either be patient, stay at peace, let go, and let God handle it. Or, you can allow that irritation to turn into anxiety, anger, irrational behavior, selfish thinking, and cursing those who are in your line of vision. Including something you want to happen hasn't been quick enough for you; possibly, the answering of your prayer begins to fester in your flesh. Causes your heart to start making stones from your anger, impecuniousness, and impatience, transferring those stones in your heart to become sinful pebbles in your mind. Corrupting your thoughts because you lack wisdom. Not understanding nor seeing the love of God as you walk in the flesh.

Allowing Satan to taint your imagination with confusion, corrupting your mind through tainted imagination, lacking in knowledge, and seeing everyone and everything before you as a problem. Having patience helps you to make wise choices, forgive others, stay composure, and see the situation through with resolve and serenity. Of course, this mindset is that of Christ Jesus, which, when you choose to follow the way, in truth and light, you become revived walking in the holy Spirit. No longer walking in the flesh, saying, "If I don't see it, I don't believe it!"

GPS>"And not only so, but we glory in tribulations also; knowing that tribulation worketh patience, And patience, experience; and experience, hope: And hope maketh not ashamed; because the love of God shed abroad in our hearts by the Holy Ghost which is given unto us." **[Romans 5:3-5]** You now see that as you think as a mere human, the things that appear good don't mean it is. You must evaluate if your motives for making choices are righteous and not self-gratifying.

Patience is a mix of different emotions, wisdom, and self-awareness. It encompasses feelings that must be guarded by having the Spiritual knowledge of how to control your emotions. It requires being unselfish, kind, understanding, and walking in the love of God. Which, with empowerment, sustains your faithful conviction in perseverance, strength, and self-control. It is accepting whatever the conditions are and the time it takes to resolve whatever you are waiting for to be done for your benefit. Be it going to the Department of Motor Vehicles, waiting in a long line at the grocery store, or waiting to be seen by a doctor. Waiting is not desired when you are living in worldliness, having a "Fast food mentality" of "I want it now!"

Impatience consists of selfishness, ego, arrogance, ignorance, and having a sense of entitlement. While you take a stand, make a scene, exposing your annoyance and unwillingness to wait whenever you think you have waited too long for results. Sometimes, lengthy durations of waiting are hard for you to endure, as you have your own expected timeline for others. Having anxiety, feelings of questioning why something or someone is not acting quickly enough to satisfy your want or need. Igniting the fuse that exceeds your time limit before you fly off the handle, saying something angrily, possibly becoming physically violent, to the point of damaging property, before storming out of the building, or the area in which your display of having a lack of patience is shown.

Your patience is noted by many, seeing you as the peacemaker, the one to come to for counseling, and understanding whenever help is needed. It means that you are able to address any heated issue or matter in a respectable, wise, calming, Christ-like manner. Not showing anger, rage, annoyance, or irritability when challenges occur. Patience itself is a test that shows maturity in Spiritual growth. It is a means of confirming if you are a true Christian or not. When something is made by man, such as machinery and other man-made items, it must be tested and tried in order to determine if it meets the qualifying standards set forth before the item is put on the market for use.

The same is true when testing the properties of metals and gems, as an example. It is through the purifying of the various metals that increases its value increases. This is the same concept when you strive to gain both knowledge and understanding that establishes wisdom. You must be purified in the grace and love of God, through the testing of your faith, by way of trials, issues of life. Staying rooted and grounded in love, believing that Jesus Christ is your Lord and Savior. Daily, the need for patience starts the moment your feet are placed on whatever solid surface your environment consists of. If you are in your house, it is the floor.

When you're camping out, as soon as you place your feet on the tent's floor, ground, sand, or whatever. Patience is needed for survival in this fallen, broken world. Stay focused on Jesus through scriptures, prayers, songs, singing praise, worship, and servitude. Giving thanks for all God does is "Very Good." You are to think about things that are Honest, Just, Pure, Lovely, Excellent, and worthy of conversation. While you are here in the earthly realm, your mind must be renewed to the Lordship of Christ as one of His disciples, agents, and ambassadors. You walk by faith, not by sight, by not letting problems and circumstances override you, usurp the authority that God has given you through Jesus Christ, your Lord and Savior. You are being led by the Holy Spirit, meaning there is a guide that is on your side, that is truthful, faithful, powerful, and of God.

The Holy Spirit, in its wisdom, convicts you to remember what you have read of the Word of God. Applying them to your life journey daily. Patience is a virtue, and you must remain in your peace and not fall to pieces, not allowing fleshly emotions to bind you in sinfulness. Patience has the ability to say, "I will not sign for the devil's packages today, using tenacity to stay obedient!" Have you ever noticed how a Sloth moves? It sooo slow, yet the Sloth stays focused on its main target, yet not in a rush to reach its goal, in patience, tenacity, and perseverance to accomplish its feat.

The same is what you must do: take it slow, simmer down, trust that you are on the right path with God, and see that all things work together for good. "Having patience is not easy, for you are still being worked on by God to attain this important character. You are, as a babe, learning to get nourishment in the form of liquid. After a while, you begin to mature in the Word, gaining your spiritual teeth so that you are able to chew on the meat of the "Good News of the Bible," receiving Jesus as the "Bread of Life, and living water, for your Spiritual growth. In general, most people are not patient, they often have the "fast food mentality" "I want it now!" I want it my way! Hurry up! "This is taking too long! "Time is money! "I can't wait; I'll do it myself.

This attitude is dangerous for you in several ways; it takes your peace, making you offended if it doesn't work out your way. In other ways, it is damaging because you have stress; you become anxious, worried, and lusting after whatever it is to materialize immediately. You ponder how long you must be patient toward others, dealing with various circumstances and confrontations. When it comes to patience and timelines, they are not yours to determine; it is God's will and timetable, not yours ever! Therefore, you are to pray to the Father, giving Him all your burdens and concerns, trusting in His faithfulness, and wait on the Lord! When you lose your peace, you are not in the kingdom of God; you are in worldliness.

Remember, the Kingdom of God consists of Peace, Righteousness, and Joy. You have found that there are many places where more patience is needed, along with common sense. Do you know that the solution for combating road rage is Jesus? Yes, it is; how about praying before, during, and when you arrive?

Leaving early so you won't be in a rush, or feel you will not reach your destination in a timely manner. How about being part of the reason why everyone arrives safely? Embrace the opportunities that God gives you to learn, grow, and thrive in various life lessons regarding patience. Patience is a virtue, which means that it is a good quality to be able to tolerate something that takes a long time to manifest. Even with your family, friends, and co-workers, patience is needed to bring improvement to relationships. So it is only right that you have patience with God's line, which is always on time. You must realize that you are his beloved child and that it is in His time and His will that all is done.

God is your source of patience every time in your life. To many, this clique "time is money." This mentality is usually that of someone who feels that what they want to do must be swift and speedy in the effort to gain money. Having it "your way" is not the correct mindset to have. Everything requires some duration of time. Being patient requires empathy, understanding, and unselfishness. Before you learn patience, many times you act like a baby. Not actually saying wah, wah, wah, but behaving like one, but in an adult's body, being demanding and impatient. Patience is not just given; it takes self-awareness of yourself, knowing your wickedness and triggers that set you off. Causing you to become an ugly o gar or having the appearance of a swollen-up Puffer fish.

Being patient requires maturity, discipline, inner peace, putting yourself in the shoes of others, and having empathy. Some people are blessed to have patience through genetics, but being a child of God, you have an abundance of patience in Christ Jesus. There is also the concept my husband taught me, "If you don't mind, it doesn't matter," being a mind over matter method. In the medical field, there are doctors, nurses, and "patients," yes, indeed, you are the one who needs to be patient! How about that? All these years, scheduling and visiting doctor appointments, you hadn't realized the irony of the word patient, which in itself is telling you to be patient.

The word "patient" is telling you to wait to be called and receive service from them, tolerating the time it may take. Being patient in your daily life journey is essential; it can bless you when you use it wisely, showing that you care means a lot to others. There is a reason why patience is a virtue: it requires faith, understanding, morals, respect, and wisdom. Becoming patient may not be easy for you, but it does take the grace of

God, trusting Him to help you in every area of your life, to work all you lack to become what He wants you to become. Often, the results of your impatience cause more problems and dilemmas, needing help to get out of the muck you have put yourself in.

Waddling in worldly manure, dying spiritually, emotionally, and physically due to the issues of life. Crap (manure)also helps make the flowers grow as an additive. Both mankind and plant life are seeds, are Divinely Designs. Plant life has to be buried in dirt, die, and be resurrected as buds, to flowers that blossom after beginning life as a seed, completing the process of becoming a unique, beautiful flower, which is all from the patience of God.

GPS>[Romans 8:31, 12:2; John 16:33; Proverbs 3:5-6; Matthew 14:22-33; Titus 2:11-14]

WAIT ON THE LORD

Waiting on the Lord is part of your life journey as you run your race to receive Eternal Life through Jesus Christ. Waiting on the Lord helps you to grow in patience. It is also a period that humbles you to see just how much God is needed in your life. Providing you with a gateway that allows you to take a break from the hustle, stress, and useless noise of the world while still letting God be God. Seeing the impatience in you, which has given you a sense of entitlement, that you think, ensures a quick, speedy, satisfying, and immediate response(s) to whatever you desire. This attitude is an issue with both your heart and your mind, needing development in forbearance and tolerance.

Waiting on the Lord strengthens you in faith, trusting that all will be well with you. During this period, you are able to see God, the ultimate supernatural power and limitless authority as Jehovah, your Creator, who is omnipresent, omnipotent, controlling all. God has already preordained what He wants you to do. In order for you to accomplish what He desires for you requires you to learn obedience through the Word of God, putting hope in His word, becoming closer to Jesus, and letting him be your example, teaching you how to want you to show you that your needs are all being met by your heavenly Father, on his selected, time, and way. Waiting on the Lord prepares you for what is coming, helping you to renew the way that you think, from foolishness to having the mind of Christ, to help you understand the lesson(s) and gift you are going to receive, teaching how to be satisfied, wanting nothing, only what God provides.

After you submit your request(s) to the Lord, wait in expectancy, never doubting but believing that God has heard you. Speak as if you have already received your request. While you wait for God, draw closer to the Lord God, having a more intimate relationship. In giving praise, worship, honor, acknowledgment, and thanksgiving, seeing your desires in fruition. Waiting on the Lord does require submission to the Lord, in patience, humility, obedience, trust, and discipline, which you will find to be well worth it, teaching you wisdom and that nothing last forever; these are seasons in your life Journey. God will bring you through in abundance of grace, love, mercy, understanding, knowledge, and wisdom.

GPS>"Wait on the LORD; be of good courage, and he shall strengthen thine heart; wait, I say, on the Lord." **[Psalm 27:14]** Why does God make you wait so long? You may ask; it could be because you have not asked the Lord for help, thinking you can solve your issues yourself in the world. When you do turn to the Lord for help, it is during this period of waiting that you learn how to endure, becoming strengthened in faith, along with other non-flesh attributes, changing your attitude, helping you grow in the areas that you need, wisdom, love, and renewal, to help you on your Life Journey. Sometimes, answers and rescues take long durations because you are not yet ready to receive them. Possibly, what you want is for the wrong motive; it could be that it is selfish. Maybe you are not ready to receive the item(s)because you are not ready mentally, physically, emotionally, or spiritually.

When you ask God for things, you should think about how and what the outcome would be if you did receive that prayer request. Your Abba Father knows just what you need, and he will provide it at the right time. Delayed answers to prayer requests don't mean that it is a "no" from God. This, too, is a way to strengthen your faith, to grow on both spiritually and physically levels. God, Your Heavenly Father, is your earthly dad, knowing your needs and providing for you, including disciplining you when needed. **GPS>**"Spare the rod, spoil the child." "He who spares the rod hates His Son, but he who loves him is diligent to discipline him." **[Proverbs 13:24]** For example, you are 7 years old, and you keep asking for a 10-speed bike when you are barely able to ride or pedal a 3-wheel bike. Suppose you ask for a million dollars. If God gave it to you in the mindset that you are in now, what would you do with it? Your mind must be renewed to encompass what God provides to you in the light, with you being in righteousness.

Not walking in the flesh, understanding in wisdom that things you see in the natural "are temporary; they are mere props that God has provided for your earthly journey. In waiting, you learn patience and wisdom through experiences that have taught you how to do without contentment, not complain in acceptance, and trust in God's Will. Teaching how to be a good steward with whatever God gives you in his time. **GPS>**"Not that I was ever in need, for I have learned how to be content with whatever I have. I know how to live on almost nothing or with everything. I have learned the secret of living in every situation, whether it is with a full stomach or empty, with plenty or little." **[Philippians 4:11-13]** Things that you cannot see are spiritual, and that is what you are to be seeking, your way of returning home, which is in the heavens, receiving Eternal Life, in your new heavenly body, as Christ has.

GPS>[Acts 4:11-12; Micah 7:7; Psalms 15:3, 27:14; Hebrews 13:5; Luke 12:15]

CHAPTER 26

Beware of Distractions and Confusions

While traveling on your life journey, you are constantly bombarded with distractions. Distractions have many forms, names, and methods. Regardless of what they are called, they all come from Satan, the "Purpose Killer." Which is what he comes to do: steal, kill, and destroy. Stealing your hope, killing your Spirit, and destroying your life in one way or another. Distractions are called many different names and come in many different forms. Such as pain, pleasure, procrastination, technology, or anything that pulls your attention away from God is a diversion.

In the world are many issues of life, such as worries, circumstances, loss, uncertainty, financial concerns, and stress. There are distractions that cause you to be afraid; the devil knows them all. Distractions cause chaos, confusion, and interference with your peace. It is the worshiping of such things as video games, television, internet, making them idols. Technology influences your ability to rest quietly before God. Think about what having a cell phone contributes to your life: mere absorption of more worldly issues. None are beneficial for your spiritual growth; neither provides you with Peace and true peace of mind.

This is what distractions do. You can't do two things at the same time, and both subjects receive the same attention. **GPS>**"No man can serve two masters; for either he will hate the one and love the other, or else he will hold to the one and despise the other. You cannot serve God and man." **[Matthew 6:24]** Distractions are a killer, yes, a killer of time for God. It's amazing how you can watch television, play video games, and do everything else, but it seems to be hard for many to just say thank you or pray.

These hindrances affect your mind, causing you to become stressed, anxious, unable to sleep, make decisions, and be productive. Your mind uses them to make you fear whatever you are facing. Deceiving you, making things look so impossible as you look around in your circumstance(s), distorting your vision, causing you to see things in hopelessness, having no help, to being defeated. Distractions are to bind you, blind you, and keep you unfocused on God. Often causing you to miss blessings.

Distractions are continually noisy, wanting your attention, saying, Look at me, Come do this, you don't have time, you have to go here, you have to drive there, and anything else that will keep you occupied mentally, on other things, rather than God. While you wear the sinful blinders of Satan, you think about how you are going to push past your dilemma and resolve the issue(s). There is no way you can push anything along, for you are not strong enough, powerful enough, nor have both supernatural and omnipotent ability to stop any issue(s) of life alone.

You must remember just who Jesus is; He is the power and authority of God. It is because of His pulling you through, in the Way, the Truth, that you receive Eternal Life. Whatever path you choose to fulfill your calling is contingent on what Spirit you are walking in, sinfulness or righteousness. You have been called to serve God; don't let interference get in the way of your doing something good. The root cause of distractions is evil; knowing that your brain is trying to multitask, obey God, and trying to please the world causes confusion.

The Latin root words for the word "distraction" are dis, meaning "apart," and Trahere, meaning "drag." The word "distraction" means to be dragged away from a task or worry. For example, a loud, crying baby in the movie theater. Many disturbances consist of noises that cause you to pay attention to them rather than do what God has called you to do. These constant interruptions used by the enemy are to do just that: disrupt your mind, overloading it to the point where you have wandering thoughts and stress.

Other ways of distraction are when you don't know your purpose. Pray to the Holy Spirit and ask for to help you focus on God's will and block any distractions from it. Life itself, work all day, every day, you are bombarded by distractions. You may say it's hard to focus on God when you are working, caring for the kids, doing housework, running errands, driving, catching a bus, practicing sports, and watching television. Well, God isn't asking for you to stop what you're doing. All he is asking is that you acknowledge him and say a few thank yous, such as "I love your Lord," throughout the day. You don't have to shout it out loud, but you can think it or whisper the thank yous and praises to him.

Get out of the habit; when you do pray, always ask for something, basically begging. **GPS>**"If you are going to ask for anything, ask for wisdom." **[James 1:5]** God is not a vending machine or wishing well where you either put a coin simulating a prayer request for something that is material. Nor is He a genie, where "your wish" is His command. You should realize that some things you don't need, and your heavenly Father knows better than you what you need. Give God equal time, if not more than a television show, being that he is your creator.

The enemy wants you to be ignorant of the benefits of having a relationship with the Heavenly Father, which can be done by reading your Bible and other spiritual doctrines and resources. You have an allocated amount of time to be here on the earth, and the enemy knows this, so he and his minions are doing all they can to keep you from knowing the truth about Jesus Christ, our Lord and Savior. Distractions are interferences to prevent you from blessings, wisdom, peace, the delay of prayer requests, and help with the issues of life.

Here are some ways to avoid distractions:

1. Make God your first priority in each thing that you do, place you go, words you speak, and staying in grace and humility. GPS>[Proverbs 3:6]

2. Practice discipline in denying yourself of fleshly wants and worldly desires. Avoid going to places that, you know, distract you because of what it is, something you find appealing, such as shopping sales, new things, new adult toys, all props to seduce you. Including invites to restaurants, especially when you are going to be treated, and it is not your birthday, stay focused on God. GPS>[1 Peter 5:8]

3. Pray to God, asking for help through the Holy Spirit to remove all unrighteous distractions in your heart and mind. GPS>[Psalm 119:37]

4. Reflect on what the purpose is that God has called you to do. In belief, trusting God to provide you with all you need to complete the task at hand. GPS>[Philippians 4:19]

5. Allocate time to communicate with God, telling him that you are willing to be obedient to his will, thanking him for the opportunity to serve Him. GPS>[Micah 6:8]

6. Read scriptures reaffirming your faith, removing any fears that you may have regarding your calling by renewing your mind and following the Word of God. GPS>[Romans 12:2]

7. Be alert for different schemes of distractions from the enemy. Remembering that Jesus, too, was tempted by the devil and defeated him. GPS>[Matthew 4:1-11]

8. Keep your task always as a priority, making time daily to accomplish it. GPS>[Psalm 90:12]

9. Protect yourself from loud, intrusive forms of noise, technology, and talkative people, use headphones, are leave the area that you are sharing. GPS>[James 1:5]

10. When you feel defeated and unmotivated, take a break and pray to the Holy Spirit and your angels for help in strengthening. Staying strong in the power and the might of God. GPS>[Hebrews 12:1-2]

11. Avoid people who always want you to go somewhere; do something whenever you are in your peace. Be more social with those who are followers of the teachings of Christ Jesus. GPS>[1 Corinthians 11:1]

12. Evaluate yourself and your environment to find a quiet place among those that don't cause interruption to your thought process and what you are doing for God. GPS>[1 Corinthians 5:11]

13. Remember that all things are possible with God. GPS>[Matthew 19:26]

Avoiding and being aware of distractions does require discipline, patience, wisdom, and the Word of God, guiding you through the Holy Spirit, walking in the Spirit and not in the flesh. Make having time to do God's will a habit, like washing your face daily. Use this same concept to speak with God in thanksgiving, obeying His Will for you and others. God is always faithful to you; He never sleeps; he is always available in His magnificence of meticulous organization.

GPS>[Proverbs 4:23-25; Luke 10:38-42; John 1:9; Proverbs 4:25; 1 Corinthians 6:20]

CONFUSION

Confusion is from the devil, all of it. God is not a God of chaos. He is a God of peace and order. Anytime you find yourself saying, "I'm confused." Know that it is not from God. Stop immediately, take a breath, and pray, asking God to guide you, to help you discern His will, and the mind of Christ.

Living in a fallen world, full of confusion by the second, it's easy to become confused because it is a part of this world's structure. Earth is a ball of confusion, with Satan running over what's happening on it. Although God has given him authority to rule the earth, Satan still succumbs to the will of God, knowing the rules, regulations, and jurisdictions he is subject to obey. Confusion is a state of disorder, bewilderment, and perplexity. A situation in which people do not understand what is happening, what they should do, or who someone or something is.

In Christianity, confusion appears in many forms, each causing difficulty in worldliness. Yet, confusion may be a way of helping you grow in the word of God because you are lost in your thoughts of what is righteous and what is sinful. If you lack knowledge, you can miss the path that you should take in helping receive Eternal Life. Not having an understanding of why and what is going on in your life journey could prove detrimental to your challenges with the issues of life. Having you walk around aimlessly in a fog, confused about who you are, what you are to do, where you are, where you are going, and what your purpose is, whatever it is, it's causing confusion. Even on the television, when you hear something and you get confused after reviewing it several times to get the correct understanding.

If you cannot understand it by using Google, dictionary, thesaurus, and the Bible, you know through decrement that this is a work of the devil. Remember, his main purpose is to steal, kill, and destroy; that means your family, your finances, your peace, your health, your relationships, your marriage, and the list goes on. Whatever you care about, he wants to take it from you. Now, on that note, I would like to tell you that God is a jealous God. He does not want you to idolize anything. He is above all things in the world and not of this world, so loving your car, house, money, clothes, yourself, television shows, phones, and all material things we treat and give more attention to than go can be taken away, including your children we put on a pedestal, your boyfriend, your computer, nothing is to be above God.

These are idols, which is why good clergy and church leaders instruct their congregation not to trust what they say but to look things up in the Bible themselves. Ensuring that you receive the Word in truth, it is always a blessing to know things for yourself in evidence of truth. Put away any envy and strife; these sinful thoughts and actions lead you to confusion; that is what the world gives you: confusion, chaos, mayhem, indecision, doubt, ignorance, uncertainty.

GPS>"My people are destroyed for lack of knowledge." **[Hosea 4:6]** In Christianity, it is important that you know who you are in Christ Jesus, which is being a child of the highest God, highly favored, blameless, free, loved, and redeemed by the blood of Christ. It is also important to know who God is and who Jesus is. Christ is His, who is not only the Son of God, but He is both your Lord and Savior. Providing you with the Word of God, shedding his blood and body as the ultimate living sacrifice, that through his death on the cross and His resurrection from the dead, freed you from damnation, bringing salvation, redemption, and deliverance to receive **Eternal Life**, returning you back to the heavens where you belong.

Not understanding your purpose for being on earth is a very difficult state of mind to be in. Keeping your loss in what you are to do, how you are to act, and what you have to help you on the course of your journey. You are just like a blank sheet of paper, that is just lying on a table. Through hearing the Word of God, you receive faith to learn of God's will and Way for you. Through the knowledge of Christ, understanding will come from the presence of the Holy Spirit in your life. Teaching you to walk by faith, and not by sight, as you submit your mind, soul, body, and Spirit to follow in obedience, wisdom, and righteousness. Now, having the ability to recognize confusion and how it can operate in your life. Sometimes, God allows confusion so that you learn to trust Him, strengthening your faith through tests where confusion is so prevalent that you must call out to the Lord, seeking help in dealing with the puzzlement of why things are happening and how to find the solution.

Here are several ways to avoid confusion:

1.Spend more intimate time with God, listening to worship music, singing, and praising God. GPS>[Psalms 149:3-9]

2.Read and meditate on the Word, daily reading scriptures, and devotionals. GPS>[Joshua 1:8]

3.Pray with friends or others of the Body of Christ. GPS>[1 Corinthians 12:27]

4.Trust God in prayer, committing your situation to Him, seeking the solution. GPS>[Isaiah 43:19]

5.Stay in humility, patience, and obedience by walking in the Holy Spirit. GPS>[John 15:10-14]

6. Focus on the benefits of being free of confusion. GPS>[1 Corinthians 14:33]

7. Thank God for allowing you to grow through confusion, teaching you wisdom. GPS>[James 1:5]

8. Keep a journal of your activities, growth, and pain. GPS>[Jeremiah 30:20]

9. Look things up if you are not sure to clarify issues. GPS>[2 Corinthians 13:5]

10. Release past hurts, avoiding anxiety, triggers, and stress. GPS>[Philippians 4:6-7]

11. Look at nature and the beauty in it, lots of greenery, with hues of burnt orange. GPS>[Revelation 4:11]

12. Avoid toxic, recklessness, bafflement, and disorder. GPS>[Proverbs 3:5-6]

13. Avoid people who have so much drama in their lives that it makes you feel uneasy. Pray for them, and when stronger, lead them to God with others. GPS>[Romans 16:17-18]

14. Realize things that you cannot control, let go, and let God. GPS>[Ephesians 3:20]

When you allow Jesus and the Holy Spirit to be your guides, you are becoming strengthened in your faith and virtuous in patience, and you await instructions in complete reliance on the light of wisdom in love from the heavens. In humility, remaining rooted and grounded, receiving your blessings and solutions, in Jesus' name. Often, the enemy uses confusion to keep you off balance so that you do not know what you are chosen for or your weapons of power to defeat him. Removing all forms of confusion from your life as you walk in the Spirit, no longer walking in worldliness, accepting the ways of the flesh, leading to death. Permitting the world to tear you to pieces through confusion. Silence is golden, **GPS>**"Be still and know that I am God." **[Psalms 46:10]** The effects of distractions and confusion prevent one from gaining knowledge, wisdom, blessing, and truth.

GPS>[Deuteronomy 28:20; Timothy 5:8; Hebrews 13:8; Matthew7:7; Isaiah 41:10]

CHAPTER 27

The Organization of God

God is a God of order. God has created an organization called the "Body of Christ." The Body of Christ is established by having Jesus as the Head of the Body. There is one body, but it has many parts that make up one body. Consisting of acknowledging each member of the body part, which is a vital part, in order for the body to function properly. Just as the human body needs different body parts to sustain it, these gifts and talents which God has given you are an intricate part, in order for the "Body of Christ" to function properly.

Being in the Body of Christ, there is a system organized in order to suggest a straightforward elimination of disorder and pretense. There are many who pretend to be Christians. In the organization of the Body of Christ, you are to follow "God's Organizational Ways." It will get you to the place called Eternal Life. You must be in prayer, as God has put a seed in you, and the Word waters the seed. You are nourished and watered every day. Something must be in your mind that leads and chooses order. As a part of the "Body, your contribution is part of it. It is to work together in harmony with the other parts of the Body, which are other members. Making the "Organization of God," which is an organized body of a group of people who work together with a particular purpose. Such as a charity, a union, a firm, a business, a society, or an association, to form and establish something. The establishment of the "Organization of God." **GPS>** "Which is built on the foundation of the apostle prophets, with Christ Jesus being the cornerstone." **[Ephesians 2:20]**

In the organization, you are to pray, care, connect with others, and contribute to them, edifying everyone each time you speak. As part of the Body of Christ, the church, you are to be organized in your minds, in your way of speaking, which is always in love, and in your actions. You are to read the Word and apply it to your life journey. You are not to just read the Word; you are to be doers of the Word, being led by the Holy Spirit of Truth. In order for the "Organization of God" to function orderly, you must first have heard the Word of God so that you can find your purpose.

The Holy Spirit brings the stirring of the Lord inside you, spreading as a fruitful vine, in "God's organization the church, **GPS>** "The steps of a man are established by the Lord when he delights in his way; though he falls, he shall not be cast headlong, for the Lord upholds His hand." **[Psalm 37:23]** Order is how God operates in everything, meticulously, with pure perfection and organization.

Some of the characteristics of being a member of this organization require you not to be selfish; you are to be ready to give your all at any time. When you are in an organization, you have to pledge allegiance to the cause of that group. You are to be on time and in person when you are supposed to be. In the "Organization of God," there is no place for selfishness, saying things like this when asked to participate in some activity promoting the Love of God. "I'm not going to do it," or "I'm sick," which is every time you are called on by a church member.

Having this state of mind is not acting as part of the "Body." How would it be if the foot told the leg, "I am not moving today," or I want to be an arm? As you can see, this would cause dysfunction in the organization. Just as God placed you where he wants you to be, he has also placed you in the body to be the part that he has given you. It is not your place to say what's right and what's wrong; you are not to judge; you are a chosen section of the blessed "Organization of God," being part of the "Body of Christ." Wherever you are located in the organization, be it as a preacher, evangelist, teacher, pastor, deacon, a prophet, you are needed and have a purpose in the ministry.

God has given you this purpose to serve Him by helping others. **GPS>**"God gave some to be apostles, some prophets, some evangelists, and some pastors, and teachers, for the equipping of the saints for the work of ministry and the edifying of the body of Christ." **[Ephesians 4:11]** You should be actively reading your Bible; something must be in your mind in order for the Holy Spirit to remind you of what you know of the Word. He, the Holy Spirit, gives you a better understanding of your life, guiding you from sinfulness.

When Christ came, your foundation was established in the Love of God, through baptismal in your life. Although Jesus was the" Light of the World," due to the disorganization of the world, this was the cause of His death, due to worldly sinfulness leading to disorganization. You must hear the Good News of the Gospel, for it gives you faith through prayer, hope, and the love of God when you follow Jesus, who is "The Way." **GPS>**"Jesus says, I am the way, and the truth, and the life. No one comes to the Father except through me." **[John 14:6]**

GPS>[1 Corinthians 12:12-27, 14:40; John 14:26-27; Proverbs 6:16-19; Romans 12:4-5]

ROOTED AND GROUNDED IN LOVE

"God is Love." You are a seed that needs to grow. Spiritually. Your growing as a seed will require more dirt to strengthen your roots, which have already started to sprout but aren't strong enough to stand up straight. You are not yet ready to use all that God has placed in your divine design. God gives love, with His Words being Spiritual seeds that help nourish, strengthen, encourage, and sustain you. While your roots are not surrounded with pebbles of sinfulness, you allow the air of God's "Breath of Life, taking in the air of the Holy presence of God, keeping you saturated with the "Fountain of Living Water," as you, the seed, absorb, the "Light of the World" all in Jesus.

Causing your roots to be rooted and ground in Love. Having a heart filled with pebbles of disobedience, bitterness, anger, and wickedness of the world.

Soon turns to become a Stoney's heart, if you have this type of heart, you are not able to receive God's Agape love. Jesus brought to you to use as Blessed guidance for you, both your physical and spiritual journey. You, too, are a precious seed that is trying to grow in this fallen world. Sometimes, as a flower growing through the concrete, is how you feel when you are faced with various situations, events, circumstances, and disappointments, to name a few.

253

Being "Rooted and Grounded in Love" means that you are strong in your faith in God. You are unable to be swayed, having no doubt, fear, or lack of anything. You are determined to stand in the strength, truth, and power of God, having your understanding in obedience to God's will. Not wavering in circumstance(s), event(s), or peril. Your belief is steadfast, grounded in the Love of God, in devotion, faithfulness, steadfast obedience, and truth. Being rooted in God's love, intimacy, dedication, admiration, worship, and honor. Firmly and with instability, deep in God's love. Praying, reading the Word, letting your conversation and speech be about Jesus. Continually in faithfulness, having a firm grip and understanding of who Jesus is, what He did for you, and why He did it.

When you are "Rooted and Grounded in Love, you are able to face pain and hardships, knowing that this season of your life has meaning and that through the Word, teaching and preparing you for such times, you are position to be a warrior in the battle, letting Jesus fight your fight, in His way. Knowing that you will always be victorious. **GPS>**"Be of good cheer; I have overcome the world." **[John 16:33]** As you are rooted and grounded in love, your mind has been renewed, causing you to walk after the Spirit, not seeking anything of the world. Being rooted and grounded in Love means you love, trust, and submit to God's will. In other words, "Let go and let God! Here is a prayer for Spiritual Strength as you travel on your Life Journey.

You stand as a mighty Oak tree, not looking to the left nor to the right but straight up, meditative, on all things that are above, that are honest, just, pure, lovely, things that are of good report, virtuous, praising God, for the beauty He beholds. You are a warrior for Christ, being an ambassador leading others to truth, accepting His agenda, salvation, and redemption through Jesus, and receiving Eternal Life. You have a heart full of love, which you give as it has been freely given to you.

Your mind, heart, Spirit, and soul are all bound in the grace and mercy of God, bearing fruit. You are not double-minded; you are a genuine, True Christian," who has been tested and tried in the fires of the world, emerging unburned, standing strong in the power of God and his might, trusting God completely. Being a seed, you need water, sunlight, and manure to help you grow into the beautiful, unique gift that you are. Through the presence of the "Resurrection of Christ Knowledge." As a God-fearing Christian in humility and piousness, you fall on your knees to pray to God, be it for help or just to have a personal conversation with your Abba Father.

GPS>"For this reason I bow my knees before the Father, from whom every family in heaven and on earth is named, that according to the riches of his glory he may grant you to be strengthened with power through his Spirit in your inner being, so that Christ may dwell in your heart through faith-that you, being rooted and grounded in love may have strength to comprehend with all the saints what is the breadth and length and height and depth, and to know the love of Christ that surpasses knowledge, that you may be filled with all the fullness of God." **[Ephesians 3:14-19]** In the divine design which God has given you, there is light.

GPS>[Philippians 4:8; Matthew 10:8; Ephesians 3:20; John 14:6; 1 Thessalonians 5:16-22]

CHAPTER 28

The Sinful Spirit Of Pride

What is Pride? Pride, in the Biblical definition of Pride, is improper and excessive self-esteem, as conceit or arrogance. Your attitude is that of only self-respect for yourself and no one else. You have the "me, myself, and I, mentality or mindset. "Self-respect type of pride is sinful as it is; vanity, which is also considered a deadly sin, can lead you to think more highly of yourself, opening a way for immoral behavior to ensue. The sin of Pride comes in many forms, and signs of pride displayed in the world. Pride can be defined as elevating one's opinions and thoughts above God's authoritative Word.

Having the spirit of Pride is thinking that you are above all, not required to live as the majority of people do. Your existence is that of having a sense of entitlement, setting you above everyone else. Pride makes a selfish heart and mindset, feeding an egotistical spirit. Leading you to believe that you are in control of your life destiny, as if you were God. Even though you have no supernatural, malevolent, or miraculous power, pride causes you to forget your identity, which is a "child of the Most High God, loving you unconditionally, covering you in mercy, grace, compassion, and forgiveness.

As you walk blindly in worldliness, needing the "Word of Light, in your spirit to help you seek and find Jesus, who is "The Way, the Truth, and the Life, through Him, you receive

Eternal Life. Renounce the spirit of pride, as it is full of deception and ruin; when you know that you are in error, you still contaminate others with your false pretense and deceit, allowing your ego to run rampant. In the Bible, many were prideful and went against the word of God, only to end in catastrophic demise. **GPS>**"The LORD detests all the proud of heart. Be sure of this: They will not go unpunished." **[Proverbs 16:6]**

When you walk and live in Pride, it carries disgrace, because of your confused mindset, you make ridiculous choices. Pride makes a selfish heart and mindset, wanting to destroy anything and anyone that keeps you from getting the attention you want from everyone. Trying to make the world revolve around you, making yourself a god to be idolized and worshiped, is a world of foolishness and abomination to God. Bringing confusion, lies, lust, shame, immorality, and vileness to your soul through your corrupt mindset. Inducing more poison and wickedness in the world. Pride makes you think that everyone is interested in you, is jealous of you, and wants to be you. Pride makes a heart of opposing God on every level of your being, who God wants you to be.

Knowing who you are in Christ Jesus, a child of the Most High God. Not believing and making yourself a god. This type of behavior and belief always leads to destruction because there is no way you can go against God and prosper righteously. Having a haughty, stubborn spirit of self-sufficiency, not seeking God, thinking that you are wiser than God, your Creator. It is the mindset that you need to renew by surrendering all, finding Jesus, and making him your Lord and Savior. Following the entire Bible, not making it a buffet Bible, where you can pick out the parts that you like to follow when it doesn't agree with your transgressions and worldly lifestyle. Exhibiting condescension and snobbishness, as you boast in insolence and self-importance, leading to nowhere, gaining nothing, and soon to fall into the filthy pit of pretension. While in your pride of selfishness, you strong-arm others in the effort to accept your way of thinking, regardless of your not being in your right senses. Leading others into your sinfulness, chaos, and warped sense of truth. Showing your lack of knowledge, understanding, and wisdom. In order to be saved, you must relinquish your sinful mindset, repentant, and turn to God, for the Kingdom of God is at hand.

GPS>[Matthew 3:2, 4:17; Proverbs 5:5-6; Jeremiah 49:16; 1 Samuel 15:26; Esther 7:9-10]

PRACTICE HUMILITY

Humility stems from the word humble; being humble is when you place others above your needs, wants, and ideas. You edify others and are happy for others' achievements. Humility causes you to love and show genuine concern for others' well-being, no matter who they may be. Humility is being devout, faithful, God-fearing, and having morals. Characteristics of admitting when in error or world slang "wrong." Humility is a trait that some are born with; you open your heart and mind to receive it and learn from it in every area of your life in time. Humility causes you not to place value on things that can be seen. You have the concept that things are just things; they are all materialistic. Realizing that all material things are mere temporal props from God to assist you on your Life Journey Run. Humility is your trait that denounces pride. You are rooted and grounded in love. Speaking truthfully in love and never meant to cause any offense to anyone.

You are not judgmental; you let go of the past and move on. You are not egotistical nor confrontational; you realize your own inferiority. You are objective and give from your heart. You try to understand what each individual needs, placing yourself mentally in the painful situations that they are experiencing. Humility causes you to be supportive of others, being both contented and satisfied with your life, in repose, peace, following the Word Jesus, whom you love. In humility and love, you are patient, having meekness in you. Believing that the Holy Spirit of God will teach and lead you in how to travel your Life Journey, although there will be times when you sin, God gives you more grace, providing you a way out in a way that is blessed, helping in avoiding temptations. You become an eyewitness testimony, giving Glory to God for all he has done, giving you victory in time, defeating sin.

Scripture says, **GPS>**"God opposes the proud but shows favor to the humble." **[James 4:6]** In being humble, you allow yourself to be placed in a low status, not exalt yourself; you have a mindset of servitude, wanting to serve others. Through your humbleness, you don't boast, thinking yourself better than others. When we demonstrate humility, it shows that we are not ashamed to show our weaknesses.

Humility is the imitating of Jesus, as He came as a servant, giving honor to God by spreading the message of Love from God to mankind. Your humility is a shield from the temptation of comparing things that others have to what you have. Humility always focuses on being a life vest full of peace, causing you to ascend to new heights while here on earth seeking the Kingdom of God and then receiving Eternal Life. Your humility shows appreciation, having a quiet reserve, being trustworthy, camaraderie, and respecting their privacy in discretion. Having the mannerisms and characteristics of Proverbs 31:1-31, if you are a female, and if you are a male, Philippians 2:1-11, mannerisms and characteristics.

Humility is not being flashy, loud, cancerous, aggressive, nor being selfish. It is the giving of yourself in complete submission. You deny yourself (die self) of being first, willingly becoming last; it is a way of giving up your right. (Example: You are in the grocery store. You have sighted an open register, so you approach it, but from your peripheral sight, another shopper is coming to the same register you are only a foot away from. Now, you could scan the items in their shopping cart, seeing that they have fewer items than you do. But you gesture for them to go ahead of you.) When you are humble, you let others go before you in line, even though you have the right to go first. This is what giving up your rights means; it is also a good deed and acts of selflessness and kindness.

GPS>"All those who exalt themselves will be humbled, and those who humble themselves will be exalted." **[Luke 14:11]** You must put complete trust in the Lord, not deceive yourself with vanity or lust. Establishing a close, sincere relationship with the Lord. Leaning on God's understanding, wisdom, and divinity to show you the righteous path through Prayer, meditation, fasting, and other faithful, resourceful practices. Jesus was a humble King; though he had absolute power over all things, he chose to live on the earth realm, as a man on the earth. In order for you to humble yourself, the initial requirement of humility is to open your heart and withdraw from the arrogance of your ego.

GPS>"When pride comes, then comes disgrace, but with humility comes wisdom." **[Proverbs 11:2]** In practicing humility, you are all in, being completely committed to others' needs, regardless of what their need(s) may be. Because of your sincere humility, you desire to help others; in all sincerity desire to obey God and serve. You listen attentively to others; you keep your word; you are less seen by being in the background and hardly heard. You are a doer of the Word, not just a listener or reader of the Word. Humility is always shown with love, truth, honor, and ethics, never shunning away from someone's needs, be they mental, emotional, financially, or substantial. God gives you more grace, with His mighty hand lifting you up, exalting you in due time. You have your focus on Jesus' way.

You are called upon to be a humble follower of Christ, trusting in faith, wisdom, and the salvation of God. True humility is seeing yourselves as you truly are, fallen in sin and helpless without God. **GPS>**"He leads the humble in what is right and teaches the humble His way." **[Psalm 25:9]** In your humility, you use any situation or circumstance as a means to be thankful, growing in righteousness, be it bad or good. You encourage others, edifying everyone any time you can in love and truth. You give your all to strengthen others through prayer, worship, Spiritual resources, activities of a Christian nature, and righteous members for consulting if needed. In being humble, you don't hesitate, admitting when you are in error or did not comprehend something before making a mess. You do not blame others; you humbly apologize for any misunderstanding to the individual(s) immediately.

Not allowing the offense to rise up, you realize that you need time to unwind, so you do, tactfully. You have patience, you are gracious, you have a good sportsmanship attitude, and you are never rude. In your humility, you lack pride; you are modest, thinking yourself less than others. You are not possessive, petty, or jealous. Your humility causes you not to brag about what you have or show off your material items. In your blessed state of humility, you do not flaunt your wealthy status, including your accomplishments. **GPS>**"Humble yourselves, therefore, under God's mighty hand, that he may lift you up in due time." **[1 Peter 5:6]** Your humbleness doesn't relish the limelight; instead, you beg for God's mercy. Being humble consists of trusting God, following His will, and fearing the consequences of neglecting His commands for truth.

Humility is having a Supernatural heart, expressing love, having a work ethic, showing mercy, and having a supernatural heart. Mercy and beyond. Your humility recognizes the magnificent power of God and the potential retribution sin can cause. In your wisdom and humility, you understand obedience, having the spirit of a servant of God.

GPS>[James 4:10; 2 Chronicles 7:14; Proverbs 22:4; Matthew 19:29- 30; Proverbs 18:12]

CHAPTER 29

What Is Faith?

Faith is trust or confidence in a person, thing, or concept. In the context of religion, faith is the belief in God or the teachings of Christianity and religion. Faith can also refer to loyalty to duty or a person, fidelity to promises, and sincerity of intentions. It is having a strong belief in God and trusting Him based on evidence with total proof. Believing in the teachings of Christ, using the Bible as the source of doctrine, leads to Christianity. Belief in anything serves as a code of ethics and standards of merit. Faith involves hearing, learning the Word of God, and applying the knowledge of God to your life journey. As you strengthen in endurance, you stamp out any doubt, diminishing it at the root.

GPS>"Faith is the substance of things hoped for, not yet seen. Faith comes by hearing and by hearing the Word of God." **[Romans 10:17]** It is having the belief that what you are desiring will manifest through patience, obedience, and wisdom in the Lord. Faith can move mountains.

Jesus said If you would only believe, all things are possible. Whom better to trust than God, the Creator of the universe, all things seen and unseen? When you have faith, you have complete trust and confidence in something or someone. As trust is an essential part of faith, bringing you spiritual guidance from the Holy Spirit, walking in the Spirit and not in the flesh, you become strengthened in faithfulness.

GPS>"For we walk by faith and not by sight." **[2 Corinthians 5:7]** A delay in a prayer being answered does not mean no. It means that God is working it all out for good, no matter what it is that has been requested. It is God's will, not yours, and if your hopes are in agreement with the agenda of your heavenly Abba Father, your prayer request will manifest. God works on His timeline and not yours. There is a possibility that may cause you to think that God either is not hearing you or is not answering your prayer request.

None of this is true, although sometimes delays may occur because God knows when, where, and how your life journey is supposed to go. Often, when you do get your prayer request answered, it may not be what or how you wanted it to be answered, creating an "awe-amazing" moment where God's glory is manifested for you. Then there are times when you do get what you want, only with regrets, which lead to facing an additional test of mayhem, with lessons to be learned from the ordeal.

Your heavenly Father is so good, being your source for everything, including your solution; nothing is done without His approval and knowledge. It is by your faith that, through the Word of God, you have the ability to receive all that is for you, being that portion which God has placed in your Divine Design before you were conceived. Carrying the substance of things hoped for, not yet seen, gives you the ability to believe in faith. Knowing that your portion of faith is enough to receive God's blessings, mercy, and grace, for He is faithful, keeping all of the promises He has given to you.

GPS>[Revelation 22:13; Matthew 6:8; Romans 5:1-5; Titus 2:11-15; Hebrews 12:1]

HOPE AND HOPELESSNESS

What is Hope? Hope is an optimistic state of mind that is based on an expectation of positive outcomes with respect to events and circumstances in one's life or the world. It may also mean to expect with confidence and to cherish a desire with anticipation, commonly used to mean a desired wish, believing that it will manifest. GPS>"Hope deferred makes the heart sick, but a desire fulfilled is a tree of life." [Proverbs 13:12] In the Bible, hope is the confident expectation of what God has promised, and it's strengthened in faithfulness. Hope is what dreams are made of; let God's Glory be exalted all over the earth!

There have been times when you have contemplated what your purpose is here on earth. Fear not, for God has a plan and purpose for you. **GPS>**"For I know the thoughts that I think toward you, says the LORD, thoughts of peace and not of evil, to give you a future and a hope." **[Jeremiah 29:11]**

Hope means that you have faith, by having a heart that is strengthened by your mindset, and having the realization that God is your hope. It is He who directs your paths, allowing you to make your choice(s). Jesus not only came to bring hope; He is our hope. We have hope because Jesus forgives us and transforms us into His likeness. Hope is a strong motivator in helping you to stand firm in the belief that what some say matters nothing to you. Once you realize that having hope means that you are not alone in facing and dealing with worldly issues plaguing you, your hope in seeing the problem solved, one way or another, can cause you to see a problem turn to dust.

Renewing your strength is what hope does; it doesn't allow you to throw in the towel and say, "It's over; you lose." Hope drives you to keep going, even if you fail or fall. Hope encourages you to believe and trust, realizing that there indeed is something larger and more powerful than you. You cannot help yourself; you always need God's Word, Jesus. Scripture says, **GPS>**"But those who hope in the LORD will renew their strength. They will soar on wings like eagles; they will run and not grow weary; they will walk and not be faint." **[Isaiah 40:31]**

Hope calls for an infallible power that can accomplish that which you can't. Hope means you believe in God, the Creator of all things. It is His supernatural power that governs all on earth, in the earth, seas, and what's in the seas: humanity, heavens, and the universe. Your hope keeps you moving toward what seems impractical to being practical. Your hope lets you stay in peace, knowing that what you are hoping for will come to pass in manifestation if it is God's will. When others say that it's impossible, **GPS>**"Jesus replied, 'What is impossible with man is possible with God.'" **[Luke 18:27]**

Having hope means that you have the assurance that God is trustworthy and never changes. He is the same today, yesterday, and forever. Jesus is your only living hope. The Holy Spirit is your inspiration, guide, and strength. In the midst of all that happens in your daily life—the ups and downs, the pain, chaos, challenges, including the world with its array of darkness, the world, through all the heartache and pain, the ups and downs of life—Jesus is your only true hope.

How is Jesus our source of hope? Jesus is the source of all because He shows us the path of life. In His presence is fullness of joy, and in His right hand, there are pleasures forevermore. Without Jesus in our lives, we are in a dinghy without paddles, floating aimlessly on the dark waters of life in the midst of the storms. When you have hope, you believe that something is possible. Jesus not only came to bring hope; He is your living and blessed hope.

GPS>[1Peter 1:3, 5:7; Titus 2:11-14; 1 Timothy 1:1;]

HOPELESSNESS

What is hopelessness? Hopelessness is the feeling that nothing can be done to improve a situation, even though the threat may not be real. Depending on your mindset, you can think the situation is hopeless because of the fear and anxiety that you are experiencing. You may feel as if the circumstance is so large that you feel hopeless, meaning you see no help. You believe that there is no solution to give you satisfaction. Living in hopelessness is a feeling of being alone, abandoned, not loved, and having no one who understands you; you have no friends and no family to turn to. This is often what homeless people feel. This feeling has destroyed many facing dilemmas that seemed insurmountable. It is a subjective emotion that has a negative viewpoint for the future, one of losing control, confidence, courage, and the energy to carry on with no goals for your future. You feel separated from God, your family, and your friends due to letting worldly ways bring sorrow and fear, causing you to become separated from God.

Know that you are not the only one who has experienced this feeling of hopelessness. Trust in God; He can remove your fears, renew your strength to change your mind to see miracles, and restore your faith again. Believe in the one true living God, Yeshua, trusting in Him to deliver you. He worked miracles, used signs and wonders, and changed the hearts and minds of others. He, indeed, is a Way Maker, promise keeper, and Light of the World.

Having hope is much more beneficial. Consider this: you are experiencing challenges in your life journey. When feelings of hopelessness overcome you, bringing feelings of anguish, discouragement, pointlessness, defeat, and hopelessness, you have no hope. It is being in a dark place alone, with no thought of help, seeing no relief, just merely existing. It is awful when you don't know or have hope in Jesus. The feeling of hopelessness does not discriminate; even Jesus experienced it when He said, **GPS>**"My soul is overwhelmed with sorrow." **[Matthew 26:38]** Just like Jesus, when you feel hopeless, turn and cry out to the Father for His presence to come and comfort you, in the mighty name of Jesus. Trust and believe, for nothing is impossible for God.

Even Jonah expressed feelings of hopelessness when he said, "I wish I were dead." [Jonah 4:9] Possibly, you may have experienced this state of being in your life, feeling as if you were a dried leaf, just being pushed by the wind, not knowing or caring where the destination would end or be. When compared with hope, it gives you the ability to believe that some tomorrows will be better and that you are not alone.

GPS>[Acts 3:1-19; 2 Corinthians 1:3-4; Psalm 6:5-7, 40:1-3; John 14:27; Malachi 3:10]

CHARITY

Charity is identified as the highest form of love in Christianity. Having charity means giving to others and doing things that are helpful with a heart of love. Charity is the elevated embodiment of love, indicating that there is evidence of signaling the returned love between God and you. Having charity with heartfelt and sincere love, along with a willingness and obedience to help others, does establish a closer relationship with God, for you are His servant, just as Jesus was when He came to earth as "The Son of Man." Having a spirit of charity is Agape love, which is pure love. It is best described as an innocent love, that of an infant, untainted by influences of any kind—only true love, with no strings attached. Not contaminated nor corrupted by man and the world in any way, charity is unconditional love. The word charity, in translation of the Greek word agape, means "love." Having charity means giving, helping others, having compassion, kindness, generosity, and a sincere heart of love.

GPS>"Let all your things be done with charity (Love)." **[1 Corinthians 16:14]** Charity is the elevated embodiment of love, indicating that there is evidence of a reciprocal love between God and you. Charity is the pure love of Christ's sacrifice for mankind, which is the greatest of all the gifts of God, being that it is perfect and everlasting. God has commanded you to be generous, willing to share, and do good to and for others. In having a charitable heart, you are practicing love outright for all to feel and be blessed from, giving glory to God.

Charity is giving from your heart, soul, spirit, and mind; it is a complete package in exchanging love with others in truth. Charity is not selfish; it is self-disciplined, denying material things to influence the calling you have received from God. Charity is patient, focusing on the needs of others, cheerfully relishing the opportunity to give to others in abundance, as God has given to you freely. Seeing a mirror reflection of the glory of God, charity strengthens you as an ambassador of Christ. Teaching you to implement the "Fruit of the Spirit" in every area of your life journey and in others in righteousness.

The virtue of charity is unselfish, not puffed up, not boastful, nor hateful. It is moral, having unity, and showing compassion, discretion, and understanding in all that you do. In being charitable, you speak, walk humbly, and listen, for love is patient and kind. Charity is being supportive of those in need, never having a self-interested motive for your actions. Having charity with heartfelt sincerity, willingness, obedience, and dedication to helping others does establish a closer relationship with God, for you are His servant. Just as Jesus was when He came to earth as "The Son of Man," there were those who at times fed Jesus, gave Him water and a place to lay His head, and even washed His feet. All these thoughtful and loving acts were done by people just like you, showing compassion and kindness to others just like you.

GPS>"For even the Son of Man came not to be ministered unto, but to minister and to give His life for a ransom for many." [Mark 10:45] Jesus is the epitome of love in servitude while He humbly lived on earth in the form of man, making Himself nothing but giving His precious life to save all of humanity. His mission was to serve you by bringing the Word of the Heavenly Father. This is the love, "charity," which is taught in Christianity, to treat your neighbors as you want to be treated; it is divinely infused in the soul, bringing hope and residing in your will. In compassion, mercy, empathy, and concern, you are to help others as they are all your brothers and sisters in Christ Jesus, for charity is forever.

GPS>"Whoever sows sparingly will also reap sparingly, and whoever sows generously will also reap generously. Each man should give what he has decided in his heart to give, not reluctantly or under compulsion, for God loves a cheerful giver." **[2 Corinthians 9:6-7]** Jesus was the epitome of servitude as He humbled Himself while living on earth in the form of man, making Himself nothing. His mission was to serve you by bringing the Word of the Heavenly Father. There are many ways that you can show charity, such as having compassion, caring for the vulnerable, and volunteering at different community functions that promote the love of God.

Donating and giving have tremendous effects on others, bringing hope, sharing your values, and helping to make life journeys better. The Bible instructs you to be humble and giving, having the right motive, which is to give God glory. You are always willing to help anyone in need, immediately gladly giving food, money, or whatever to the best of your capacity you can do. Being charitable may give you purpose, for you are doing as Christ said: help those who need help. You give to the needy anonymously, for you are not vainglorious, seeking rewards, accolades, or recognition for what you have done. You know that your deed(s) are a matter between you and God.

GPS>"Take heed that you do not do your charitable deeds before men, to be seen by them." **[Matthew 6:1-4]** You are always willing to help anyone in need, immediately gladly giving food, money, or whatever to the best of your capacity you can do. You are sincere in your contributions and want to help, for you understand and believe that God loves a cheerful giver. Having charity in your heart makes the world a better place.

GPS>[2 Corinthians 9:7; Luke 6:30; Proverbs 28:27; Acts 20; Hebrews 13:16; 1 Timothy 6:17-19]

CHAPTER 30

Why You Seek The Kingdom Of God

You seek the Kingdom of God because our divine objective is to return home to Heaven. Heaven is where God is, along with His only begotten Son, Jesus Christ. Being His child, you are to walk in the righteousness of God. You seek the Kingdom of God because that is where eternal life is for you.

If you are not seeking the Kingdom of God, then what kingdom are you seeking, and why? Surely, you have felt that you don't belong on Earth. You seek the Kingdom of God because your divine objective is to be a servant of the Lord, blessed with gifts to meet your calling successfully, helping others by spreading the Word of God through the Holy Spirit. You are an ambassador of Christ. You are to spread the Word of God to everyone, leaving no one ignorant of the love that is God. You are to tell others how much God loves them with unconditional love, providing their every need without asking. You must have the mind of Christ, which requires you to focus on Him, pray unceasingly, love one another, help each other, and edify everyone. You are a living well, full of wisdom, understanding, peace, and blessings.

As He prompts you to search for who you are, what your purpose is, and how to get back to the Kingdom of God, you will learn how and what it requires to get there. The only way to achieve this is by having the mindset of Christ and following the Word of God, which are your stepping stones for the paths you must take to reach the Kingdom of God. Once you hear the Word of God through the Good News of the Gospel, you will begin to see with spiritual eyes, knowing that you are a spirit living in a body that has a soul. Through this ultimate demonstration of love and obedience to the Father, Jesus became your Way, the Truth, and the Life. Through Him is eternal life.

You seek the Kingdom because that is the prize you are running your life journey for; it is your treasure in Heaven. There is nothing good that this earthly kingdom has for you to receive. It only has worldliness, full of sin, unrighteousness, and evil, which is ruled by Satan. His kingdom authority is for a specific amount of time allocated by God, whose authority surpasses Satan's. In fact, Satan is God's "lackey," bringing chaos, mayhem, and obstacles to mankind.

Your life journey back home to Heaven is not an easy one. You start off as an infant in Christ, and with each test, temptation, and consequence, you grow through the stages of pain. These stages can make a physically grown man cry because of the troubles he is facing. All are part of the journey, helping you grow in love and wisdom through your experiences, making you a witness of truth, and establishing you as an anchor to those lost in the darkness of worldliness. Each time you go through chaotic, worldly issues, they serve as a road map to the Kingdom of God.

In seeking, you find mercy, grace, love, salvation, help, and redemption. You find forgiveness of your sins, which may have caused you to be stuck, possibly forcing you to take a few steps back due to the stubborn mindset you are harboring. Seeking the Kingdom of God provides continual light on your life journey. It renews your mind, soul, and spirit. It teaches you how to walk in the Spirit, not by sight, but by faith, believing that all things work together for good to those who love God.

Seeking the Kingdom helps you maneuver through the physical world without being part of it because you are led by the Holy Spirit, which is truth. You are seated in Heavenly places where God the Father, His only begotten Son, Jesus Christ, and other spiritual beings reside. As a human living on Earth for a time determined by God, you must learn how to find your way back to the Kingdom of God.

Following the Word of God is your stepping stone for the path that leads to the Kingdom. Being His child, you are to walk in the righteousness of God, following the ways of Jesus as a catalyst, bringing you closer to achieving the highest reward offered: eternal life, which is the ultimate gift from God. This gift allows you to be with your Father, who wants you to be with Him in Heaven.

You must seek above to know that there is something far better than what is here on Earth. Seeking the Kingdom means searching for God in Heaven, which is your treasure. There is nothing physical on Earth that is better than the Kingdom of God. The Kingdom of God is your hiding place; it is your refuge, your strong tower, your haven. It is your shelter, sanctuary, and peace.

As a Christian, you must understand that you are on a life journey here on Earth, which is not your home. You are a spirit in a body on a mission for God, making His agenda your agenda. God's will is what matters, not yours, unless it aligns with His. You have to seek the Kingdom of God because that is your home. When your body dies, your spirit will return to God.

You have directions and instructions guiding you to the Kingdom of God. All the blessed instructions are God's Words, spoken by Jesus and documented in the Bible. Jesus is the way; He is the epitome of Heaven on Earth. His being on Earth was for the sake of all mankind. When Jesus walked on Earth, He was teaching you how to act: loving everyone equally, speaking the truth all the time, never changing or lying, no apologies, no mistakes, only agape love, truth, and peace.

Seeking God's Kingdom requires you to have a true, loving heart full of virtues such as kindness, goodness, faithfulness, gentleness, perseverance, love, peace, joy, and self-control. He is your protector and defender. God is all that we see and don't see in both the natural and spiritual realms.

Seeking the Kingdom of God is the only way you can walk in righteousness, pleasing God, and giving Him glory in all that you do. Seeking the Kingdom is searching for the paths predestined for you to follow, with the goal of finally reaching the Heavenly Kingdom and being a disciple of Christ. You must walk in the Holy Spirit. If you are not in the Spirit, you cannot find the Kingdom of God. If you don't seek the Kingdom of God, then what are you seeking? Nothing on Earth is greater than having eternal life in Heaven.

What on Earth will you take with you when you die? Money, house, boat, position, status, lover? If so, know this: nothing will go with you when you die. Everything you see with the natural eye will stay on Earth. While you search for worldly things, which are all temporary, nothing can guarantee you everlasting life in peace. The only way to have this is by following the Bible and its instructions.

Not seeking the Kingdom means you are living foolishly, dangerously, haphazardly, and playing with the future of your soul and spirit. After you die, God has the final say on where your soul goes. Not seeking Heaven is a sure way not to ascend because you didn't ascend while on Earth. Instead, you decided to wade into the mire and walk blindly in the darkness, encountering chaos, trials, and suffering.

The only reason you are not seeking God is that you think you don't need Him or His help. How prideful and foolish! Walking around on Earth is only temporary, and within that time period, walking around aimlessly is not the choice to make if you seek peace with God. If you go it alone, you are just that—alone.

Seek God, your Abba Father, to have eternal life in Heaven and peace. Remember, your body will not be the same.

Scriptures say that we will be as Jesus is now in heaven, whatever form that may be. Just follow the scriptures that your Heavenly Father has provided for you to get back home, which is above in the heavenly spiritual realm. Not the Old Testament; that was before Jesus came. After Jesus came, the New Testament was the guidance for walking in righteousness. After Jesus died and rose from the dead, the Holy Spirit is what guides you, reminding you of what Jesus has said, which is the truth, as a conscience. The reason why we seek the Kingdom of God is because God's Word says so. Scriptures say, **GPS>**"But seek ye first the kingdom of God, and His righteousness; and all these things shall be added." **[Matthew 6:33]** The Heavenly Father has qualified you to share in the inheritance of the saints.

Prayer, along with thanksgiving, increases your knowledge, strengthening you with all power, according to Jesus' glorious might, for all endurance and patience with joy. You seek the Kingdom of God because it is your quality-of-life force. By seeking the Kingdom of God, you let go of worldly issues that come with stress, chaos, pain, confusion, and hopelessness. You stop looking back, where the pains of the past are. You are in the now, looking toward the Kingdom of God. That is where you find light, love, peace, forgiveness, and truth. Having these things elevates you to go beyond and above all that has caused you pain, whether from making a mess through sinning. You are to look forward, not forgetting the past, but learning from it and moving on. The past is in the rearview mirror on your travels. Nothing to see except where you have been, which no longer matters because you are going forward to something new.

You can stay bogged down with baggage that you carry from the past, but that will only deter you from being freed from the weight of those things that caused you pain. Let go and let God! You must admit it's not easy to let go of despair and the anguish that has you in a yoke. Seeking the Kingdom of God gives you hope through faith that the Kingdom of God is a better place to be than anywhere on this Earth, being part of and caught up in unrighteousness, defeat, and loss. The

Kingdom of God does not have any of the stuff that the world gives you, consisting of worry, offenses, hate, envy, and the list goes on.

The Kingdom of God is a place of peace, where your portion is to believe, trust, and obey the Word of God. It does not make demands on you that cause you anxiety, fear, or destruction. Seeking the Kingdom of God requires you to renew your mindset from worldliness to spiritual, seeking good things and thinking on things that are above, not earthly matters that are often led by the flesh. It rejuvenates your soul, spirit, and mind, causing the flesh to take a back seat on your quest to find the Kingdom of God, with all the promises, blessings, and benefits that are included. It is better to seek the Kingdom of God than to be stuck in a slime pit. That is what it is like when you have no heavenly guidance.

You are to seek the spiritual things of God as a priority over the physical things of the earthly world. Being saved, you must seek things that are above in Jesus' name. Foolishness speaks in this mindset: "I don't have anything, I don't get anything." When your way of thinking is full of hopelessness, it causes your heart to be stingy; it causes your heart to be sick. **GPS>**"Hope deferred makes the heart sick, but when a desire is fulfilled, it is a tree of life." **[Proverbs 13:12]**

Not able to give any love. Christianity is receiving the love of God and then giving that love to others. Seek and find the Lord, and He will be found, blessing you with righteousness, compassion, strength, love, wisdom, mercy, and victory. God wants you to want Him, acknowledging that He is in you, for without Him, you can do nothing. In the book of

John, Jesus explains what it means to be connected to Him in belief, faith, trust, love, and giving all your cares to Him.

When you seek the Kingdom of God and find it, the Holy Spirit will cause you to have a hunger and a thirst for the Word of God, causing you to be a witness of both the truth and love of God. Seeking the Kingdom of God, in itself, is spiritual; it requires faith and conviction. You should seek the Kingdom of Heaven because the other alternative is to die, either spiritually, naturally, or maybe even both. Why not seek the Kingdom of Heaven? You're going to the movies, buying a house, a car, getting married, having a family, traveling, and all sorts of things have you seeking them. So why not Jesus? **GPS>**"But without faith, it is impossible to please Him; for he that cometh to God must believe that He is and that He is a rewarder of them that diligently seek Him." **[Hebrews 11:6]**

God is in the heavens, and you will find Him there, above in the heavenly realms, waiting for you to come to Him. When you seek the Kingdom of God, it is showing and confirming that you believe in God, in Heaven, good, evil, and Satan. Why do you seek God? Because God said, "Seek Me." If you are not seeking God, then what are you seeking, and why? There is nothing that you can do without God's power, including Earth and all of the universes, not excluding what happens to your spirit after your body dies.

If you are not seeking God, then your mind is on something that is worldly, and that is not walking by faith and not by sight. You already know, feel, and see what the world has to offer you: destruction, darkness, fear, hopelessness, unrighteousness, deceit, illness, chaos, unwanted situations. Not one of these listed gives life or makes your life better on

Earth, nor in the heavens, which is where God is. Think about things that are above, seeking the Kingdom of God, for the Kingdom is at hand, as close to you as your Bible.

GPS>[Matthew 6:33; Romans 14:17; John 3; Acts 28:31; Galatians 5:19-21]

CHAPTER 31

Thanksgiving

"Thanksgiving," what a universal word. It holds so much and tells you everything there is to know about Thanksgiving. In America, this is an annual national tradition, bringing families together to partake in the festivities of dining. Having a traditional holiday meal, which includes turkey, has been marked by religious observances. "Thanksgiving" commemorates a harvest festival celebrated by the Pilgrims in 1621. The first "Thanksgiving," associated with Pilgrims and Native Americans, has come to symbolize intercultural peace, America's opportunity for newcomers, and the sanctity of home and family. Thanksgiving is held in the United States on the fourth Thursday in November. A similar holiday is held in Canada, usually on the second Monday in October.

To give thanks to anyone is one of the most loving ways to acknowledge what a person has done, and it convicts you to say "thank you," no matter the language or place on earth or in the world. The word "thanks" means "I appreciate you." Giving thanks is so remarkable; it brings joy to the recipient, who, in turn, gives thanks for the acknowledgment expressed by someone or others regarding a task they've done.

Whenever you think of "Thanksgiving," you should think of how much God has given you, done for you, and is doing for you right now. Even when you don't see Him, God is working, including His Angelic Host, in obedience to participate in whatever position He has assigned for each of them. God has even made Gargoyles to help in your fights against the ugly, evil ones of Satan, be it in another realm, world, or in the natural.

GPS>"The Lord has made everything for His purpose, even the wicked, for the day of trouble." **[Proverbs 16:4]** Whatever you receive from God, you should give thanks, for it has given you peace of mind and not left you in pieces, Amen.

Whether it seems bad or good to you, it really doesn't matter; it is how you handle whatever challenge or circumstance(s) you are facing. You should be thankful to have such a mighty God who is with you going through both worldly and spiritual storms. In this period of growth, through pain, fear, chaos, and suffering, your behavior plays a big role in the outcome. You learn to trust God and believe that Jesus is the way, following what the Word says in the Bible. This is the way that you grow into being a better person and follower of Christ in victory.

Or, in your lack of knowledge, you attempt to face all these things alone, using worldly mindsets and ways, believing that you can resolve your problems on your own. **GPS>**"Enter His gates with thanksgiving and His courts with praise; give thanks to Him and praise His name." **[Psalms 100:4]**

Have you ever heard the saying, "It's a jungle out there"? Well, indeed it is, and in order for you to grow in wisdom, character, forgiveness, love, integrity, patience, and love, you must become strong in the Lord and in the power of His might. Walking by faith, and not by sight, submitting all to God in Jesus' name. Putting on the whole Armor of God so that you can take your stand against the devil's schemes.

Giving thanks was always taught in my family, to say "thank you" whenever you receive anything, basic manners 101. Including whenever someone does something for you that causes a stirring inside of your being that makes you want to express acknowledgment, appreciation, and gratitude for what you have received. You were taught to say "thank you" whether or not you liked the present, gift, or blessing of kindness that the issuer had in mind and heart to bless you with.

This is also what is expected of you—to give thanks to God with homage and gratitude daily throughout the day. You can never say too many "thank yous" to your Creator. Trust the Lord and His mighty power; worship Him always. Just start thinking about yourself and those you know. Your life so far has been prosperous, good, safe, planned, and blessed, causing you to be filled with thanksgiving to Almighty God, your Heavenly Abba Father.

In the same mindset of respect, love, honor, appreciation, and gratitude you express whenever you get gifts from your earthly parent, you say, "Thank you," dad, mom, or whomever. God, your Heavenly Father, loves you more than any earthly father could. There are so many things to be thankful for in your life—just waking up in the morning is a gift, and that's why it's called the present.

Scripture says that you are to walk in a manner worthy of the Lord, fully pleasing to Him, bearing fruit in every good work, and increasing in the knowledge of God. You are to give thanks to the Father, who has qualified you to share in the inheritance of the saints in light. God has delivered you from the domain of darkness and transferred you to the kingdom of His beloved Son, in whom you have redemption and the forgiveness of your sins. Each new day, you receive new Mercy, leading you to Salvation from God your Father, meaning He is so loving and forgiving that He does not hold grudges. You are to give thanks in the truest and most heartfelt sense of the biblical word as you offer God your praises, acknowledging to Him that He is the Giver of all good gifts.

You are to worship Him with the highest esteem, for He is your Heavenly Abba Father. There should be offerings to God in love, expressing an overflow of sincere gratitude, praise, and thanks given daily. Even though you may not feel like something is going on regarding your life journey, it is, for God never sleeps. When you are sleeping, He is working. This is such an incomprehensible, mystifying gift of God's love for you continually. God is available for you 24/7—everlasting—there is no limit to His availability, being there for you, providing all your needs, help, and protection spiritually and naturally. There should be thanks for whatever is occurring in your life, be it good or bad. It always is good—whatever God does is for your betterment.

Thanksgiving should be a daily praise, not an occasional expression of thanks. God meets your needs daily and has in the past, so why shouldn't you say thank you daily? God reassures your heart of His constant love and faithfulness in meeting your needs, both spiritual and physical. Don't bargain with God; be direct—ask for what you need. This is not a cat-and-mouse, hide-and-seek game you're in.

Don't you think the Father who created you in love will give the Holy Spirit to you when you ask Him? Thanksgiving for you, as a Christian and ambassador of Christ, is to be a recruiter for God, being an example to others, helping them to learn about God and His love for them, for God is love. God saw everything that He had made, and behold, it was not only good but was very good. This includes you; you are good. The world wants you to think that you are a nobody, but God says that you are somebody, and He wants you to tell everybody about Jesus, the Word, and what God has done for you. Some will depart from the faith, hating and doubting the existence of God, but you stand firm, following the Holy Spirit.

GPS>"For everything God created is good, and nothing is to be rejected if it is received with Thanksgiving." **[1 Timothy 4:4]** Thanks and appreciation for how much God loves you. He has even provided a way not to fear what you are about to consume in your body. God offers a covenant with you. Your Heavenly Father has given you authority to bless your food. As you "give thanks" to God for what you are about to consume, you are acknowledging that He is the Creator of all things. Saying grace to bless your food gives honor to God, showing that you trust Him, praise Him, worship Him, and need Him in every area of your life. God is your existence; acknowledgment and acceptance are so deserving of your Heavenly Father. He gives you food because He created it for you to thrive.

Each day you rise, you should be giving thanks for your daily bread, including acknowledging the Holy Spirit that dwells in you, which is another reason for Thanksgiving. God is so deserving of all the praise, worship, trust, honor, love, respect, complete surrender, and heartfelt Thanksgiving, which is due Him. Saying grace shows that you trust God and that you respect Him, knowing the omnipotent power that He has over all things, visible and invisible. You've been given the Spirit, having no fear and power authorizing you through Jesus Christ. **GPS>**"For God hath not given us the spirit of fear but of power and of love and of a sound mind." **[2 Timothy 1:7]**

When you bless your food, you are acknowledging the power of God. First, thank God for blessing you, deeming you worthy to receive His bounty, which He has created and caused to grow for your earthly body nourishment and, at the same time, feeding your spirit. Say, "Bless me, O Lord, with these Thy gifts which I am about to receive from Thy bounty through Christ our Lord. Amen." Thank God for giving you a Spirit that is of power and of no fear, empowering you to face any obstacle, having no fear because He is your redeemer and protector. Don't bargain with God; be direct and ask for what you need. This is not a cat-and-mouse, hide-and-seek game you're in. If your little boy asks for a serving of fish, do you scare him with a live snake on his plate? If your little girl asks for an egg, do you trick her with a spider? As bad as you are, you wouldn't think of such a thing—you're at least decent to your own children. Don't you think the Father who created you in love will give the Holy Spirit when you ask Him?

Thanksgiving for you, as a Christian and an ambassador of Christ, is to be a recruiter for God, being an example to others, helping them to learn about God and His love for them, for God is love. You are to give thanks in the truest and heartfelt sense of the biblical word as you offer God your praises and acknowledge to Him that He is the Giver of all good gifts. Even though you may not feel like something is going on regarding your life journey, it is, for God never sleeps.

When you are sleeping, He is working. This is such an incomprehensible, mystifying gift of God's, displaying His love for you continually. God is available for you 24/7; everlasting, there is no limit to His availability, being there for you, providing all your needs, help, and protection spiritually and naturally.

There should be thanks for whatever is occurring in your life, be it good or bad. It is always good, whatever God does. Even when God saw everything that He had made, and behold, it was very good. You are good, and the world wants you to think that you are a nobody, but God says that you are somebody, and He wants you to tell everybody about Jesus, the Word, and what God has done for you. Some will depart from the faith, hating and doubting the existence of God. **GPS>**"For everything God created is good, and nothing is to be rejected if it is received with Thanksgiving." **[1 Timothy 4:4]** Giving thanks and blessing your food before you eat is a blessing indeed, showing again thanks and appreciation for how much God loves you.

GPS>"For God hath not given us the spirit of fear; but of power, and of love, and of a sound mind." **[2 Timothy 1:7]** When we bless our food, we are acknowledging the power of God. First, ask Him to bless you by deeming you worthy to receive His bounty, which He has created and caused to grow for your earthly bodily nourishment and, at the same time, feeding your spirit. Before each meal, say, "O Lord, bless us this day with Thy daily goods which we are about to receive from Thy bounty through Christ our Lord. Amen." You have communication with your Father anytime, anyplace. Being that you are a little less than the angels! There are many ways in which Thanksgiving may be expressed.

GPS>"Enter into His gates with Thanksgiving and into His courts with praise; be thankful unto Him, and bless His name." **[Psalms 100:4]** You should be thanking Jesus for empowering you with a Spirit of no fear. Jesus is your redeemer and protector. There should be offerings to God in love, expressing an overflow of sincere Thanksgiving to Him daily. You are to worship Him with the highest esteem, for He is your deliverer. Through Jesus's sacrifice of His body and blood, there is now no more condemnation to those who are in Christ Jesus. God has chosen you, giving you a blueprint of the map to finding eternal life. Created in the "Elegant Design of God," being a spirit, living in a body, having a soul, on earth, doing the will of God. Modeling as a created masterpiece, giving thanks, seeing God all around above you! What could be better?

GPS>[1Timothy 4:4-5; 1 Chronicles 16:11-34; Psalm 121:1-8; John 10:10; Isaiah 12:4-5]

BE THANKFUL FOR ALL YOU HAVE

In most families, basic and wise upbringing trains you to be appreciative of what you have. This type of home training provides discipline for individuals to grow into realizing that, whether it be tangible objects that you can see or a sense of gratitude for things of nature and the unseen realm. Thanksgiving is not just for "Thanksgiving Day," which comes once a year in November. It is something that you should feel each day—thankful. When you are thankful for what you have, there is a tendency for you to be at peace. You don't have that anxious or selfish attitude of "me, myself, and I." Giving thanks to God for all that you go through and whatever experience is a blessing to you and others around you.

All material things are temporal props that your Heavenly Father has given you to use and enjoy on your life journey. But they all will eventually break, rot, depreciate, be stolen, or lost, even eaten by moths and other sources. Even your body is temporal. Once the life source leaves your body, the soul and spirit return to God, having the fleshly body return to its original form—dirt and ashes. Yet, having eternal life when you die physically is the best gift ever given—that of Jesus giving His life for you in love, making a way for you to get back home where you are loved, free, at peace, no bills, no worries, no negativity at all. No drama, no pain, nothing to hurt you, disappoint you, leave you, lie to you, betray you, no debt, and the list goes on.

Here on earth, everything that you see with your natural eyes is nothing worth having, really. Those things can't give you peace of mind forever. Sure, they look nice, smell nice, and make you feel important, having others envy you. Many of these material things are mere distractions that keep you from praising your Father. I remember one day, I was going through something, and I said softly, "I'm tired of praying." I immediately heard, "What if I get tired?" Wow, what an awakening! From that day on, I don't say that anymore because I realized what would happen if I didn't have Jesus with me or have the Father looking out for me.

The same is true for you. God never sleeps; He is so organized, your life is like a tapestry—on the front, it is so very beautiful and neat, but once you turn it over, you see an array of color threads, some with knots, some dangling, all woven into fabric showing the divine design of threads going this and that way, all by the organized, integral hand of God. God and His angels work in your life behind the scenes, preventing you from the dangerous potholes of life in the form of temptations and worldly issues. Though tests and trials are meant to grow you, if you do not understand and have no growth of wisdom, the lesson may be a downfall for you.

GPS>"Lay not up for yourselves treasures upon earth, where moth and rust doth corrupt, and where thieves break through and steal. But lay up for yourselves treasures in heaven, where neither moth nor rust doth corrupt, and where thieves do not break through nor steal." **[Matthew 6:19-20]** Never compare yourself with anyone, for envy steals joy; focus on your own growth and find true contentment.

Be grateful for what you have; focus on your heart, mind, and soul. It is important to be thankful for all that you have in your life and all that is going on in your life, whether you see it as good or bad. All is done because of God's will, not yours. Once you realize that you are where you are supposed to be at all times, then your journey here on earth provides clearer paths to spiritual growth. You have what God wants you to have at that time, and you must be thankful for whatever that is.

Have you ever wondered why so many celebrities, wealthy people, and famous people commit suicide? Possibly, it is because they are not connected with their Abba Father, their Creator, God. You see, they have all these material things and beautiful possessions, but they don't give time to God or have a relationship with Him. All those items will be left when they die. The Egyptians are a prime example of having riches and being buried with them. The outcome was grave robbers because you can't take anything with you when you die. Only your spirit and soul return to heaven. The things you see are merely props God has given you to use on this earthly life journey. True riches are the ability to walk in the spirit and not be lured by fleshly desires and wants. You have a purpose here on earth, and that is to receive the love of God and share it with your brothers and sisters, no matter what their skin color is.

Trust the Holy Spirit, for He knows what you want to say when you can't find the words to speak or know what to pray for. **GPS>**"Likewise, the Spirit also helps us with our infirmities: for we know not what we should pray for as we ought: but the Spirit itself makes intercession for us with groaning which cannot be uttered." **[Romans 8:26]**

GPS>"For where your treasure is, there your heart will be also." **[Matthew 6:21]** Learn how to be content. Being satisfied is one of the best feelings; to have contentment is like a baby with a bottle—such serenity and pleasure, right? That is how you are supposed to be, like a baby feeding on the milk, which is the Word of God, in contentment. Seeking more knowledge and graduating in understanding, you reach a level of revelation of Christ's knowledge, which provides meat for your hunger for the Word of God as spiritual nourishment, feeding your heart, mind, and soul.

GPS>"LORD, my heart is not haughty, nor mine eyes lofty: neither do I exercise myself in great matters or in things too high for me. Surely I have behaved and quieted myself as a child that is weaned of his mother: my soul is even as a weaned child." **[Psalms 131:1-3]**

Although you face trials, circumstances, and issues of the world, don't let them overpower you. Surrender all to God, having no fear. You have the same peace that is found in the eye of the tornado. Therefore, when you are in the eye of the tornado with God, there is peace, but when you are out of the eye of the tornado without God, everything is in pieces. There are things flying around you while your mindset and situations are all in pieces. Be thankful for the supernatural love of God, for in it lies all that you need. Having no lack, ask, and you shall receive. **GPS>**"These things I have spoken unto you, that in me ye might have peace. In the world, ye shall have tribulation, but be of good cheer; I have overcome the world." **[John 16:33]**

GPS>[Hebrews 13:5; Matthew 6:19-21; Philippians 4:11-13,19; James 1:17; 1 Timothy 6:6-8]

KNOWING THE DIFFERENCE BETWEEN WANT AND NEED

Want and need—there is a distinct difference between the two. Want is to desire something that you think or feel will please your flesh and worldly lust. Take this example of "want": you see a television set that is 65 inches wide, and you start to think about getting a 65-inch-wide television set when you already have a 45-inch television that works perfectly well. In fact, it satisfied you last night before bed and this morning while you watched the news. Now, because you are in the store, you ponder getting a larger television set. This mindset is worldly, as you already have what you need, yet you want to buy something else, not because the television is broken, but because you've seen it and now want it. Want is a wish to have, but it is not necessary for your survival.

Both start with the letter "W." Want is to wish. To want is like a child who sees something in a store, you already have games, toys, bikes, and everything that makes you happy when you are at home. But once you are in the store, your eyes are lured by seeing something else that is appealing to you, causing you to desire it. You make it known to whoever is with you who has the power to get it for you. You really don't need it; you just want it.

Now, when you get it, a few days later or a week at most, you are not even playing with the item you purchased. This type of behavior or thought pattern is due to being spoiled and allowed to be selfish, creating a feeling of entitlement. Some of you (children) are great debaters and negotiators for getting or having your way. The difference between want and need truly must be taught early to everyone. Having this wisdom will make you wiser, less selfish, and more conscientious and will give you a practical mindset that will cause you to be more Christ-like.

How to address this and get free of seeing and wanting? A tip that may help you determine the difference is self-control and discipline in your life, following the ways of Jesus. **GPS>**"Therefore do not worry, saying, 'What shall we eat?' or 'What shall we drink?' or 'What shall we wear?' For after all these things, the Gentiles seek. For your heavenly Father knows that you need all these things." **[Matthew 6:31-32]**

Need, on the other hand, is something that is necessary to enhance your quality of life. A need is something that affects your life—your shelter, your health, food, and gainful employment. When you need something, it is essential for your survival, such as how you need air to breathe in order to stay alive or food to sustain your body with nourishment. Having a place to live provides you with shelter from the elements, being your physical safe haven. Having transportation and employment is a necessity in order to pay your bills and purchase essential items such as clothing and food, including gasoline for your automobile or money for other various means of transportation required for you to reach destinations such as your employment or to travel from point A to point B.

The letter "N" is the first letter for both the words "Need" and "Necessity." Learn the difference and utilize this knowledge to have more peace in your life and less stress, which may cause you to fall to pieces. Often, this behavior is due to having selfish thinking about only what you want, leading to sinfulness, as you will do anything to get what you want.

This should not be. What you should want is to know Jesus more and have Him as your treasure here on earth, for "Heaven is at Hand." As a Christian walking in the Holy Spirit and righteousness, you have no anxiety about wants and needs because you trust God. He provides all of your needs. Learning to be content offers you a way of having no worries, no additional cares, and no pressures of life. You are able to walk in truth, knowing that all your needs are met and that things are as they are supposed to be, obeying God's will.

GPS>[Philippians 4:19; John 6:35; Psalm 23; Isaiah 41:10; Malachi 3:10]

COUNT IT ALL JOY, WHATEVER CHALLENGE
YOU EXPERIENCE

Every day here on earth, you will interact with others on the same journey as you. Some know their purpose and goal, while others are clueless, knowing nothing about having Eternal Life. Through these encounters lie your experiences in the forms of tests, trials, chaos, and circumstances. Catapulting you into the worldly mindsets of others and their ways, requiring you to daily put on the "Whole Armor of God," for you are constantly in a spiritual battle, and just like wartime, some information is given on a need-to-know basis to those who are at the level of righteousness and wisdom in which clear transmission of the Holy Spirit's guidance is heard, understood, acknowledged, and accepted.

Taking up the "Shield of Faith" to stop all the "arrows or darts of the enemy" defensively and offensively covering the body, as Satan's design is to corrupt your mind and heart. Unrolling the fiery darts (arrows) of disobedience, fear, guilt, lust, anger, and any sinfulness that has found a way into your soul, spirit, and mind. When you wear the "Whole Armor of God," you are protected in the garb of a blessed "Warrior of God's Army," being covered from head to toe in the Spiritual Armor to wear continually, for you are not fighting against flesh and blood, but the principalities of this world, seated in high places.

GPS>"Stand firm then, with the belt of truth buckled around your waist, protecting the private area of your body, then putting on the 'Breastplate of Righteousness,' protecting your chest cavity and your heart. Next, place on your feet the 'Shoes of Peace,' saturated with the Good News of the Gospel, then pick up the 'Shield of Faith' to stop all the fiery darts of the enemy, defensively and offensively covering your body. Then, put on the 'Helmet of Salvation,' protecting your head and mind. Finally, picking up the 'Double-Edged Sword of the Spirit,' which is sharper than any two-edged sword, cutting through both bone and marrow, being a discerner of the heart and the Word of God, covering you from head to toe in the 'Whole Armor of God.'" **[Ephesians 6:10-24]**

Being that there are two sets of eyes working on your life journey, you see differently when using the eyes of the body. It causes you to see danger in your circumstances, causing fear to ensue, as fear can change your focus, making the ordeal more unbearable and frightening. When you use your eyes of faith, you see all the promises, provisions, and protection of God. Having "no fear," for you know that "greater is He that is in you than He that is in the world," bringing life in abundance to you in peace, modifying your perspective, blessing you with the ability through wisdom to count all your challenges as joy.

In the renewal of your mind, in faith, you understand where you are positioned, which is under the promises of God. The key to having the ability to count trials, non-pleasurable events, and issues of the world in joy depends on your attitude and understanding. God is working through your trials, where some of the most painful issues have purified you through the forgiveness of your sins, bringing you salvation and delivering you from sin and death. Showing how each trial and test has a purpose, everything is working out for your good, showing God's presence, glory, and miraculous power. You know that it could always be worse, so you count it all joy, for this too will pass; nothing lasts forever.

Counting everything that happens to you in joy is hard to do, especially after being programmed all your life to respond to things that don't give your flesh satisfaction and interfere with your mindset, making them seem like a problem. You really need to have the attitude that you are learning, being molded, growing stronger from these situations and experiences, and taking refuge in God. As a child of the Most High God, you have become freed from the snares of the devil; you have gained wisdom and strength, along with blessings, the ability to recognize blessings when they are in disguise, to help you on your life journey. You are linked to others for the endgame, using the Words of God and your faith as ammunition, being armed with the weapons from the Lord to speak, to do, and to teach others, using it in your life through Christ Jesus.

Those times you feel weak and things go against your liking, lean on the grace and mercy of Christ to sustain you. Those darts of the devil fly nonstop in an effort to cause you to fall into sin of some sort, enslaving you in the bondage of sinfulness when you follow worldliness. It is inevitable that you will have to face some dilemmas while on your life journey, but through patience and the Word of God, you will be victorious. God's agenda should be your agenda because you are here to serve, just as Jesus came to serve mankind.

Whenever you are disobedient, you are really fighting against God's will for you, and your arms are definitely too short to box with God. Count it all joy when you are threatened by the troubles of the world, issues, chaos, and calamities. Even Jesus was tempted by Satan when He was fasting in the desert for 40 days and nights. Through the power of the scriptures, Jesus was able to resist Satan's temptations. God is above all, and He has made ways for you to pass through whatever it may be that is causing you turmoil.

There are some things that can't be explained in this realm or time, but there is comfort in knowing that you will find peace when you decide that you are ready to let go and let God be still. Having patience, contentment, humility, and trust in the living hope of Jesus, which is perfect love, casting away all fear in faithfulness. **GPS>**"My brethren, count it all joy when you fall into various trials, knowing that the testing of your faith produces patience. But let patience have its perfect work, that you may be perfect and complete, lacking nothing." **[James 1:2-4]**

Rejoice, for your life has already been planned by God, so whatever you have in your life or experience, it is already known by your Heavenly Father, providing His Spirit in all your needs, granting you liberty, needing nothing but His presence. **GPS>**"For I know the thoughts I have toward you, thoughts of peace, to give you hope and a future." **[Jeremiah 29:11]** Here is a prayer: Thank the Lord for gray days, busy days, and even days when everything seems to go wrong! Thank you for the storms of life, bringing calmness to my being. Thank you, God, when it looks grim, for I am looking toward you, for you are my joy.

GPS>[Matthew 4:1-11; 2 Kings 6:16; James 1:2; Philippians 4:13; 1 John4:4]

CHAPTER 32

How To Receive Eternal Life

Many ask how you can receive eternal life. Here is the answer: you must believe that there is only one true living God. You must accept Jesus Christ as your Lord and Savior. You must be born again through being baptized in the name of Jesus Christ. You must be willing to put away the things of the world and serve the Lord with all your heart, might, mind, and strength. This way of walking is called "walking by faith and not by sight. This means your faith, belief, and hope are all geared toward being a disciple of Christ, walking in the spirit and not by material things that you see. You are in the world but not of this world; in essence, you have become part of a peculiar people.

GPS>"For thou art a holy people unto the Lord thy God, and the Lord hath chosen thee to be a peculiar people unto himself, above all the nations that are upon the earth." **[Deuteronomy 14:2]** God sees you as a living stone that was once rejected by the builders, now being built up as a spiritual house, to be a holy priesthood, to offer spiritual sacrifices acceptable to God through Jesus Christ, as a Holy person. Like a newborn infant, longing for the spiritual milk, that by it you may grow up into salvation, tasting indeed that the Lord is good.

GPS>"Everyone who believes on Him will not perish but have eternal life." **[John 3:16]** Eternal Life is a gift to live in God's presence. After you die physically, your spirit will be exalted to immortality. There are other factors required in order to receive eternal life that you need to know. You must be convinced, believing that Jesus Christ is Lord. The Holy Spirit will convict you of this.

Eternal life means that after your body dies, your spirit is released no longer on earth. Your essence [soul/spirit] will continue on in another realm, returning to God, as all souls belong to God. **GPS>**"All souls-to-me they belong. As the soul of the father, also the soul of the son-to-me they belong. The soul who sins is the one that will die". **[Ezekiel 18:4]** You will exist looking as Jesus did after He ascended to heaven. When you believe in your heart that you are saved, that assurance is in the Salvation that God gives you.

The Holy Spirit tells you every day that you are a child of God and that you can be saved. This is based on the principles of God's love. Through baptism, the righteousness of God has made you perfect because of Christ in you. Following the 10 commandments shows obedience, showing the love of God. Purified by the renewing of your mindset, now able to walk by faith, and not by sight. In order to receive eternal life, you must also be born again in Christ Jesus through Baptismal. Believing that Jesus is the Son of God, who came down from heaven, is your Lord and Savior. Through the Living Water of Christ, there is a rejuvenation to your spirit and in your life journey.

GPS>[John 3:5; Romans 1; Matthew 25; 1 Peter 5:10; Acts 13]

BAPTISMAL

Prior to Jesus' arrival at the site, "Bethany beyond Jordan" (Al-Maghtas), where he found His cousin John the Baptize, He, in humility and obedience, started his ministry only three to four months prior, baptizing his followers with water in the name of Yeshua, telling each one to repent of their sin(s) in preparation for the coming of Jesus. John the baptized said, GPS>"I am baptizing you with water, but one mightier than I is coming. I am not worthy to loosen the thongs of his sandals." **[Luke 3:10-18]** John was led by the "Fire of the Holy Spirit, causing him to be a lit fuse, igniting the way for the arrival of Jesus Christ, the Lamb of God, and Savior of the World. Many don't understand the process, nor the reason for getting baptized, and its importance.

The water baptismal signifies the death of Jesus and resurrection. In obedience, as you stand in the water, it represents Jesus' death on the cross. When you go down into the water, you are being buried as Jesus was, then, in coming out of the water, your sins(s) are washed away, causing you to be purified, rising from death as Jesus' resurrection. Baptismal is so important that Jesus told the Pharisee Nicodemus how important it is to be baptized. Baptismal means that you are "being born again"; it is the renewing of your mind, heart, and soul to think, speak, walk, and live in the Spirit of God.

Following the Holy Spirit and not the flesh in righteousness, being baptized means that you are publicly acknowledging your faith, love, and belief in Jesus as your Lord and Savior, being forgiven, having your sins washed away, and receiving eternal salvation. Becoming a family member through Christ, no longer a part of the world and its ways, walking by faith and not by sight.

Through the miraculous power of baptismal, you are being born again, cleansed of your sin(s), having a renewed mindset, and seeing the Kingdom of God. All Baptismal has the power for you to see the Kingdom of God, at hand. This is the blessing wisdom and blessing that the Pharisee Nicodemus came in the dark to visit Jesus; speaking in riddles, Jesus said, **GPS>**"Jesus answered him, "Truly, truly, I say to you, unless one is born again, he cannot see the kingdom of God." Nicodemus said to him, "How can a man be born when he is old? Can he enter a second time into his mother's womb and be born?" Jesus answered, "Truly, truly, I say to you, unless one is born of water and the Spirit, he cannot enter the kingdom of God. That which is born of the flesh is flesh, and that which is born of the Spirit is spirit. Do not marvel that I said to you, You must be born again." **[John 3:3-12]**

Scriptures say that Jesus, while in Galilee, told the eleven apostles and others to go and make disciples of all the nations, baptizing them in the name of the Father and of the Son and of the Holy Spirit, teaching them to observe everything that He had commanded them, and that He would be with them always, even unto the end of the world, which is part of the, "Great Commission." In the Book of Acts 2:328, Jesus commanded baptisms to be done "in the name of Jesus Christ.

GPS>[8:14-17; Matthew 22:46, 28:19-20; John 1:29-34; Numbers 4-9]

Chapter 33

In Summation, Follow Earnestly

REPENT

Psalm 51

"Create in me a clean heart, O God, and put a new and right spirit within me."

Luke 18:13-14, Acts 2:38

RENOUNCE

Titus 2:11-15

"Let us renounce this world and set before us the will of God, as it is manifested and opened unto us in his word."

Proverbs 28:13, Luke 14:25-33

RENEW

Isaiah 40:31

"Do not be conformed to this world, but be transformed by the renewal of your mind, that by testing you may discern what is the will of God, what is good and acceptable and perfect."

Psalm 51:10, Ephesians 4:23

**YOU HAVE REACHED YOUR DESTINATION------>
ETERNAL LIFE IS STRAIGHT AHEAD**

GOD BLESS YOU

REFERENCES

Some of my resources were from different versions of The Holy Bible. Consisting of several versions. The King James; KJV, New Living Bible; NLT, New King James Version; NKJV, New International Version; NIV, New American Bible; NAB, Amplified Bible; AB, Contemporary English Version; CEV, Good News Bible GNB, New Testament; NT, American Standard Version; ASV, New Living Translation; NLT, Christian Bible; CB, and the English Standard Version; ESV.

https://www.christianstudylibrary.org
https://anglicanfocus.org.au >
https://www.touchinglives.org > devotionals >
https://www.bible.com >
https://www.thingsofthesort.com
https://www.bible.com > compare
https://quod.lib.umich.edu
Oxford langages.oup.com https://www.biblestudytools.com
https://www.churchofjesuschrist.org
 https://www.britannica.com > Definition from Oxford languages
https://www.quora.com > what-are-the-three-basic- types-of-sin Christian views on sin – Wikipedia
https://www.thesaurus.com > browse sinless
https://commons.wikimedia.org/wiki/File:Recent_Trinity_Shield.svg
https://boonecenter.pepperdine.edu/blog/posts/understanding-agape-love.htm

https://en.wikipedia.org/wiki/Binding_and_loosingRef:
https://www.bible.com/reading- plans/21895-the-benefits-of-forgiveness/day/1
https://www.google.com/search?sxsrf=APwXEde8-5cQUKr5BlnkHw8dAaRiqmISSg%3A1683429247476&q=what%20is%20forgiveness%20in%20the%20bible&ved=2ahUKEwiOn7PSnuL-AhX8lWoFHXz_AIwQmoICKAB6BAgGEAs&biw=1405&bih=766&dpr=1.22
https://www.linkedin.co m/pulse/3-biblical-reasons-why-you-shouldR
https://en.wikipedia.org/wiki/Binding_and_loosingRef:
https://www.bible.com/reading- plans/21895-the-benefits-of-forgiveness/day/1
 https://www.google.com/search?sxsrf=APwXEde8-5cQUKr5BlnkHw8dAaRiqmISSg%3A1683429247476&q=what%20is%20forgiveness%20in%20the%20bible&ved=2ahUKEwiOn7PSnuL-AhX8lWoFHXz_AIwQmoICKAB6BAgGEAs&biw=1405&bih=766&dpr=1.22
https://www.linkedin.co m/pulse/3-biblical-reasons-why-you-shouldRepentanceepentanceinChri.
https://en.wikipedia.org> wiki https://en.wikipedia.org> wiki of Christ https://www.churchofjesuschrist.org> gospel-principle https://faithgateway.com > blogs
https://en.wikipedia.org/wiki/Repentance_in_Christianity biblegateway.com
https://en.wikipedia.org> wiki > word by word
https://dictionarycambridge.org
https://cancer.org
https://en.m.wikipedia.org.wiki
https://christianity.com>wiki

https://www.bible.com> Meriam-Webster
https://biblestudytools.co: Oxford Languages -Learn moreBiblehub.com
https://www.volcabulary.com >Bible.com
hhttps://www.bibletolife.com
https://www.countryliving.com org...
https://www.bible.com/reading-plans/21895-the-benefits-of-forgiveness/day/1
https://www.google.com/search?sxsrf=APwXEde8-5cQUKr5BlnkHw8dAaRiqmISSg%3A1683429247476&q=what%20is%20forgiveness%20in%20the%20bible&ved=2ahUKEwiOn7PSnuL-AhX8lWoFHXz_AIwQmoICKAB6BAgGEAs&biw=1405&bih=766&dpr=1.22
https://www.linkedin.co m/pulse/3-biblical-reasons-why-you-should-Repentance_in Chri.
https://www.churchofjesuschrist.org> gospel-principle
https://biblereasons.com/reasons-for- fasting
https://www.biblegateway.com
https://www.biblestudytools.com
https://thetruthlover.wordpress.com Praying the Temple Prayer with Pastor Cho Wikipedia
https://en.wikipedia.org > wiki > Rehema_(doctrine)rhema will be our general term to refer to all of these means of God communicating His specific will to an individual." Hamon states "A rhema is an inspired ...What is Rhema?
https://itsyonobi.com
https://advice.theshineapp.comCho
https://www.lords-prayer-words.com/famous_prayers/god_grant_me_the_serenity.html

https://www.google.com/search?

https://www.biblegateway.com

https://quod.lib.umich.edu>kjv-idx

https://www.christianity.com

https://www.thegospelcoalition.org>

https://www.dictionary.com > browse

https://www.britannica.com > topic

https://www.churchofjesuschirist.org >... https://
www/bible.com > PSA 49:8-9 https://www.face2face.org.za
> rec...

https://www.face2face.org.za

https://minimalsismmadesimple.com

 https://www.christianity.com/wiki/christian- terms/what-
does-humility-mean-in-the-bible-why-should-we-be-humble.
html https:

q=pride+in+bible+meaning&sca_esvsclient=gws- wiz

Reference: https://www.mindtools.com >the danger of
arrogance

https://biblesumo.com different types of pride

https//www.learingreligieon.com > defeating confusion

https://www.cgg.org>biblestudy

https://ladiesdrawingnigh.org

https://www.google.com/search?

wikicollinsdic.what+is+resurrection+power&biw=1405&bih
=766&sxsrf=APwXEdfPJg_ClRPrfuBp5w

vr1994cKyGIw%3A1683066165239&ei=NY1RZIbDoipqtsP

gPGhyAg&oq=what+is+resurrection+p&

gs_lcp=g&sclient=gws-wiz-serp

https://www.google.com/search?

https://www.bible.com/reading-plans/21895-the-benefits-
of-forgiveness/day/1

https://www.google.com/search?sxsrf=APwXEde8-5cQUKr5BlnkHw8dAaRiqmISSg%3A1683429247476&q=what%20is%20forgiveness%20in%20the%20bible&ved=2ahUKEwiOn7PSnuL-CC=what+does+resurrection+power+mean&biw=1405&bih766&sxsrf=APwXEdd5ljHvpKzdY6TkJyiX1P0eiRqqhglient=gws-wiz-serpResurrection/

https://itwministries.org/living-iin- resurrection-power/

Macmilliandictionary.com/us/dictionary/american/resurrection

https://en.wikipedia.org/wiki/Resurrection/

https://itwministries.org/living-

https://www.bible.com >bible > LU

https:// www.bible.com >

https:// condolencesmessages.com

https://www.churchofjesuschirst.org > httpsiffinfirst.org

https://www.choctawnation.com > a>

https://https://en.wikipedia.org> wiki > Repentance in Chri.

biblegateway.com https://en.wikipedia.org> wiki >

https://en.mwikipedia.org > wiki wikipedia.org wiki wikipedia.org > wiki >Sal...

https://www.churchofjesuschrist.org › ftsoy ›crosswalk.com 2022/04 >ftsoy > 2022/04

https://www.britannica.com> topic

https://search.yahoo.com/search?p=WHAT+IS+PATIENCE&fr=yfp- t&fr2=p%3Afp%2Cm%3Asb&ei=UTF-8&fp=1/

https://www.encyclopedia.com/religion/encyclopedias-almanacs-transcripts-and- maps/patience-bible

DayspringSilom Springs

https://www.vocabulary.comAhX8lWoFHXz_AIwQmoICK
AB6BAgGEAs&biw=1405&bih=766&dpr=1.22
https://www.linkedin.co m/pulse/3-biblical-reasons-why-
you-should-
https://onlinelibrary.wiley.com› doi › pdf › j.17…
https://www.nationalshirine.org >blog
https://manchesterinkink.com > the
https://www.learnreligions.com > c…. https://rasining
everydaydisciples.com
Wikipediahttps:q=pride+in+bible+meaning&sca_esv=56012
4145&sxsrf=AB5stBhcZ3M7tCagkHsk
BPwqFhLnPTWQQg%3A1692989285314&source=hp&ei=
ZffoZKzlD5PIkPIP_fWR0AU&iflsig=AD69kcEAAAAAZ
O kFdQgmh3nkWxlFPt3X-
unulqs7NWf&oq=PRIDE&gs_lp=Egdndsclient=gws-wiz
the danger of arrogance gotquestions.org different types of
pride
https//www.learingreligieon.com > defeating confusion
biblestudy
 https://www.google.com/search?

www.ingramcontent.com/pod-product-compliance
Lightning Source LLC
Chambersburg PA
CBHW060410130626
46555CB00005B/2022